The Wall Street Reader

Selected and edited by
BILL ADLER *and*
CATHERINE J. GREENE

The
Wall Street
Reader

The World Publishing Company
New York and Cleveland

Published by The World Publishing Company
2231 West 110th Street, Cleveland, Ohio 44102

Published simultaneously in Canada by
Nelson, Foster & Scott Ltd.

First Printing—1970

Library of Congress Catalog Card Number: 71-96929
Printed in the United States of America

WORLD PUBLISHING
TIMES MIRROR

ACKNOWLEDGMENTS

Acknowledgment is made to the following authors and publishers for permission to reprint the material listed:

"Support and Resistance" from *How Charts Can Help You in the Stock Market* by William L. Jiler. Copyright © 1962 by William L. Jiler. Reprinted by courtesy of *Trendline*, publisher of *How Charts Can Help You in the Stock Market* by William L. Jiler.

"The Ever-Liquid Account" and "Tip to the Investor: Always Write it Down" from *The Battle for Investment Survival* by Gerald M. Loeb. Copyright © 1935, 1936, 1937, 1943, 1952, 1954, 1955, 1956, 1957, 1965 by G. M. Loeb. Reprinted by permission of Simon and Schuster, Inc.

"The Careless Capitalists" and "Beware of Barbers, Beauticians, and Waiters: The Financial Press" from *20 Million Careless Capitalists* by Carter

The following page constitutes a continuation of the copyright page.

F. Henderson and Albert C. Lasher. Copyright © 1967 by Carter F. Henderson and Albert C. Lasher. Reprinted by permission of Doubleday and Company, Inc.

"Adventures in the Land of the Red-hot Tip" from *Wall Street Made Easy* by Ellen Williamson. Copyright © 1965 by Ellen Williamson. Reprinted by permission of Doubleday and Company, Inc.

"Commodity Futures Trading" from *Choosing Tomorrow's Growth Stocks Today* by John W. Hazard. Copyright © 1968 by John W. Hazard. Reprinted by permission of Doubleday and Company, Inc.

"Mutual Funds" from *How Women Can Make Money in the Stock Market* by Colleen Moore. Copyright © 1969 by Colleen Moore Hargrave. Reprinted by permission of Doubleday and Company, Inc.

"The Penny Stock Market" from *Anyone Can Make a Million* by Morton Shulman. Copyright © 1966 by McGraw-Hill Company of Canada, Limited. Reprinted by permission of McGraw-Hill Company of Canada, Limited.

"Buy on the Rumor: Sell on the News" from *The Sophisticated Investor* by Burton Crane. Copyright © 1959 by Burton Crane. Revised edition copyright © 1964 by Sylvia Crane Eisenlohr. Reprinted by permission of Simon and Schuster, Inc.

"Can You 'Beat the Market'?" and "The Folklore of the Market" from *How to Buy Stocks* by Louis Engel. Copyright © 1953, 1957, 1962 by Louis Engel. Reprinted by permission of Little, Brown and Company.

"'Cashing In'on Population Growth" from *Financial Independence Through Common Stocks* by Robert D. Merritt. Copyright © 1952, 1953, 1957 by United Business Service Co. Reprinted by permission of Simon and Schuster, Inc.

"The Low-High Spread" from *The Low-High Theory of Investment* by Samuel C. Greenfield. Copyright © 1968 by Samuel C. Greenfield. Reprinted by permission of Coward-McCann, Inc., from *The Low-High Theory of Investment* by Samuel C. Greenfield.

"What to Avoid in Over-the-Counter Securities" from *Increase Your Profits in the Stock Market* by Frank B. Diamond. Copyright © 1967 by Frank B. Diamond. Reprinted from *Increase Your Profits in the Stock Market* by permission of Cornerstone Library.

"GMAC's—'The Pause That Refreshes'" from *The Fine Art of Making Money in the Stock Market* by Frank B. Diamond. Copyright © 1968 by Frank B. Diamond. Reprinted from *The Fine Art of Making Money in the Stock Market* by permission of Cornerstone Library.

The following page constitutes a continuation of the copyright page.

34823

Contents

Introduction

To most people the name "Wall Street" brings to mind a crowded and frantic two-block area, where people race madly from tickertape to telephone making countless millions by buying and selling "hot stocks" known only by those "in the know"—whose secret network of "contacts" reaches far and wide.

Of course, this is a myth. As the most successful Wall Streeters themselves know best, the real lure and excitement of the stock market lies in the very fact that there is no way to know what tomorrow will bring. No two years, no two days, are alike, no two stocks are alike, no two people have the same investment needs, and *no two people ever agree on how to invest in the stock market.*

There has been an overwhelming amount written about the stock market. Every newspaper, local and national, radio and television program has news each day to tell the public, and the world, about Wall Street. Almost every American man, woman, and child—in fact anybody who pays even the most minimal insurance premium or has $1.00 in a savings account—is, if only indirectly, investing in the stock market.

But corporate and institutional investing do not give us much food for thought. What is thought provoking, however, are those true stories we often read about of individuals—men and women—who, on their own initiative and often no nearer to Wall Street than we are, and working with a relatively small amount of money, have accumulated small fortunes by sound investment decisions.

Decisions is the key word. The sophisticated investor works from a predetermined logic or method. Because of this he or she is prepared for any kind of market activity. The market, or a stock, may very well go up or down, but it is what you have already decided to do at these points that will, in most cases, bring you profits. The performance of the market should not decide for you. The stock market will always fluctuate—but your self-confidence should not. And self-confidence is the one trait common to all sophisticated investors—they know *when* to buy and *when* to sell. *What* specific companies to buy or sell changes from day to day and year to year—today's popular company may be next year's wallflower.

The Wall Street Reader will be of invaluable help to the experienced and novice investor alike. The selections have been chosen from the best-selling and most informative books on the subject of investing in the stock market and were written by highly respected authors known for their pertinent and timely advice. Each of these selections will educate you in a new aspect of investing. Gerald Loeb, Louis Engel, Burton Crane, and "Adam Smith" are among the many successful investors who will share with you the wisdom they have attained from many years of experience, and the advice of these professionals will enable you to evaluate and understand the good—and uncover the bad—points of the stock you hope will make you money.

Wall Street is a fertile ground for making money. *The Wall Street Reader* will generate the excitement to be found in this type of investment. You may be surprised to discover the many points on which the experts themselves disagree. The investment opportunities on Wall Street are as many and varied as the ways to investigate them. Choose from the following what best suits *your* needs.

Bill Adler
Catherine J. Greene

The Wall Street Reader

The Folklore of the Market

LOUIS ENGEL

How to Buy Stocks *by Louis Engel was first published in 1953 and became a national best seller. Since then there have been four revised editions. The key to its success lies in its clarity and in Engel's sound investment advice. In the following selection from this popular book Engel discusses eight common clichés most often heard regarding the stock market. Using actual examples, he shows when and how these axioms can mean profits for you.*

*T*HE cheapest commodity in the world is investment advice from people not equipped to give it.

Many a man who doesn't own a share of stock still fancies himself as something of an authority on the market, and he's ready and willing to deliver himself of an opinion about it on the slightest provocation. If he actually owns stock himself, chances are you won't have to ask his opinion. He'll tell you what to buy, what to sell, and what's going to happen to the market. And you can't stop him.

The more a man knows about the market, the less he is willing to commit himself about it. The wisest of them all, old J. P. Morgan, when asked his opinion of the market, always used to reply, "It will fluctuate." He wasn't just being canny. He knew that was the only provable statement that could be made about the market.

Nevertheless, over the years a number of generalizations about the market and about investing have come to be accepted as gospel. Actually, these homespun axioms must be accepted as little more than folklore. And like most folklore, each of them has a certain element of truth about it—and a certain element of nontruth.

For instance:

"Buy 'em and put 'em away."

This would have been a fine piece of advice if you had happened to buy $1,000 worth of General Motors stock in 1923. By mid-1966 that stock would have been worth more than $60,000, and you would have collected over $40,000 in dividends.

But in the early twenties the car everybody was talking about was the Stutz Bearcat, and there was a great deal of speculative market interest in Stutz stock. You might very well have decided to buy $1000 worth of that. How would you have made out on that purchase? The answer is that you would have lost all your money, and furthermore you would never have collected a penny in dividends.

Of course, there is a measure of sense in the axiom. If you start worrying about fluctuations of a point or two and try to buy and sell on every turn, you can pay out a lot of money in commissions needlessly and maybe end up with less profit than if you'd "bought 'em and put 'em away."

Nevertheless, it's only good sense to remember that securities are perishable. Values do change with the passage of time. Industries die, and new ones are born. Companies rise and fall. The wise investor will take a good look at all his securities at least once a year, and he could do worse than to ask his broker to review them with him then.

"You never go broke taking profit."

That's obviously true. But you can certainly get hurt badly. Suppose you had put $50 into Sears, Roebuck in 1906. By

1940, the stock that you had bought would have been worth over $4300, and by mid-1966, that same stock was worth almost $20,000.

Or consider another classic case. In 1914, you could have bought 100 shares of stock in International Business Machines for $2750 and in just eleven short years you could have sold out for $6364. Certainly you can never go broke taking profits of nearly 250%.

But as far as IBM stock is concerned, you certainly would have taken a licking if you had sold in 1925. For by the middle of 1966, your original 100 shares would have grown to 28,409 and they would have had a market value of $9,900,000.

Of course, a profit *is* always a nice thing to have—in the pocket, not just on paper.

"Buy when others are selling. Sell when they buy."

This sounds like a neat trick, if you can do it.

Obviously, you can't make money if you consistently buck the trend of the market. Where, for instance, would you have been if you had been selling stock all through the bull market since 1950?

So the trick lies in anticipating the action of all the others— in buying just before the crowd decides to buy and selling just ahead of them. This is just exactly the trick that the exponents of various formula plans try to turn by hitching their buying and selling operations to some arbitrary decline or advance in the market.

Others, less scientific, simply try to sell at the tops and buy at the bottoms. But how do you know when the market hits bottom? How far down is down?

Make no mistake about it. Anyone who tries to practice this fine art is "playing the market" in the purest sense of the phrase. He's speculating; he's not investing.

"Don't sell on strike news."

There's some truth to the old adage. Nowadays, labor troubles in any big company or in any industry are apt to be pretty well publicized. Consequently, the market is likely to have discounted the possibility of a strike during the time it was brewing; the stock will already have gone down in price, and it may even advance when the strike news breaks.

Again, many people think that a strike doesn't really damage a company's long-term profit picture. They contend that while a strike is on, demand for the company's products is only deferred, and as soon as the strike is over, the company will enjoy better business than ever.

But such a theory is often little more than wishful thinking. After all, most strikes end with the company facing a higher labor bill. And many times the demand for its products which a company couldn't fill while its employees were on strike has been happily filled by a competitor.

"Don't overstay the market."

A fine piece of advice, but how do you know when to sell and take your profit—if that's what you are interested in?

Sometimes you can tell by watching those basic business indicators that show what's happening to production, distribution, and consumption of goods. But sometimes you can't, because the market doesn't seem to be paying too close attention to them. That was certainly true in the years after World War II, in 1962, and in 1966.

Nevertheless, if business appears to be on the skids, and the stock market is still boiling merrily upward, sooner or later there's going to be a reckoning.

"Always cut your losses quickly."

Nobody wants to ride all the way downhill with a stock if the company is headed for bankruptcy, but at the same time you don't want to be stampeded into a sale by a price decline that may have no relationship to the fundamental value of the stock.

Remember, the price of a stock at any time reflects the supply and demand for that stock, the opinions and attitudes of all the buyers and all the sellers. If a stock is closely held, if its *"floating supply"*—the amount usually available in the market—is limited, the price of that stock can be unduly depressed for quite a period if some large holder is selling a sizable block of it, just because he may need the cash and not because he thinks less of the stock.

The market on any given day is made by just a tiny handful of all the people who own stocks. On the exchange as a whole ten million shares may be traded in one day, but that still represents only $\frac{1}{10}$ of 1% of all shares listed on the exchange. The 99.9% who aren't selling have some reason for holding on—or think they do.

Of course, there is much truth in the observation that unsophisticated investors do tend to sell a stock too readily when they have a profit in it and hang on to a stock in which they have a loss, hoping that it will come back.

"An investor is just a disappointed speculator."

This cynical observation has a measure of truth in it. Every stock buyer hopes for a big fat profit, even if he won't admit it to himself. So when the market drops, he does the best he can to assuage his disappointment by assuring himself and everybody else that of course he never expected to make a killing—he was just investing on the basis of the fundamental stock values.

This is especially true of that congenital bull—the odd-lot buyer. As a class, the odd-lotters almost always buy more than they sell. And all too often, they finally decide to buy only when the market is already too high.

So often does this happen that some speculators gauge their own actions by the relation of odd-lot buying to odd-lot selling. When that ratio increases—when the proportion of odd-lot purchases rises—the speculators sell.

But in the long run, the small investor often has the last laugh. After all, the stock market has gone pretty steadily up for 50 years, hasn't it? And since the odd-lot man is a heavy buyer of the market leaders—the 100 stocks that usually account for two-thirds of the exchange volume—he has made out pretty well over the long pull.

On the other hand, many a big speculator, like Daniel Drew, has died broke.

"A bull can make money. A bear can make money. But a hog never can."

That's one to remember.

The desire to make money leads most people into the market.

Call it ambition or greed, it remains the prime motivating force of our whole business system, including the stock market.

But greed is always dangerous. It's an engine without a governor.

So you made a killing once in the market. Good. You were lucky. Don't think you can make one every day.

If you own a good stock, one that's paying you a good return on your money and seems to go on doing so, hang on to it. Don't keep looking for greener pastures, bigger profits. And forget about the other fellow and the killing he made—or says he made. Maybe he can afford to speculate better than you can.

In short, if you're an investor, act like one.

The Careless Capitalists

CARTER F. HENDERSON and
ALBERT C. LASHER

Do you, as an investor in a company, have any influence in management's financial decisions? Can you, a single individual, in any way protect the price of your stock? Two experienced financial consultants, Carter F. Henderson and Albert C. Lasher, answer such inquiries in the following selection. Using several examples they illustrate how one single shareholder has gained the attention, respect (and fear) of a corporation's directors.

*I*F you are one of the more than twenty million Americans who own stock in U.S. corporations, chances are you only know one fact about your investment—how much your shares were worth at the close of yesterday's stock market.

You probably don't know the size or trend of your companies' sales and profits, the amount of their dividends, the names of their presidents, the range of the products they make, or that you have the power to influence the way they are managed.

To put it quite bluntly, you are a careless capitalist.

Even if you earn a relatively high income of $10,000 after taxes it still takes you an entire year to save $500 or $600, according to the United States Department of Commerce. You are able to save this money because you have decided to deny yourself some of the good things of life today so you can build a portfolio of investments that will grow in value and help make tomorrow's dreams come true. A college education for your children, a new home, a small business of your own, security in your old age, these are the kinds of things you can look forward to if you have capital working for you in the form of common stocks.

There's a good chance that your investment in stocks represents one of your largest single assets, possibly the largest, ranking with your life insurance and the equity in your home.

Common sense suggests that you would devote at least as much time to these hard-earned investments as you do to cleaning the family car, mowing the lawn, or watching television. But the fact is that the average American stockholder seemingly couldn't care less about what's happening to the corporations whose shares he owns.

A famous survey, for example, has shown that a staggering percentage of stockholders can't name a single one of their companies' products. To make matters worse, many stockholders who do name them guess wrongly, i.e., Swift & Company makes trucks, General Motors makes gasoline.

It's a newsworthy event when more than 1 per cent of a corporation's stockholders turn up at the annual meeting. Many of those who do attend come for the free lunch, sample products, or the lack of anything better to do. When American Telephone & Telegraph told its stockholders that luncheon would be served at their 1960 meeting, more than 11,000 people jammed the hall. Several years later, when lunch was eliminated, attendance collapsed to less than 3000.

Not long ago, there was a sudden flurry of buying activity in the stock of a little-known company called Data-Control Systems, of Danbury, Connecticut. Wall Street was dismayed until someone realized that many people were apparently grabbing the company's shares thinking they were investing in the Control Data Corporation, of Minneapolis, a big and successful computer manufacturer.

United States Attorney offices across the nation are flooded with an unending stream of complaints from casual capitalists who have bought stock in companies solely on the basis of high-pressure solicitation. The treasurer of a large Midwestern bank, for instance, purchased $8000 worth of Canadian mining stock after a ten-minute telephone call from Jersey City, New Jersey. Four months later, the banker sold his shares for 25 cents on the dollar.

Every time American Telephone & Telegraph gives its stock-holders the right to buy additional shares below the going market price, thousands of A.T.&T. investors casually allow hundreds of thousands of dollars worth of their "rights" to expire despite repeated warnings from the telephone company's management.

And in New York, Delaware, Pennsylvania, and other states where large numbers of companies are incorporated, a king's ransom in dividends cascades into the states' coffers every year because the stockholders legally entitled to these payments have lost or abandoned their stock certificates and have disappeared from sight without bothering to leave forwarding addresses.

Some cynical brokers who have grown rich buying and selling stock for America's share-owning millions brand the average stockholder as far more than a careless capitalist. They call him a downright boob. "What would we do without them," says the thirty-eight-year-old vice-president of one of the biggest broker-age firms on Wall Street. "They buy when we're ready to dump, and they sell when we figure the market has bottomed out and is ready to turn around."

One of the favorite stock market barometers, as a matter of fact, is the odd-lot index that measures the buying and selling of less than one-hundred-share lots of stock. This index, in effect, reflects the activities of the Wall Street equivalent of the two-dollar bettor. When the little man is buying, many Wall Street pros figure the market is about to go lower. But when he gets scared and starts to sell, these same pros figure that's the time to jump in and grab the bargains before the market heads for higher ground.

In the face of evidence such as this, it would appear that the careless attitude of American stockholders would rule them out as a force in shaping the destinies of the companies they own. This conclusion has indeed been espoused over the years by a number of well-known students of business and finance.

Adolf A. Berle, Jr., and Gardiner C. Means were among the first to outline these views in their book *The Modern Corporation and Private Property,* published in 1932. Messrs Berle and Means concluded that the widely dispersed ownership of most large corporations has resulted in a shift of operating control from the people who own these companies to the hired hands who manage them. This, in turn, makes it extremely difficult for stockholders to throw an inept management out on its ear, and extremely easy for these highly paid executives to retain effective control of the company until they retire or die.

"The stockholder in the modern corporation is neither willing nor able to exercise his legal sovereignty," says economist and management consultant Peter F. Drucker in *The Future of Industrial Man.* "In the great majority of cases he never casts his vote but signs a proxy made out beforehand to and by the management. He exerts no influence upon the selection of new managers who are chosen through co-option by the management in power. The stockholder exercises no influence upon the decisions of management. As a rule he neither confirms nor repudiates them; he does not even know about them and does not want to know about them."

In his provocative book *The Paper Economy* lawyer David T. Bazelon proclaimed, "Large publicly-held corporations are not private property and they are not controlled by their stockholders. Where did anybody get the idea that they were?"

It would be outrageously naïve to suggest that stockholders control the corporations they legally own. But it would be equally naïve to say that they have no control over them at all.

Consider the following random examples of how stockholders have influenced decisions affecting corporations whose shares they own:

General Baking Company stockholders rejected a one-third increase in the number of shares available for purchase at a discount by company executives, while the share owners of the

Sayre & Fisher Company vetoed a similar executive stock option plan altogether.

Owners of New York's Oakite Products, Inc., rejected a management proposal to merge their company with Calgon Corporation of Pittsburgh.

Stockholders' objections caused Grow Chemical Company and Chris-Craft Industries, Inc., to break off merger talks before even bringing the proposal to a vote. Adverse stockholder reaction was also responsible for the collapse of merger plans between Consolidated Foods Corporation and United Artists, Inc. Said Consolidated's Chairman, Nathan Cummings, "The figures were right, but some of our stockholders thought it would be too radical a move."

After stockholders of Boise Cascade Corporation voted overwhelmingly in favor of a merger with Rust Craft Greeting Cards, Inc., Rust Craft's share owners turned it down.

Stockholders of the well-known Paramount Pictures Corporation and the lesser-known Elgeet Optical Company of Rochester, New York, were each able to gain representation on their companies' boards of directors by threatening long and costly proxy fights.

And an increasing number of stockholders of firms such as Atlantic Research, Transcontinental Investing and McCrory Corporation have used legal action—or the threat of legal action—to get members of management to reimburse their companies personally for what the owners insisted were costly business blunders.

The significant test is what you or any other individual stockholder could do on your own to influence the fortunes of a giant corporation in which you have an infinitesimal interest—say less than .0006 per cent of its outstanding shares.

One stockholder who took this test and passed it with colors flying is a pepper-pot Detroit lawyer in his sixties named Sol A. Dann, who apparently thinks of himself as the Don Quixote of the corporate world. He even has a Sancho Panza in the person of Karl S. Horvath, a small stockholder and disenchanted former employee of the Chrysler Corporation—the auto giant against which Dann rode to battle. (Mr. Dann has a propensity for auto companies as adversaries, having previously tilted with General Motors, American Motors Corporation, and the old Studebaker-Packard Company.)

Sol Dann owned 5100 shares of Chrysler's stock, or less than .0006 per cent of the company's 9 million shares outstanding when he stood up at Chrysler's 1960 annual meeting and held forth on the big corporation's ills for one hour and twenty minutes.

In the course of his harangue, Dann noted that Chrysler had lost more than $34 million in 1958, and $5 million in 1959, and had run up $250 million in long-term debt from a standing start in 1953. As if that wasn't enough bad news, the company had slashed its dividend from $4 in 1957 to $1 in 1959.

Mr. Dann accused Chrysler's top brass of a variety of generally undocumented sins, not the least of which were cupidity and stupidity. One of the few specific charges he made was that Chrysler's management was in cahoots with some of its suppliers. He accused the company's executives of paying "up to $300 a ton for steel while its competitors are paying only $150."

This charge was one of several that Chrysler Chairman L. L. "Tex" Colbert attempted to refute—the rest he ignored. Mr. Dann was also largely ignored by Detroit's daily newspapers, which failed to mention, not only his lengthy exchange with Mr. Colbert, but the fact that he was present at the meeting in the first place.

Sol Dann's obscurity did not last long. As it turned out, at least one member of Chrysler's top management group had been a stockholder in a supplier company. Chrysler's newly appointed president, William C. Newberg, had held important interests in two of the auto maker's suppliers and resigned two months after the meeting.

Some of Dann's charges, loose as they were, seemed to have hit home. Suits and countersuits were filed in the Delaware courts by Dann, Chrysler, and an assortment of Chrysler stockholders, officers, and former officers, including Mr. Newberg. (The main legal battle emanated from Delaware because Chrysler, like many other U.S. companies, is officially domiciled in that state.) Recriminations were exchanged in the press between the battlers. On July 27, 1961, about a year after Newberg's resignation, Tex Colbert himself resigned as chairman and president of Chrysler and became chairman of the company's Canadian subsidiary. A new top management team was installed with ex-accountant Lynn A. Townsend as president.

A good many observers thought there was little that Townsend and his men could do to turn the ailing Chrysler Corporation around. The company's 1961 sales fell to $2.1 billion, compared to 1957's record $3.6 billion. In February 1962, Chrysler's shares of the new car market sank to a postwar low of 8.3 per cent. Stringent cost-cutting produced some profit, but the $1.24 a share Chrysler earned in 1961—down from $3.61 the year before—did little to assuage stockholders' fears that their company might be riding down the road to ruin.

But the new management took hold and Chrysler started hitting the comeback trail. The year 1966 was the most successful sales year in the company's history with volume at a record $5.6 billion, and its share of the new car market at a solid 16.7 per cent.

Today, Sol Dann, who spent most of the five years between 1958 and 1963 engaged in a legal war against Chrysler, is satisfied with the way things came out, even though his claims against the company were thrown out by the courts. "When St. Peter asks me what I've done with my life," he says, "I'll tell him I've raised a good family and saved Chrysler."

But the rewards have been far more than spiritual for Chrysler stockholders who refused to ditch the company during its years of adversity. Mr. Dann, for example, paid about $350,000 for his 5100 shares. The stock was split twice in 1963, a 4 per cent stock dividend was declared the following year, and if Sol Dann had sold his shares when Chrysler hit its high he would have received the $350,000 he originally paid for his shares plus a bonus in excess of $1 million—not counting dividends.

The Chrysler case illustrates, among other things, one of the most important levers that stockholders have to pry concessions from management; the ability to embarrass the officers and directors personally by uninhibited public criticism. A pointed question raised at an annual meeting by the owner of ten shares, for example, is no less pointed than one asked by the owner of ten thousand shares. And management's handling of the question—be it brilliant or ludicrously inept—may, within hours, be relayed to every corner of the nation by private wire, news ticker, and the press.

There is no all-embracing reason why American stockholders are so lackadaisical about their painfully acquired investments.

Some stockholders say they don't understand what business is all about even though the federal government, stock exchanges, brokerage houses, enlightened corporate management, and the press have made it possible for today's investor to follow the fortunes of his shares with consummate ease.

Other stockholders take the position that the managements of their companies know best and should be left alone to run the business as they see fit. These investors would do well to pay more attention to the financial sections of their daily newspapers, which carry a steady flow of stories about management mishaps, such as the $250 million the Ford Motor Company lost on its Edsel, and the $425 million the General Dynamics Corporation frittered away on its 880 and 990 jet transport planes.

Still other stockholders simply don't want to be bothered looking after their investments, an attitude well calculated to produce only one kind of payoff—a bundle of beautifully engraved stock certificates ideally suited for papering the family playroom. . . .

Support and Resistance

WILLIAM L. JILER

/

There are innumerable ways to devise charts depicting the
behavior of the stock market and of individual stocks.
Chart analysis is a complex and often misunderstood
subject. The best known and respected chart expert and
market technician is William L. Jiler, the President of
Trendline (a Division of Standard and Poor's Corporation).
A valuable chart pattern for investors to know is that of
"support and resistance." Jiler, in the following selection,
explains why this is so valuable and illustrates how it can
be used to best advantage.

HAVE you ever bought a stock, watched it decline in price, and yearned to sell out for what you paid for it? Have you ever sold a stock, watched it go up after you had sold it, and wished you had an opportunity to buy it again at the original price? Well, you are not alone. These are common human reactions, and they show up on the stock charts by creating *support* and *resistance*.

A support level is that price at which one may expect a considerable increase in the demand for a stock, or buying. A resistance level is that price at which one may expect a considerable increase in the supply, or selling. Such levels are not hard to find: for example, any price level where a great deal of stock has changed hands may be pegged as a support or resistance level (the terms are interchangeable, as will be seen). Heavy turnover in a given price area produces what analysts call a congestion range on the chart, as in Figure 1.

Figure 1 How Resistance Forms.

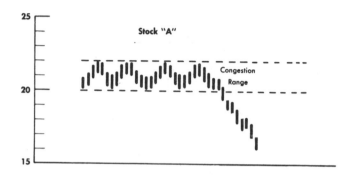

Let's assume that you and hundreds of other investors bought stock A at a range between $20 and $22 a share, and then saw it slip down to $16. The first reaction of the typical buyer will be to hold on, in hope that the stock will rebound, climb above $22, and show a profit that will vindicate the buyer's judgment. However, if stock A remains depressed, many buyers will begin to think it would be great just to break even. So if the stock finally heads back upward, the disposition to sell will grow stronger as it gets closer and closer to the breakeven point. Naturally, the more trading (or congestion) that occurred in the $20–$22 price range, the greater the supply of stock for sale. *Hence, the greater the resistance at that point to a further advance.*

Now, suppose that, after all those investors bought stock A between $20 and $22, it went *up* instead of *down*. The analyst will peg that zone as a *support area*. That is, he would expect that, if stock A, having risen to $25 a share, or more, should slide back, it would meet new buying demand as it returned to the $20–$22 range. There are a number of reasonable explanations. For one thing, those who *sold* out when the stock was at $20–$22 have been kicking themselves all the time it was moving up, and many may be eager to buy back the stock at the price at which they sold it, and thus get "back on board" without embarrassment. They may then say that they were right all along about the great prospects of stock A. Another group—among those who *bought* in the $20–$22 range, or who thought of buying at the time but saw the stock *"get away"* from them—may plan to buy any time it gets back to that price. A third type of major buying may develop from traders who sold short on the rise, and purchase stock to cash in their profits when it falls back.

The analyst usually draws support and resistance points or zones in horizontal lines on his chart. For example, referring to Figure 2, if a stock trades for some time between $20 and

Figure 2   How Support Forms.

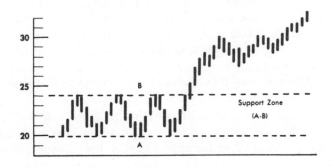

$24, the support level becomes outlined at $20 (line A) and the resistance level at $24 (line B). Once prices break above the resistance level of $24, the entire former range (between A and B) becomes a support area, or zone.

As the market develops, a support level may become a resistance level, and vice versa. (See Figure 3.) Suppose that

Figure 3   Old Resistance Becomes New Support

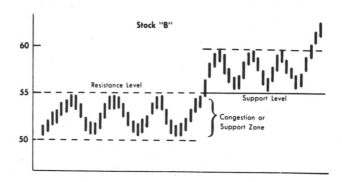

stock B has seesawed between 50 and 55 for several months. During this period, we would correctly label 50 as the support level and 55 as the resistance level. Now, if prices one day break through and close* above 55, this former resistance level automatically becomes a new support level. The many investors who *bought* the stock at 55 at last have found that their judgment was sound, because now they have a paper profit, and some may be willing to buy more at that level. The many who *sold* at 55 may be eager to "get on board again" at that price, for the reason given above.

If the breakout had been *down*—that is, if stock B had fallen below 50, then 50 would switch from a support to a resistance level. All buyers at 50 and over would then have losses and many might want to "break even" if prices get back to 50 or over.

---

* It might be noted here that analysts regard the closing price as more significant than the "inter-day" high and low, largely on the ground that the average investor looks for, and reacts to, the closing price in his morning newspaper. Stock manipulators have been known to exploit this fact by rigging the last deal of the day, at a price quite different from the bulk of the day's trading.

An individual stock (or an average, for that matter) may well meet support or resistance at certain other price levels established in the minds of investors, either historically or quite recently. How often does one hear someone say, "I always make money buying such-and-such stock at 20 and selling at 40."* A study of the cyclical stocks (those whose fluctuations follow the ups and downs of the business cycle most closely, such as steels and other basic industrials) reveals that many of them have favorite historic turning points.

Even on the short range, the highs and lows of a stock's fluctuations may have a psychological effect on investors, and thus become minor levels of support and resistance. To illustrate, suppose you held some stock that was rising in the market, and had just about decided to sell, when suddenly it began to drop from new highs. Wouldn't you feel you had missed a golden opportunity to "sell at the top"? And if, while you were brooding about it, your stock rallied to the previous high, wouldn't you be inclined to get out there? If enough buyers feel that way, this high point can form a potent resistance level, even though the first time around, it was reached on very light trading.

The 50% Rule

When a stock, or the market as a whole, has swung violently up or down, professionals look for a "technical rebound" or "technical reaction." That is, stocks tend to snap back, a third to two-thirds of the way. If stocks have jumped, the quick-trader sells to cash in on profits; if they've dropped, the "bargain hunters" rush in. Then, the stock may resume the original trend. In longer-range swings, there is a tendency for support or resistance to develop when the stock retraces half of the ground won, or lost, in the last move. For example, if a stock has advanced from

---

* The round number is another common support or resistance level—simply because many investors set their goals in multiples of ten, or even five.

20 to 60 without serious interruption and then goes into a down-trend, there's a good chance that it will find support at a level midway in the previous advance. Therefore, half of the 40-point gain, or 20 points, can be subtracted from the high to find a potential support level at 40. (See Figure 4.)

Figure 4   The 50% Rule.

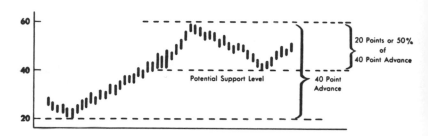

Unusual Volume

We have noted that a "congestion range" on the chart shows that a lot of shares have changed hands at a given price for a relatively extended time, and makes this price a probable support or resistance level. Logically, it should not matter too much, however, whether the trading took weeks, or occurred more or less in a relatively short time, as long as trading activity is heavy. A brief flareup of volume during a price movement, *even though it does not appear on the chart to have interrupted the price trend,* often discloses a potent support or resistance area which later proves effective in checking a decline or a rally.

For example, a stock may be rising on average volume and hit, say, $14 a share, whereupon trading suddenly expands sharply. Without any extraordinary acceleration, the price continues to rise, but at about 16, the volume subsides to "normal," or the rate prevailing before the flareup. The price may now continue upward, fall back or move "sideways," but in any case, the chartist will mark this 14-to-16 area as a *High Volume Zone*, and will look for support or resistance in this area. The principle works just as well on a decline, of course. (For examples of High Volume Zones, see the charts at the end of this [selection].)

When the volume of trading expands sharply as a stock reaches an unexpected support or resistance level, the *potency* of that level tends to be increased. Paradoxically, a sharp *drop* in volume sometimes appears to have the same significance! Why this should happen is problematical; perhaps many of those interested in a stock withdraw from the market at what they regard as a significant turning point to see which way it will jump. The drop in volume therefore would be a tip-off to a shift in market psychology associated with a specific price level. In any case, while volume goes *up* more often than *down* at support and resistance levels, it goes down often enough to warrant the consideration of the analyst.

Another note on volume: when a stock breaks out of a congestion zone in which it has been trading, the analyst will, as always, watch the volume to help determine whether the breakout is "valid," rather than just a flash in the pan. It is helpful to know that a valid breakout on the rise (penetrating a resistance level) usually is accompanied by an increase in volume. On the other hand, a valid "downside" breakout (penetrating a support level), usually occurs on light volume first, which must be confirmed by an increase in volume as the price continues to decline.

Like trendlines, support and resistance can be found at almost any time and on any chart. In fact, they are the basic components that make up all the more sophisticated patterns that chartists look for in trying to predict price movement. An object in motion (a trend) will continue in motion until it meets an opposing force (support or resistance). The chart reader continually works with both these tools, and he finds that they help each other. Trendlines help confirm support and resistance levels, while support and resistance levels help confirm and anticipate new trendlines.

On daily charts,* it is prudent to consider the *bottom* of a support zone as more valid than the *top*. Very frequently, a rising stock will react back *into* a support zone and then resume its advance. (See Figure 5.) A new support level may then form

Figure 5 Valid Support Levels.

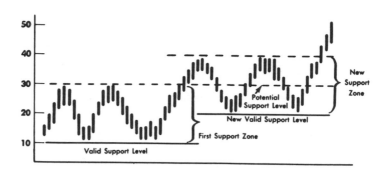

within the previous support zone, and become the next valid support.

The study of support and resistance can tell the investor whether his ship is on course. As long as support levels hold firm, he can feel that his stock is doing well, and he may buy more. If his stock breaks through a support level, he has cause for concern, and may consider selling out.

Some traders use their studies of support and resistance to set up practical trading systems. They *buy* when stocks have fallen

* Weekly and monthly charts also reveal support and resistance levels, and are convenient for spotting long-established, or "historic" levels of individual stocks. . . . The potency of resistance and support levels has a tendency to fade with time, but the chartist will find many surprising examples which have proved to be significant even after several years have elapsed.

to support levels, or when stocks have risen and broken through resistance levels. They sell when stocks hit resistance levels or fall through support levels.

Another technique may be as follows: If a stock breaks out of a trading range of 50–55 and climbs, say, to 58, the previous resistance point of 55 becomes a support zone. The short-swing trader may not wish to hold on to the stock if, on a downswing, it penetrates the 55 level. Longer-range traders may be content to hold the stock as long as the lower level of the support zone (50) is not broken.

The sophisticated investor uses the support-and-resistance concept to help him decide in advance at what price he should instruct his broker to sell, in order to cash in his profits on a market rise. In a major downtrend, he uses it to find a level where a rally is likely to develop, at which point he may close out a short position (buy stock cheaply to replace shares he sold short at a higher price), or he may plan new investment buying.

Screening the Hopeful from the Hopeless at the $2 Window; and Some Thoughts on When to Sell

IRA U. COBLEIGH

Author Ira U. Cobleigh is a director of six corporations, a popular lecturer on finance, and a frequent guest on television and radio programs. Very low-priced stocks have always been a controversial subject among investment professionals, and all would agree with Mr. Cobleigh that these are the "riskiest of securities." However, since there have been so many successful speculations in these "cheap" stocks, there must be some method with a chance at winning. This article presents Cobleigh's analysis of the best approach for making profits in this area.

. . . **S**TOCKS at the $2 window can pay off; and . . . to neglect this market sector may be to miss priceless opportunities for gleaning profits.

Before plunging rashly into these dangerous and deceptive market waters, however, it is important to develop some effective method or technique for selection of those minishares that offer legitimate prospects for growth and gain; and the rejection of the corporate weaklings, the poorly managed, the woefully under-financed and the tired and deeply troubled ones with no place to go.

At every stage of the market there is a long list of issues quoted at low prices. In mid-1962 there were thousands of stocks on display at the $2 window due to (1) the sharp market decline in June of that year (23% on the Dow Jones Industrial Average) and (2) the hundreds of issues of shares of new companies offered a year earlier, many of which declined dismally. (Nineteen sixty-one was a peak year for "Regulation A" Underwritings—corporate issues raising $300,000 or less.) Of course minishares appear in greatest profusion in the early phases of bull markets, and after sharp market declines. These are in fact the ideal times for low-altitude shopping.

Regardless of the time in which you enter this bargain basement, however, there are certain basic things you should know about the issues you are considering. You must develop satisfactory evidence that the company you're speculating in has (1) the essential ingredients for survival, (2) potentials for growth and gain and (3) capability of attracting market sponsorship and an animated speculative following. You must also bear in mind that regardless of the fundamental values in any stock—sturdy or flimsy—if it doesn't attract more buying than selling, it won't go up! Indeed, many stocks go up spectacularly without any persuasive statistical motivation simply because they have become popular and are "touted" in board rooms from coast to coast. This sudden popularity stimulating strong price uptrends is often due to nothing more substantial than a rumor—of an oil strike in Australia, of a new patent or process; of possible acquisition or merger; of entry into an exciting new product or service field. Almost anything that whiffs of romance, glamour or hope can make a low-priced stock advance madly when enough traders "get the message."

Therefore, in listing criteria for the selection of possibly rewarding ministocks, we must make ample allowance for this unknown and mystical element—the fad or fashion for a given industry, or issues within it at a particular time. Riding the tide or trend of market fashion can reward a trader far more richly than the buying of an an issue on the basis of a good balance sheet and a defined uptrend in earnings in an unglamourous or non-popular industry. Remember how baby uranium shares soared in 1956? (There were 400 new uranium issues that year.) Most uranium companies founded in 1955/6 are now out of business, but while the industry was hot, share gains within six months of 500% to 1,000% were by no means uncommon. In 1961, bowling was erroneously assumed to be the coming major pastime of mankind. The leading stocks here, American Machine & Foundry and Brunswick, soared, followed by a spate of satellite issues—Bowl-Mor (pinsetters), Bar-Cris (alley builders) and a dozen sizeable bowling alley chains. AMF descended from a 1961 high of 63⅝ to a 1966 low of 13½. Brunswick dipped from 74⅞ in 1961 to a 1966 low of 6. (At this point Brunswick became a "turnaround" situation.) Bowl-Mor and Bar-Cris went bankrupt, and several alley chains were reorganized and their shares descending to the $2 window—near the sill! In 1967/8 silver and computer stocks could do no wrong. In the spring of 1968 shares in nursing homes, and vendors of fried chicken and hamburgers were all the rage.

Accordingly, with all your hopes and dreams of killings in penny stocks, be mindful of the capricious influence of market popularity on share prices. Riding a fad can often produce exciting market gains regardless of the condition of the economy; but you must be ready to jump out nimbly before your modish stock goes out of style or you may be left holding "a cluck." In the stock market, "nothing recedes like excess."

Having highlighted this major psychological phenomenon, the whims and caprices of speculative markets, let us now move on to those more logical elements that influence stock prices. What should you know about a company to formulate an opinion as to whether to buy or bypass its modestly priced stock?

You should know:
1. Where the company is located.
2. How long it has been in business.
3. How many shares it has outstanding and where they are traded.
4. Kind of business the company is in, and something about

its products, processes, services, its customers and markets.

5. Latest 12 months' earnings (if any) and recent balance sheet figures.

6. The present officers and directors and something about management capability. (Has new management taken over?)

7. Market price range of common stock in past and current year, and some estimate or record of daily trading volume.

8. Current economic factors that might stimulate the earnings potential of the company and its industrial sector.

9. Whether new capital must be raised to assure corporate survival.

10. Does management own a substantial amount (20% or more) of stock?

11. Is there a thin floating supply of shares?

Most of this information can be obtained from the latest annual report of the company or from a prospectus, in the case of a new issue. Supplementary statistical material may be obtained from reports or market letters prepared by brokers, and by investment services such as Standard & Poor's; and possibly from current articles or items about the subject company in the daily financial pages or in one of the investor periodicals (*Commercial Financial Chronicle, Forbes, Barron's, Financial World,* etc.). The National Quotation Bureau's "Black Book" supplies information on many small companies. Writing the company president requesting information about its position and prospects is also suggested; although sometimes the president won't answer.

Armed with useful data gleaned from these or any other available sources, you are ready to formulate a decision about the attractiveness (if any) of a particular stock at its prevailing price. Before reaching this decision, you should ask yourself these questions:

1. Does the company have enough working capital to survive? Three out of five new companies are not alive on their fifth birthday; and insufficient money is, next to man-

agerial incompetence, the principal cause of demise. If the company can survive, even though its present plight is desperate, a day may come when its stock will be enthusiastically sought and bought by speculators.

2. Is it in a rapidly growing industry? And does it offer products or services in great present or potential demand?

3. If it is a metal or mineral enterprise, are these natural resources in a rising demand and price trend?

4. If it's an oil or mineral exploration, are the company's properties close to proven ore bodies or existing commercial production?

5. Have the men in management records of earlier business success?

6. Are patents or processes involved properly protected? Does the innovation have promise of a genuine breakthrough in a major market?

7. Could the company be attractive "takeover bait" because of (a) a tax loss carry forward, (b) a patent or process or established market, (c) realty holdings, forest or mineral resources?

8. Is there a responsible underwriting or brokerage firm actively interested in the stock and providing market sponsorship for it?

9. Is it a fledgling new company or a possible turnaround situation? (Turnarounds generally involve less risk.)

10. Has the stock shown any evidence of manipulation? (If so, you may be "sucked in" and "left holding the bag" after the manipulating vultures have unloaded.)

11. What is a reasonable estimate of net profits per share two years hence?

If a majority of the answers to questions 1–8 are affirmative (negative on 10 and adequate on 11), then you probably have a stock that will at least give you a run for your money. Your chances may be further improved if you have the guidance of some seasoned investors with capability and judgment who may also have looked into this company, and evaluated its prospects. In any event, there'll be plenty of risk. They're never "blue chips" at $2 a share!

These are some of the bench marks that might well be applied in the appraisal of low-priced shares. They should help to steer you away from flimsy ventures or outright frauds. On that last point, under no circumstances buy over the telephone an unknown issue at an unchecked price from a total stranger. He may eagerly convince you that "the property adjoining the acreage of this company has increased 1,000% in value in the past year." The guy trying to lay off this stock on you is a crook, a hustler, a boiler-shop operator intent on selling you "moose pasture." Hang up on him, because he may be fatally persuasive, if you listen to him long enough!

Where Should You Do Your Shopping?

The next question is "where to shop?" Not on the New York Stock Exchange because, as this was written (August 1, 1968), not a single share trading there was selling as low as $5. The next stop is the American Stock Exchange where 25 issues were still on display (also August 1, 1968) at the $2 window. As mentioned earlier, the AMEX authorities in May 1968 urged some 30 companies (whose shares were listed there) that they reverse split their common stocks so that these issues would no longer sell in the $5 price range (and hence be theoretically less attractive targets for witless and uninformed speculation). There were 19 issues below $5 on the National Exchange; none on the Boston, Cincinnati, Detroit, Philadelphia-Baltimore-Washington, or Midwest Exchanges; one on the Pittsburgh Exchange; a few on the Pacific Coast Exchange, and a batch of them, mostly mining issues, on the Salt Lake City and Spokane Exchanges. There are also, of course, droves of penny stocks on the Toronto and Vancouver Exchanges but we are not including them because meaningful information about many of them is difficult to obtain; and speculators have become quite disinterested in trading in Canadian issues because of the 18¾% Equalization Tax charged American investors.

We conclude then that the main arenas for low-priced trading today are (1) on the AMEX, (2) National Stock Exchange, (3) Salt Lake City and Spokane Exchanges and (4) the vast and nationwide over-the-counter (OTC) market.

We should logically divide this OTC market into two sections— new issues and seasoned ones (which of course are far more numerous).

The New Issue Market

There has never been such a golden time for original subscription to new issues as in 1967/8. Hundreds of companies have brought their common stocks to the public for the first time, and subscribers have had a field day with over 90% of all new issues showing an advance over subscription price in the past 18 months. To illustrate the recent profit windfalls gleaned in this section of the $2 window, just glance over the following tabulation of new issues and their market performance OTC, in the first seven months of 1968.

New Low-Priced Stock Issues
January–August 1968

Company	Offering Dated	Offering Price	July 23, 1968 Bid Price
Alden Electronic & Impulse Recording Equipment Co., Inc.	Mar. 19	5	8¼
Allied Aero Industries, Inc.	Mar. 5	4¾	8½
Applied Synthetics Corp.	May 22	1¾	13¾
Astrosystems, Inc.	Jan. 4	5	17½
Automation Sciences, Inc.	June 11	4	15
Basic Leasing Corp.	Mar. 6	3	8
Brogan Associates, Inc.	Apr. 26	3	13
CSI Computer Systems, Inc.	Apr. 24	5	9¼

New Low-Priced Stock Issues (Continued)
January–August 1968

Company	Offering Dated	Offering Price	July 23, 1968 Bid Price
Childhood Productions	Jan. 2	5	12
Citation Manufacturing Co.	May 22	5	12
Comark, Inc.	June 20	3	13½
Commercial Programming Unlimited, Inc.	June 20	5	9
Comp-U-Check, Inc.	Apr. 24	3½	6½
Comptran Computer Corp.	July 2	2.35	8
Computer Environments Corp.	Apr. 18	5	13
Data Systems Analysts, Inc.	July 12	5	10¾
Datatronics, Inc.	June 10	4	8½
Doktor Pet Centers, Inc.	June 11	5	14
Electron-Machine Corp.	July 3	2	3⅜
Federal Data Processing Corp.	Apr. 5	4	8½
Gamma Process Co.	Jan. 31	5	34¼
Goody's, Inc.	July 11	5	11¼
Ground/data Corp.	June 24	2	4¼
Hydro-Ski International Corp.	Apr. 29	2	5
International Computing Service, Inc.	July 8	4	7¼
Juness Industries, Inc.	Feb. 14	5	4
Leasing Consultants, Inc.	Feb. 29	2	12½
Lectro Computer Leasing Corp.	Mar. 7	5	9¾
Life Sciences, Inc.	May 7	5	8½
M.P.C., Inc.	Apr. 4	5	5⅝
Mechtron Corp.	May 21	3¾	16½
Medi Card, Inc.	June 19	5	6¾
Mr. Swiss of America, Inc.	June 17	5	13
Northern Precision Laboratories, Inc.	Feb. 8	3	9
Old Florida Rum Co.	July 15	2¼	2¾
Petrodyne Industries, Inc.	July 2	5	10½
Pharmaceutical Savings Plan	Feb. 14	5	9½
Plain 'n Fancy Donuts of America, Inc.	June 18	5	6

January-August 1968
New Low-Priced Stock Issues (Continued)

Company	Offering Dated	Offering Price	July 23, 1968 Bid Price
Private and Computer Schools, Inc.	April 17	5	18½
Radiation Machinery Corp.	Jan. 9	3	44
Radioptics, Inc.	Apr. 5	5	7
Radix Corp.	Mar. 12	5	16¼
Republic Systems & Programming, Inc.	Feb. 5	2¾	8⅞
Rex Plastics, Inc.	Apr. 16	4	9¾
Saucy Susan Products, Inc.	May 7	2	3¼
Sierra Silver Mining Co.	Mar. 18	1	3⅜
Stanlift Corp.	June 25	5	6¾
Sun-Glo Products Corp.	May 9	3½	6½
Thermo Nat'l Industries, Inc.	Jan. 4	4½	8¾
Trio Laboratories, Inc.	Feb. 21	5	6¾
Unico Environmental Instruments, Inc.	June 14	5	8¾

Many of these stocks spurted not because their future was so notably glamorous but because of simple demand-supply forces. If the issue is 100,000 shares and the underwriter has orders for 600,000, it's bound to zoom!

This list was not screened or handpicked. It was taken from a tabulation of new issues published by the *OTC Chronicle* (of which the author is Feature Editor). There were, in addition to these, many other issues (including Regulation A issues of $300,-000 or less) which have not been included because they were too small and their trading markets too limited and regional.

It is apparent that buying these new issues has recently been an almost sure-fire way to glean swift market profits. To buy these newcomers, you must learn about them well in advance of public offering so that you know where to place your subscription. Information about securities in registration is given, often months in advance, in the columns of *Investment Dealer's*

Digest and the *Commercial & Financial Chronicle*. You should also acquaint yourself with the underwriting houses bringing out new issues. Some of these firms have been in business for years and have established good records for origination of offerings of dynamically growing companies whose shares have gained dramatically. A good underwriting name is, however, no guarantee that the company will survive and prosper, but it does offer some insurance that the issue has been carefully investigated.

You should also know how to derive useful information from a prospectus (which is about the dreariest piece of literature you'll ever come across!). The prospectus of a young company will play down any romance in its stock. It will usually depict meager sales and earnings (often losses) and a weak working capital position (to be corrected presumably by the infusion of capital from the underwriting). You must convince yourself that the company has products or services that can generate increased sales and profits. The list of officers and directors given may give you some basis for confidence in management. Assure yourself, too, that the money being raised will permit the company to operate for at least two years even though no net earnings may be reported during that period.

Place your order as far in advance as possible, and try to buy from more than one house so that your desired subscription can be filled. Even if you cannot buy the amount you wish at the offering price, or do not get allotment of your order in full, you may wish to buy shares in the after-market; although you may have to pay a higher price. Again, in these new issues, it's the popular or fashionable ones that soar; you may want to sell in a hurry if the issue more than doubles in a few days. So buy what's in vogue.

Seasoned Issues

While in recent months probably the most assured gains have been made in the OTC market by subscription to these new issues, the OTC market in existing issues has also been responsive to eager buying. Excellent results have been achieved in oils such as Clinton which rose in 1967/8 from 1 to 14; White Shield from 2 to 20; and in many junior electronics, industrial and mineral shares; and in motels, food service and computer-oriented shares.

Panoramic Diversity

In the broad OTC market, as well as on the exchanges where low-priced issues trade, the leading categories of speculative issues are usually oils and minerals. This is probably owing to the fact that such companies are easy to start and often require rather modest amounts of capital. Many hopeful mineral companies are in fact not in operation but have ownership of mineral rights on acreage, which may some day be worth a lot of money if somebody else starts drilling successfully nearby. The problems for mineral companies usually come when the decision is made to drill extensively or possibly to build a mill. These operations take capital, and, of course, if after funds have been raised the drilling program proves unproductive, and the company exhausts its capital in pursuing it, the subject stock will dive and the company may even go out of business. These are some of the many risks you take in mineral shares. One thing you must say about these companies is that there's plenty of stock around! It seems fashionable to capitalize mining companies with millions of shares of stock of a penny or no par value.

In "taking a shot" at a mining or mineral stock, you should first consider the demand for the subject element. Right now, for example, the worldwide demand is strong for silver, nickel, sulphur, platinum; but less urgent for lead, zinc and iron. On the Spokane Exchange (renowned habitat of the silver mining shares) any stock you would have bought in the past 18 months would have shown a handsome gain, because the price of silver soared from $1.29 to $2.40 an ounce. Many expect the price of silver to continue to go up as new industrial uses for it create more urgent demand. Gold may one day leap from its official world price of $35 an ounce to $70. If and when it does, gold shares will zoom. There are scores of them at the $2 window, but most of them are Canadian companies. In the U.S. many gold mines with proven reserves have been closed down because they simply could not earn a profit at $35 an ounce. These marginal companies might reopen and operate profitably on $70 gold. Shares in such, bought in advance, could in that event pay off handsomely.

The search for nickel is going on intensively around the world, and some of the baby nickel stocks might reward you. The big daddy here is, of course, International Nickel, responsible for around 70% of the North American production.

Oil In Demand

The global demand for oil continues unabated and petroleum still supplies roughly 55% of the world's energy. Oil shares, traditionally highly speculative, should surely be on your low-priced shopping list. Dozens of them started out at the $2 window and many hopefuls are still there. Mesa, Clinton, White Shield, Basin, Occidental, Coastal States, Hess, Banff, Canadian Homestead and a bunch of land companies with oil beneath have all prospered and showed great market gains. In selecting a low-priced oil stock, assure yourself about honesty and competence of management, make certain that the company has enough money to stay alive and offers legitimate hopes that the land under exploration may turn out to be part of an oil field as Leduc, Cook Inlet or Williston Basin. Some of the best gains in oils occur in little, early phase companies that through good fortune have staked out lease holdings in areas where big strikes by big companies (who have plenty of money for drilling) have later occurred.

Industrial Shares

In selecting industrial shares there are no set rules. Each company is a law unto itself. Most of the speculation here is in newer companies (less than 5 years old) because older ones have either "made it" and their stocks have risen, or they've gone broke. Among newer companies are those in electronic parts and components, toys and gadgets, mobile homes and trailers, small appliances, cosmetics, metal castings, furniture, fried chicken, hamburgers or steaks, restaurant or motel chains, shopping centers, licensing and equipment rentals; plus companies in widely assorted fields: nursing homes, scientific and instrument companies, warehouse and trucking, sporting goods (skis, fishing tackle, etc.), ice cream and soft drinks, and service companies (laundry, employment agencies, computer schools, car washing, rug cleaning).

In insurance there are still quite a few casualty, fire and life companies whose stocks trade at the $2 window. And in computer leasing, software and service, there have been dozens of newcomers in the past two years, quite a few starting out at $5 a share or less.

Many real estate stocks, highly leveraged by mortgage debt ahead of the equity, are found among the lower-priced issues. Disc, Inc., American Land, and Pickwick Organization, all in business for several years, had low-priced common stocks available as this was written.

The shares of companies whose prosperity has waned often sell at the $2 window. Sometimes these will prove to be miserable speculations, even at a dollar or two a share, because they are on their way to the financial flophouse. Others may hover in a twilight zone of survival (possibly Chapter XI of the Bankruptcy Act) and, by fortunate infusions of new capital or management or both, or by a take-over bid be brought back to life. Avien Corp., an electronics company, in 1962/3 sold at 50¢ a share and was in Chapter XI. Its business improved in time, and Avien common sold on AMEX in 1968 as high as 8. An even more dramatic "return from the grave," financially speaking, was Oil Recovery Corp. This company in the 1960's was highly favored by speculators, and its stock sold on April 24, 1961 at $75 a share owing to its imputed prospects for its flooding process for oil recovery. The great promise faded fast and on September 7,

1965 Oil Recovery Common sold at 18 cents! The hopes for its success had been deferred and deferred until, in 1966, Oil Recovery had debts it couldn't cope with; and the assets were about to be sold for account of creditors. At the last minute, a new group put up a little money, extended the debt payments and, a year later, a merger was effected with Basin Petroleum Corp., with Oil Recovery holders winding up owning a share of Basin for each 4 old OR shares held. Basin sold at $13 in August 1968! Quite a reprieve!

In both of these cases, Avien and Oil Recovery, dramatic speculative gains were scored by those bold souls who bought these tired stocks while they were virtually waiting on the undertaker's steps.

Warrants

Another native group of minipriced dwellers in the subway market includes "warrants." These are the will o' wisps of Wall Street. They're not stocks, bonds, debt or equity. They never share in earnings, pay dividends or represent claims on assets; yet they can create some of the most exciting of market gains on very little money invested.

For instance, you could have purchased Jefferson Petrochemical warrants in 1962 at 1⅞. They sold in 1967 as high as 53¼. Between 1966 and 1968 National General warrants rose in price from 2⅝ to a high of 47.

A warrant offers the holder the right to purchase, directly from the subject company, a share or shares (or fractional share) of its common stock at a specified price and during a certain time period (usually from three to five years). There are a few perpetual warrants. Warrants always sell below the price of the stock to which they relate; and they nearly always sell at more than they are mathematically worth. The best time to buy them is when they have no real value at all. For example, there exists a warrant to buy Atlas Corp. common at $6.25 a share without any limitation as to time. On January 5, 1967, Atlas common sold at $3 a share and the warrant (to purchase a share at $6.25) sold on the same day at $1.75! Why? Because if Atlas stock advanced, the warrant would go up parallel with the common stock; and you, the speculator, could in effect make the same trading gain on 100 warrants costing $175 as on 100 shares of the common stock costing $300. In roaring bull markets, warrants do in fact rise faster than the common stocks they're tied to.

The main points to observe in buying warrants are: (1) to get as "long" a warrant as possible—five years or ten years away preferably; (2) to get a warrant in a company, however minuscule or early phase, that offers hopes for rising earning power; (3) to buy your warrant hopefully at one-third or one-fourth of the (then) price of the common stock.

To offer guidance in this exciting area of warrants, here are a few at the $2 window as this was written:

				Aug. 15, 1968
Company	*Stock Purchase Provision*	*Year Expiration*	*Common Stock*	*Price Warrant*
Atlas Corp.	1 share @ $6.25	Perpetual	5⅝	3¼
Brun Sensor Systems	1 share @ $6 to 4/69, then @ $8	1970	4⅜	2¼
ᵀChemcell	1 share @ $10	1970	8¾	2⅞
ᵀClairtone Sound	1 share @ $6.50	1970	5	2⅜
Colonial Acceptance	1 share @ $10	1974	11	3¾
First National Realty	1.15 shares @ $6.75	1971	4¼	2⅝
Hoerner Waldorf	1 share @ $30	1973	20¾	3⅛
Henry's Drive-in	1 share @ $9	1970	8⅞	3¼
Life Investors	1 share @ $12.50 to 2/70, then $15	1975	8½	2
Mitron Research & Dev.	1 share @ $13	1970	8¾	2⅞
Puritan Fashions	1 share @ $13	1981	14	5⅛
ᵀQuebec Natural Gas	1 share @ $15	1976	13⅛	4¼
ᵀTraders Group	1 share @ $15	1972	9¼	2⅛

Note: ᵀ denotes Toronto Stock Exchange.

These warrants are under no circumstance to be construed as recommended, endorsed or offered. The list was presented for illustrative purposes only.

. . . We couldn't begin to cover here the entire range and amazing assortment of stocks and warrants found in industries represented at the $2 window. We have merely endeavored to supply a rough road map to guide you.

The actual task of evaluating the penny shares that attract you, and of deciding which ones are in companies that can generate swift gains—that is your task! Your quest can be fun, it can add excitement and adventure to your life; and it may reward you generously. There are no absolute rules, however, and you may have to play this game of speculation a lot "by ear"—letting out a few sour notes on occasion.

Market Tactics

After you've followed the program set forth—a scanning of the low-priced list, screening of a few interesting-looking ones, gathering needed information about them and exercising your judgment in selection of the likeliest long shots—then you're ready for actual market operation.

Don't scatter your fire. Plan to buy no more than five issues, maybe only two or three that you like very much. Buy "at the market" and buy for cash. Use a well-regarded and responsible broker, preferably a seasoned firm with a long-established reputation for integrity. Spend only money you can afford to lose, because you're buying the riskiest of securities. Have a price target or objective. Decide if you are buying a certain stock for a trading profit within a year or for long-term holding if the company looks like a baby Solitron. Many "old pros" use "operation bait back." They sell half of their holdings if and when they can realize a gain of 100% or more after taxes; and keep the other half which then costs nothing. There are in truth no absolute rules about when to sell, and it is probably true that most traders are shrewder at buying than in timing their selling.

Many people owned Xerox, Occidental Petroleum, or Coastal States Gas ten years ago but sold out too early, missing the major advances in these fortune builders. You'll have to develop your own selling philosophy although as a formula unrelated to conditions or market climate, this bait back idea seems to have merit. A quite uninformed building contractor of my acquaintance made a great deal of money in the market (which he seemed to play by ear). Asked how he decided when to sell he replied: "When my hand itches!" This may be as good a rule as any until we get computers to give us the "sell" answer.

Whenever you make a buy or sell decision, don't cry over it. Everybody goofs in an area as uncertain as the speculation. "He who looks back in the market dies of remorse!"

The Ever-Liquid Account

GERALD M. LOEB

*Every investor has certain needs (other than making
profits) and these can vary from person to person. Some
investors look for peace of mind in their stock portfolio;
for others the stock market can mean excitement and
perhaps the opportunity to try a little risky speculation.
Gerald M. Loeb, one of Wall Street's most respected
authors, is aware of the wide variety of investors' emotional
needs. For the cautious, and particularly those who are
apprehensive about being "fully invested," Loeb describes
one approach to stock market investing.*

*T*HERE is a philosophy of handling investments that perhaps is quickest described by dubbing it "The Ever-Liquid Account."

The name is completely descriptive. Handled in this way, one's funds are *always* liquid. Briefly, in its operation, an ever-liquid account is normally kept fully uninvested; i.e., in cash or equivalent only. "Equivalent" means any kind of really liquid short-term security or commercial paper. Book values and market values are always kept identical. Income is real income; i.e., interest, dividends, capital gains realized and realizable, less capital losses taken or unrealized in the account, which is always marked to the market. Investment and speculation are merged.

My experience with this philosophy of investment is that it gives some people great peace of mind. It seems to prove more profitable in deflationary periods and less so otherwise. I do think that it has a place in certain types of investor thinking. By the nature of the world, everything is today less safe and sure. This method recognizes that fact and does not tend to lull people into false security. In fact, in *apparently* bringing diminishing current returns, it may actually be protecting against large capital losses to be suffered in the future by the always "fully invested" class.

Income and appreciation are obtained in the ever-liquid account by entering the stock market as a buyer when a situation and trend seem clearly enough established so that a paper profit is present immediately after making the purchase. In order to keep the account truly ever-liquid, one must use a mental or an actual stop on all commitments amounting to some predetermined percentage of the amount invested. There are those who have used 3% and others up to 10%. Of course one does not make a purchase unless one feels rather sure that the trend is sufficiently well established to minimize the possibility of being stopped out. Yet it will happen occasionally anyway.

The decision of what and when to buy is made on a personal basis using various yardsticks best understood by individual investors. More or less, I use all of the accepted sources of information, including a general understanding of economics, statistical research, etc., together with material gathered through personal contact with corporation executives and observation of the character of buying and selling orders, etc. However, the stock finally selected must of necessity be a very liquid active market leader or give extremely strong promise of shortly entering that class; and in order to buy and hold it or increase one's line of it, it must be advancing in price. To that extent, technical factors are vital but otherwise they are only incidental.

This investment philosophy leads into concentrated purchases of single issues rather than diversification, because one of the primary elements in the situation is that one must know and be convinced of the rightness of what one is doing. Diversification as to issue and type of investment is only hedging—a method of averaging errors or covering up lack of judgment.

This ever-liquid method also rarely calls for attempts to buy at the bottom, as bottoms and tops are actually impossible to judge ordinarily, while trends after they are established and under way can be profitably recognized.

It is a method that leans towards pyramiding; i.e., towards following up gains and retreating before losses. Such an account, properly handled, bends but never breaks. "Averaging down" is, of course, completely against its theory.

In normal markets, by which I mean active markets with broad varied participation and not unusually subject to unpredictable news developments, the belief that it is the right time to buy a certain leader will be so positive in the competent operator's mind that he will not hesitate to take a rather large position at once in one selected leading issue. This position will be much larger than if it were a segment of a diversified list, but, on the other hand, it will tend to employ a far more conservative percentage of one's capital than would ordinarily be spread about the board by orthodox speculation or investments. There might be times when an investor would use 20–25% of the account in such a single issue, though this percentage would not apply in special cases where the amount of capital is very large or very small. There naturally must be a relationship between the amount of capital, the breadth of the market in a particular stock, and the tax bracket of the owner of the account.

If the market advances as expected, more of the same stock will probably be purchased. If the markets are narrow and highly dependent on news, little or nothing will be done. What is done will be on an ever-smaller scale as far as the initial commitment in any particular issue is concerned. If the shares go down, the loss will be small. If they go up, more can be bought. The theory calls for such large profits, if successful on the small amounts employed, that the account can get a satisfactory average return with a large part of its capital seemingly sterile. And there is always a generous reserve to try again in case of losses.

It offers complete protection against holding investments that seem very sure on the basis of all the known facts and yet decline marketwise. After a small decline, the ever-liquid method forces liquidation regardless of other facts. The fact of the market decline itself is the ruling fact of the situation. More often than not, many months and many points lower the real causes of the decline become evident to the "transfer it into your own name and lock it up" class of buyer.

At times, of course, a stock will decline for temporary reasons, and then start on a real advance. There is no rule against repurchase lower or higher as far as the ever-liquid account is concerned. In fact, repurchases at higher than the original or first liquidation price tend, in my experience, to return profits rather more than the average buy. The reason for this phenomenon is that the market, in getting stronger when the general expectation suggests it will get weaker, is, in fact, giving an A-1 buying suggestion to those who will see it and are not afraid to follow it. However, the ever-liquid account, having taken a loss and being out of the market, is in a preferred position because its owner goes back into the same stock only if conditions justify. He is not just locked in and hoping. In the interval of time, another issue may, on the revival of an uptrend, seem far more attractive. There is a lot of meat in these last two sentences.

This procedure puts a premium on ability. It is not easy. Lack of knowledge shows up quickly. Luck plays no part in it. The accounting reflects the real situation, and one is never kidding oneself with a taxable income from gains on a few coupons clipped, dividends received and profits taken while actually there exists a far greater unrealized loss in issues still held and "too low to sell."

The ever-liquid account is the acid test of successful investment or speculation. There are many other ways of making money in the security markets of course, but none that I know is so little dependent on luck or chance or where the results are more accurately reflected from an accounting standpoint.

I may as well anticipate someone saying "inflation." The fact is that liquidity and mobility are the great allies of safety against change. Intelligent capital is like a rabbit darting here and there to cover. Fixed investments, like real estate anchored to the ground, are far too inflexible for real protection against any hazard whether it is a tax hazard or a war hazard or political or style hazard or what have you.

Hence, the "Ever-Liquid Account."

The Penny Stock Market

MORTON SHULMAN

*Canadian Dr. Morton Shulman is a dynamic and highly
successful investor. In his exciting best seller* Anyone Can
Make a Million *he dispels many common myths about
investing in the stock market. One myth he disagrees with
is that there are great profits to be found in penny stocks.
With some amusing examples of typical behind-the-scenes
activities in some penny mining stock dealings, Shulman
draws vivid conclusions on how a potential investor should
evaluate this often irresistible temptation.*

Consolidated Dominion went from 20¢ to $50.
Quantro went from 3¢ to $20.
Triangle went from 10¢ to $19.

*T*HE dream of every stock-market gambler is to buy just such a vision—to invest $1,000 and see it turn into $500,000. Because of these dreams, thousands of men have become millionaires—not by buying penny stocks, but by selling them. It is now standard promoter practice to pay a few hundred or a few thousand dollars to buy a property within a short distance of a producing mine or a "hot" prospect and then to issue up to a million dollars worth of stock at anywhere from 30¢ to a dollar to the gullible public. Of every million dollars worth of stock issued, far less than half will be used for actual exploration of the property, and in some cases none of the money is so used. A portion of the cash will go into the treasury of the company, a large amount will go to the telephone and telegraph companies to pay for the long-distance calls to the suckers, and the vast majority will go to make new millionaires of the promoters.

The myth of the fortunes made from the penny stock that finds a rich ore body and goes to $20 to $30 has been carefully fostered by a mining industry which depends on the promotion type of financing for its vigor. Unfortunately, it is a complete myth. *There is not a single member of the public living in North America today who has made a sizable sum of money by investing in the penny mining market.*

The Irish sweepstakes persuade millions of North Americans to make a donation to Irish hospitals by giving back a portion of the "take" and by making a few of their benefactors rich beyond their dreams. The penny mining market has never made a member of the public rich, and yet through extremely clever publicity has persuaded the supposedly intelligent professional classes of North America to continue to annually donate millions to this very uncharitable group. How do they so successfully perpetrate this same fraud year after year?

The routine is as formalized as a ballet. The promoter either forms a new company or purchases control of an existing company listed on a Canadian stock exchange. A typical example was Fax Mines,* a company with a listing on a Canadian stock exchange trading at 5¢. The company had no assets and had sold its total capitalization of 5 million shares. A well-known Canadian promoter, Edward Collins, purchased one million shares of the company's stock for $70,000 from the original or-

---

* Fax Mines, Jenny Mines, Jerrett Motors, Canadian Jefferson Securities, Edward Collins, George Crawford, Fred Gora, Henry Severn, Heather Investment Services, and Strang Advisory Services are fictitious names used in this . . . chapter to illustrate an often-repeated situation. Any resemblance to living persons or firms is purely coincidental.

ganizer of the company. This gave him effective control of the company, as the remaining four million shares were widely distributed, with no individual holding more than ten thousand shares. A promoter never attempts to move a stock when in this situation, because the other shareholders may begin to sell their stock to him. Instead, Collins called a special meeting of the shareholders, which because of the company's inactivity was attended only by himself and his associates. At this meeting he called in all of the company's stock and changed the company's name to get rid of the old tired Fax Mines image. The shareholders were given one share in the new company for every 10 shares they had held previously. The new company, Jenny Mines, had an authorized capital of five million shares, but there were now only 500,000 outstanding, of which 100,000 were held by Collins.

At this time there was a very active uranium boom in Canada. Several companies near Elliot Lake had discovered ore bodies and were going into production to supply ore to the United States. Collins arranged for his brother-in-law, George Crawford, to purchase a piece of bush land ten miles from Elliot Lake and 25 miles from the proven mines. Crawford paid $250 to the prospector who staked the property and promptly sold the land to Jenny Mines for $50,000.

Jenny Mines had no money, however, so Collins underwrote (purchased) 200,000 shares of stock from the treasury of the company at 25¢ a share so as to supply the $50,000. The company then announced that in return for this underwriting they had granted Collins one-year options to purchase another 1,500,000 shares at prices ranging from 30¢ to $1.00.

At this point Crawford returned the $50,000 to his brother-in-law. These men now had reached the point where, by laying out $250, they had received 200,000 shares of company stock plus options on an additional 1.5 million.

Next, Collins paid $3,000 to an employee of a large trust company, who had access to the files listing the shareholders of several large mines for whom the trust company acted as transfer agent. For his $3,000 he received 12,000 names and addresses of individuals who were then holders of successful mining stocks. The "trust" company employee didn't have to copy out all these names, for his firm had every name on a mailing plate, and the employee merely ran all the plates through the machine, thus producing a master list in one hour of overtime. (Another promoter did not wish to spend the $3,000 and rented a third-floor office on Bay Street from which he entered a trust company's office at midnight while the janitor was kept busy with a bottle of whisky. No one at the trust company ever suspected, although the promoter grumbled that he always left the plates much neater than he had found them.)

The 12,000 investors now began to receive a well-printed, glossy "information bulletin" sent out by Collins' brokerage house, which he grandly called "Canadian Jefferson Securities." The weekly bulletin expansively and optimistically described the uranium boom then going on in Canada and pointed out some of the extraordinary price changes that had occurred; stock of some companies had literally quadrupled or better in days. The third bulletin described in loving detail the romantic story of Gunnar Mines, a legitimate company which had jumped in a few days from $2.50 to $13. Along with this bulletin was a stamped postcard. The receiver was invited to sign and return it in order to receive, with no obligation, full information on a new exciting prospect near the successful mines described earlier. This company was "about to begin drilling," which could very likely send its price from its then 39¢ to over $10.

Promoters consider a 3% return from a promotional mailing to be satisfactory, and Collins expected to get back 350 to 400 postcards. To his amazed delight, he received 1,600 signed postcards, probably due to the front-page publicity given the Canadian uranium strike and the atomic bomb.

Within a few days these 1,600 individuals, practically all of whom were in the United States, received a long-distance call from Toronto which went like this: "This is your Canadian broker calling. My name is Fred Gora, and I want to tell you about what will probably be the greatest opportunity in your lifetime— to get in on the ground floor of a great Canadian mine before the sharks up here know about it. The name is Jenny Mines, and she probably has such a big uranium ore body that you can stick Gunnar and Consolidated Denison in one corner of it and you wouldn't even see them. The price is only 39¢, and although I'd like to offer you more, the president of our firm will only allow me to sell 1,000 shares to new customers. The idea is, we'll make you money on this one and then try to do more business at some future date. You want to check with your banker? Well, of course, go right ahead, but I have only been allotted 25,000 shares to sell to new clients, and you represent my last thousand. I have over 300 more people I haven't phoned yet, and my last call was to a banker in New York City; he wanted 20,000 shares, and I could only give him one. Jenny is listed on the stock exchange, you know, and we're only distributing stock at this low price because they insist on a wider distribution before it moves over $1.00. Okay, I'll send out a contract to you tonight. Please put a cheque in the mail for $390. You don't even have to pay the regular stock exchange commission."

As a result of these 1,600 calls, 400,000 shares were sold, and payment was received for 350,000. Collins now needed more stock for his "clients" and so exercised his options on Jenny Mines at 30¢. Ten days later the 400 original phone purchasers received a second call: "This is Fred Gora phoning from Canada, bringing good news about Jenny Mines. The outlook for the company has improved so much that Jefferson Securities have put another $100,000 in their treasury. The stock has been very active on the stock exchange and has now moved up to an all-time high of 65¢. Some very good news is going to be released tomorrow. I am not allowed to reveal it yet, but I can tell you this, that it will put the price of the stock much, *much* higher. Because you are now a regular client, the president has given me permission to sell you a small amount of stock at today's price; this is only because you showed faith in us before, when Jenny was 39¢. We have very little available, and only to our regular clients, but I have managed to squeeze out a maximum of 3,000 shares for you—and frankly the president said to try to talk you down to half of that, but I want to make this money for you so that we will do a lot of business in the future. So just put your cheque in the mail for $1,950, and you can skip the commission. Jenny Mines is going to make all of us very rich men."

In the meanwhile, Eddy Collins had really put $100,000 in the treasury of Jenny Mines in order to exercise his stock option, but he had no intention of leaving it there. Jenny Mines now hired "Crawford and Company" to do a magnetometric survey of the property for the sum of $85,000, two-thirds of which was immediately passed back to Collins under the table. Strangely enough, this was the good news that Fred Gora had predicted, and the company now made a public announcement that the survey was under way and would be followed by diamond drilling.

The stock continued to move higher on the stock exchange, reaching $1.00 three weeks later. By this time Collins had twelve salesmen working the phones, busily selling Jenny Mines all over North America. He exercised further options, paying Jenny Mines $250,000 for further blocks of stock at higher prices. Needless to say, most of this money quickly found its way back to Collins via the drilling company that Jenny Mines hired.

This drama was rapidly reaching its climax, and a crescendo of stock selling occurred. Announcement of the imminent drilling was made to the *Northern Miner*, advertisements were placed in the mining and daily press with a map showing the proximity of Jenny Mines to successful mines, and a tremendously high-pressure phone campaign was conducted to sell Jenny Mines at $1.00. "Jenny closed at $1.10 today. We are letting you have it at 10¢ under the market." Unfortunately, the clients did not understand the unintentional pun in that sentence.

Friday, January 28, 1963, Jenny closed at $1.20 on the stock exchange. Saturday morning Eddy Collins paid off his salesmen. They received an average of $9,000 each for the ten weeks' work. Fred Gora, his best salesman, had earned $21,000. They smiled and shook hands, and the salesmen went to look for another similar promotion.

Fred Gora boarded a plane for Vancouver with his $21,000 in $100 bills in a breast pocket. He soon fell asleep in his aisle seat, and the thick packet of bills fell into the aisle. The steward-ess could not believe her eyes and hurried forward to give the money to the pilot. His first thought was of dope pushing, and he radioed ahead to ask the Royal Canadian Mounted Police to meet the plane at Calgary. Some minutes later Gora awoke, and feeling the absence of his money pack, became volubly upset until the stewardess calmed him and returned the money.

When the plane landed in Calgary, the R.C.M.P. quickly whisked Gora into a private office and began a polite but in-sistent cross-examination as to the source of the money. Gora swears that when he refused to talk, the police corporal blurted out, "Mr. Gora, we are aware that one of your acquaintances has been smuggling hog bristles from Communist China into the United States via Canada. This is a very serious offense. We in-sist on knowing if your money is from this source."

The amazed swindler burst out laughing and replied, "Hog bristles! Are you kidding? This is my pay for selling moose pas-ture to American investors!" The constable apologized and es-corted Fred Gora back to his airplane.

On Monday, January 31, Jenny Mines opened with no bid offered at $1.00. The first trade was at 60¢, and within twenty minutes the stock sold down to 14¢, where it remained for several days while short traders (professionals who had sold stock they didn't own in the expectation of just such a collapse) bought back the stock they had sold over $1.00. Jenny then gradually declined to 3¢, and it has traded in a 3¢ to 6¢ range since that time.

Collins made a gross profit of $2.5 million, out of which he had to pay just under $400,000 to his various associates. He de-cided for reasons of health to close Jefferson Securities on Febru-ary 1, then moved to Nice, where he rented the large villa that he still occupies today. Strangely he did not dissipate his illgotten wealth in the vice traps of Nice, but being a hard-working individual, opened a new business. This was an ad-visory service, giving market advice to European investors who were interested in North American securities.

Unbelievable as this story sounds, it has been repeated hundreds of times in the past decade, and some individuals have fallen for the same fable many times. Doctors are the prime suckers, for they have excess cash with no business to put it in; they are too rushed to properly investigate any stock; and they are trusting by nature. There is probably not a doctor in all of North America who has not been stuck at least once by Eddy Collins or others of his ilk. Dentists and lawyers are a close second, but chartered accountants seem to fare better. Widows and orphans are never stuck by these operators, who avoid them like the plague, not because of innate decency, but because widows scream to the authorities and the press. The professional or businessman rarely publicly complains, because he cannot bear to have his own greed and stupidity exposed.

And indeed there is no limit to the greed and stupidity of these lambs who think they are wolves. At 11 P.M. one very cold January night, I received a phone call from a lawyer friend who said he had to see me that night on a very urgent financial matter. He explained that he had two clients with him, dentists who had invested their entire savings of $85,000 in a fantastic once-in-a-lifetime proposition, and that he intended to invest his own modest savings in the morning but first wanted my opinion.

Twenty minutes later, three excited men arrived at my home and poured forth this fantastic story: An unbelievably large iron ore deposit had been discovered in Liberia; the Sheik of Kuwait had agreed to put up twenty million dollars to finance the development and production of the ore, which was then to be shipped to Kuwait, where it was to be used in a new process for refinement of oil under the Kuwait desert. The twenty million was already in deposit in a Liberian bank, and the deal was to be closed in just five days, but the promoters and developers of the property had run short of ready cash and needed just $30,000 to pay the legal fees and close the deal. In return for loaning this $30,000, the two dentists had been given the secret information that Ross Metals,* an unlisted penny stock trading at 30¢, was for tax reasons to be given full title to the iron property.

---

* Name changed.

When this news was released to the public, the stock would be worth about $50 per share. To prove the truth of all these statements, the previous week one of the dentists had actually been flown to Liberia and had not only seen the property but had been introduced to the Sheik of Kuwait himself (or a reasonable facsimile). That week the dentists had purchased 200,000 shares of Ross Metals at 30¢.

When I expressed, as gently as possible, my doubts about this "deal of the century," the dentists' reaction was violent. They jumped to their feet, accused me of wanting to discourage them so that they would sell their stock cheaply while I bought it up, then stamped angrily from the house. I learned that night never to try to talk sense to individuals in love with their dreams. They will not tolerate anyone's shattering them.

One month later the promoters of Ross Metals had sold all their stock, and it quickly fell to 2¢. The property in Liberia unfortunately did not have enough ore to warrant going into production, and the pseudo-Sheik of Kuwait had disappeared. Interestingly enough, the two dentists are still mad at me. I guess they have to blame someone other than themselves.

Fortunately, not all penny stocks are swindles. But, as a general rule, if the stock is being sold over the phone, the chance of the client's making money is about nil.

Even those promoters who are honest (and most promoters and honesty have difficulty going together) cannot offer their clients a decent break. For even if every penny that goes into the company's treasury is spent on exploration and development, the chance of producing a mine is close to nil. Of the thousands and thousands of penny prospects that have been explored in all of North America since the war, less than half a dozen have ultimately turned into a mine and paid dividends greater than their cost. Unfortunately, even the most conscientious promoter must siphon off over half of the money he receives in order to pay the fringe expenses involved in promotion and sale of these mining stocks.

It is, of course, far easier to give advice than to follow it, and although I have no trouble turning down the phone promoter,

I find it very difficult to say no to the friend with the "hot tip"; and money is usually just as lost on a hot tip as with the promoter. The information is all too often either false or planted. A recent personal experience illustrates the temptations and pitfalls of the hot tip, even when, as in this case, the stock being tipped was an honest, legitimate one.

One evening John Hay, a mining engineer friend, phoned excitedly after the market had closed. "Mort, I have exciting news! International Copper is trading in Vancouver at 65¢. Tomorrow at two o'clock the company is going to announce a 2% copper find plus an 85¢ underwriting, and the stock is going to be listed on the Vancouver exchange. I have the information straight from a director of the company. I'd like you to buy some stock first thing in the morning, and we'll split the profits. There's no chance of this information being wrong, because he knows I can't afford to lose and he wouldn't give me bad information."

It would be a rare individual who could refuse such a story, apparently straight from a director of a mining company, and next morning I purchased one thousand shares of International Copper at 60¢.

By 11 A.M. the stock was down to 55¢, and I was mentally berating my own ignorance when John phoned to reassure me that all was well and that at 2 P.M. the announcement would be made. Sure enough, at 1:30 the stock began to move up, and at 2 P.M. I sold it at 84¢.

At 2:15 John Hay phoned frantically, "I've made a terrible mistake, I gave you the name of the wrong company! Let's get out and take our loss!" When I told him that I had already sold at a profit we both broke up with laughter.

The moral is that if you make money on a hot tip, it's an accident.

What about those penny mines that do find ore and go up so beautifully? Five years ago a typical penny dreadful was being sold over the phones at 35¢ while drilling was being done on the property. To the amazement of the promoter, a huge ore body was found, which meant that the stock was worth 20 or 30 times the price it was being sold for. No news of this strike was released by the promoter, because to his dismay he had sold almost all his stock. Instead, he went to work buying back all the stock from the phone customers at 50¢ per share. After he had it all back, he released the news, and the stock moved up to its present level of $45.

At least the clients made a little money on that one!

There is thus one general rule in relation to penny mining stocks. *Don't buy them.* The odds are impossible.

There is, however, one exception to this rule. It is a very important one and should not be overlooked.

There are some low-priced mining stocks that have made spectacular market moves and in which no promotion was involved; for example, Pine Point went from $2 to $83, and Mattagami from $3 to $22. The trouble with this type of stock is that it is uncommon; the move is gradual, unspectacular, unadvertised; and the public never buys it until *after* it has made the big move. How can these situations be recognized early? A description of such an issue will show the points to look for.

A typical example was Newconex Holdings. This was a company formed in 1962 by giant Consolidated Goldfields of South Africa. Goldfields had been increasingly nervous about their concentration of funds in South Africa and England and, deciding to place some of their funds in safer political arenas, created subsidiaries in the United States, Australia, and Canada. These subsidiaries were set up in such a way that their shareholders literally could not lose.

Newconex originally issued 700,000 shares of stock at $5 each, of which 450,000 were purchased by Goldfields themselves, and the remaining 250,000 were sold to the public by a highly reputable Canadian stock broker, Nesbitt Thomson & Company. The $3.5 million thus raised was all placed in the Newconex treasury. Each of the 700,000 shares carried as a free bonus two options (warrants) entitling the holder to purchase two additional shares of Newconex at $5 at any time within a five-year period.

Simultaneously, Goldfields concluded a unique agreement with Newconex which ensured Newconex's financial success. This unprecedented agreement obliged Goldfields through a wholly owned subsidiary to begin an active program of exploration in Canada. All losses were to be borne by Goldfields, all worthless properties were to be kept by Goldfields, but Newconex was given the right to take over any successful finds from Goldfields within one year, at cost! This meant that Newconex was now an exploration company with all the possibilities of sudden upward surges in the stock that could occur with an ore find, but without any of the dangers of attrition of capital through exploration expense. In other words, this was a company that could not lose!

One would have expected a tremendous rush from the public to buy the stock, for it is not too often that a speculator is given the chance to gamble without any risk of loss. There was no rush; in fact, there was no public buying at all. Nesbitt Thomson & Co. sold the 250,000 shares available to their clients, arranged for the stock to be listed on the Toronto Stock Exchange, and then worried no further about it. Newconex stock slowly drifted downward and in a few weeks was trading at $4.25 with the two warrants still attached. The warrants themselves were trading at $1.00, and so the stock alone was valued by the buying public at only $2.25. Yet this stock had $5 in cash behind every share, plus a guarantee against loss by Goldfields.

During the next three years, Goldfields spent close to one million dollars on exploration and found nothing. Newconex was sitting with $3.5 million, which they invested in stocks and bonds following the advice of Nesbitt Thomson and Company. They invested the funds remarkably well and within three years had increased their assets by over 50%. Each share now had cash and liquid assets behind it of $8.00. The disinterest of the public continued and the stock offered on the exchange was slowly bought up by two or three wealthy, knowledgeable investors and investment funds. The warrants continued to trade around $1.00 while the stock hung being between $4.00 and $5.00. It is interesting to note that even experts find difficulty in buying value when no promoter is spreading glamour about, and by the end of 1964 practically all of Nesbitt Thomson's clients had sold their stock. Goldfields, however, was not unaware of the tremendous value building up in Newconex, and they purchased 50,000 more shares of the company stock from Canadian Gas and Energy, a closed-end mutual fund that had purchased the stock near its lowest prices on the Toronto stock exchange.

Goldfields now compared the results Newconex had achieved in comparison with the other subsidiaries in the United States and Australia and decided that the Canadian company had not done well enough. They requested the president's resignation and brought in Mr. Bill Robinson from Canadian Gas and Energy as the new president. By September, 1965, Newconex had become a beehive of activity. It had crews exploring in many areas of Canada (at Goldfields' expense), and it was busy examining many companies offered to it for sale.

One company that approached Newconex was Pyramid Mining, who owned a very strategic piece of ground in the North West Territories, right next to the huge Pine Point Mine. Pyramid needed money to explore this property, and Newconex agreed to supply it in return for a block of Pyramid stock.

All this activity had not appreciably affected the price of the Newconex stock, which now had liquid assets equal to $8.50 per share but which continued to trade around $5.

There is always a critical point in the stock history of undervalued mining situations like Newconex where the public suddenly sees a situation which has been obvious for years but which no one has looked at. The critical day for Newconex was October 7, 1965. On that day the *Northern Miner* ran this item on the front page:

NEWCONEX, CONWEST SHARE AT PINE POINT

Newconex Canadian Exploration, exploration arm of Newconex Holdings, is getting into the Pine Point area in a big way.

At mid-week, the Northern Miner was able to confirm with company officials that it now holds about a 50% participation with Conwest and Central Patricia in that team's substantial and well regarded holdings which almost surround Pine Point Mines.

Conwest, which will continue as the operator, has been carrying out extensive geophysical work on this key ground all summer. Tentative plans are to drill this winter.

This was the first public notice that Newconex was busily searching for a mine, and the following week the *Miner* wrote up as exciting news what the whole mining fraternity had been ignoring for three years.

The Conwest-Central Patricia team, starting this week to drill some well regarded anomalies in the Pine Point area on ground they have held for years, new-highed at $6.75 and $1.82 respectively. But the market didn't take too much note of an exclusive story in this paper last week which revealed that Newconex Holdings as a full partner, now probably holds the largest single interest in this project, although it did gain 45¢ to reach its former all-time high of $6.15. This figure is still well below its liquid breakup value which now stands at about $8.50 per share. A unique feature of the Newconex setup permits the company to purchase anything found by its exploration arm for $15,000. The tab for this arm, Newconex Canadian Exploration, is picked up by the parent Gold Fields Mining & Industrial Ltd. of London, Eng. In other words, Newconex Holdings, the T.S.E. listing, doesn't have to spend its money on exploration. And it has a pretty capable associate in Conwest. On the other hand, this association could make available almost unlimited funds in the event of a success at Pine Point or elsewhere. Newconex Warrants, which give the right to buy Newconex stock at $5 per share till Feb. 28, 1967, gained 40¢ on the week to $1.65 on volume of 79,200 shares. Floating supply of both stock and warrants is unusually light, which makes for a rather explosive situation marketwise.

That did it! First the mining people, then the public jumped in. The two contracts on the following page illustrate the effect the sudden awakening produced.

As such a story should, this one ended happily. Pyramid drilled their property with the money supplied by Newconex and found a huge ore body. Body stocks passed from being ignored to being market darlings, and all those who bought and had the will power to hold on made huge profits.

HECTOR M. CHISHOLM & CO. LIMITED

MEMBERS
TORONTO STOCK EXCHANGE
MONTREAL STOCK EXCHANGE
CANADIAN STOCK EXCHANGE

GROUND FLOOR
82 RICHMOND STREET WEST
362-4731

TORONTO 1, CANADA

BRANCH OFFICE
KING EDWARD SHERATON HOTEL
363-3074

TO Γ

Dr. M. Shulman,

WE HAVE THIS DAY **SOLD** FOR YOUR ACCOUNT ON ☑ THE TORONTO STOCK EXCHANGE		☐ THE CANADIAN STOCK EXCHANGE	☐ THE UNLISTED MARKET	**DATE** Nov. 4/65	**VALUE** Nov. 9/65			
BROKERS ON REQUEST	SHARES	DESCRIPTION	PRICE	AMOUNT	COMMISSION	TAX		TOTAL
Bong	200	Newconex Holdings	9.25	1850.00	40.00	2.00		1808.00

E. & O.E.

HECTOR M. CHISHOLM & CO. LIMITED

MEMBERS
TORONTO STOCK EXCHANGE
MONTREAL STOCK EXCHANGE
CANADIAN STOCK EXCHANGE

GROUND FLOOR
82 RICHMOND STREET WEST
362-4731

TORONTO 1, CANADA

BRANCH OFFICE
KING EDWARD SHERATON HOTEL
363-3074

TO Γ

Dr. M. Shulman,

WE HAVE THIS DAY **BOUGHT** FOR YOUR ACCOUNT ON ☑ THE TORONTO STOCK EXCHANGE		☐ THE CANADIAN STOCK EXCHANGE	☐ THE UNLISTED MARKET	**DATE** Sept. 30/65	**VALUE** Oct. 5/65			
BROKERS ON REQUEST	SHARES	DESCRIPTION	PRICE	AMOUNT	COMMISSION	TAX		TOTAL
Daly	200	Newconex Holdings	5.10	1020.00	30.00			1050.00

E. & O.E.

Purchases or sales are made with the distinct understanding that actual delivery is contemplated, and are subject in all respects to the bylaws, rules, and customs of the stock exchange where the order is executed and to the customs of the brokerage business. It is agreed that all

How can other pyramids or Newconexes be recognized before their stock has moved 'way up in price? These mining prospects all have six features in common:

1. They are never sold over the phone.
2. No promoter recommends their purchase.
3. Their treasuries all contain substantial funds.
4. From 25 to 80% of their stock is held by one or more large producing mining firms.
5. The amount of stock issued to the public is small, usually less than one million shares.
6. The market price of the stock is always over one dollar and should be less than $10.

There are always a few such stocks available, trading at very low prices, and their history has been almost universally a good one. But these stocks are purchased primarily by knowledgeable people in the mining business and not by the public. These are the only situations in the mining market where the purchaser is almost sure of making a profit.

What this chapter boils down to is, never buy tips or promotions; buy value and wait. There will be many more Pine Points and Newconexes.

---

securities carried from time to time in the customer's marginal account, or deposited to protect the same, may be loaned by us or may be pledged by us on our general loans, either separately or together with securities or others, and either to secure advances within or in excess of the amount due us thereon. It is also agreed that we reserve the right to close transactions (without demand for additional margin or any other notice whatsoever) on a stock exchange or similar institution, or at any public or private sale whenever we deem it necessary for our own protection by reason of insufficient margin or otherwise.

The Relatively Unpopular Large Company

BENJAMIN GRAHAM

Benjamin Graham is one of America's most respected investment counselors. Here he suggests a promising and reasonable investment approach.

*I*F we assume that it is the habit of the market to over-value common stocks which have been showing excellent growth or are glamorous for some other reason, it is logical to expect that it will undervalue—relatively, at least—companies that are out of favor because of unsatisfactory developments of a temporary nature. This may be set down as a fundamental law of the stock market, and it suggests an investment approach that should prove most conservative and promising.

The key requirement here is that the enterprising investor concentrate on the larger companies that are going through a period of unpopularity. While small companies may also be undervalued for similar reasons, and in many cases may later increase their earnings and share price, they entail the risk of a definite loss of profitability and also of protracted neglect by the market in spite of better earnings. The large companies thus have a double advantage over the others. First, they have the resources in capital and brain power to carry them through adversity and back to a satisfactory earnings base. Second, the market is likely to respond with reasonable speed to any improvement shown.

A remarkable demonstration of the soundness of this thesis is found in studies of the price behavior of the unpopular issues in the Dow-Jones Industrial Average (DJIA). In these it was assumed that an investment was made each year in either the six or the ten issues in the DJIA which were selling at the lowest multipliers of their current or previous year's earnings. These could be called the "cheapest" stocks in the list, and their cheapness was evidently the reflection of relative unpopularity with investors or traders. It was assumed further that these purchases were sold out at the end of holding periods ranging from one to five years. The results of these investments were then compared with the results shown in either the DJIA as a whole or in the highest multiplier (i.e., the most popular) group.

The detailed material we have available covers the results of annual purchases assumed in each of the past forty-five years.[1] In the early period, 1917–1933, this approach proved unprofitable. But since 1933 the method has shown highly successful results. In twenty-six tests made by Drexel & Company of one-year holding—from 1936 through 1962—the cheap stocks did definitely worse than the DJIA in only one instance; the results were about the same in eight cases; and the cheap stocks clearly outperformed the average in eighteen years. The consistently better performance of the low-multiplier stocks is shown (see table) by the average results for successive five-year periods, when compared with those of the DJIA and of the ten high-multipliers.

---

[1] Two studies are available. The first, made by H. G. Schneider, one of our students, covers the years 1917–1950 and was published in June 1951 in the *Journal of Finance*. The second was made by Drexel & Company, members of the New York Stock Exchange, and covers the years 1933–1962. The data are given here by their kind permission.

Average annual percentage gain or loss
on test issues 1937–1962

Period	10 Low-Multiplier Issues	10 High-Multiplier Issues	30 DJIA Stocks
1937–1942	−2.2	−10.0	−6.3
1943–1947	17.3	8.3	14.9
1948–1952	16.4	4.6	9.9
1953–1957	20.9	10.0	13.7
1958–1962	10.2	−3.3	3.6

The Drexel computation shows further that an original investment of $10,000 made in the low-multiplier issues in 1936, and switched each year in accordance with the principle, would have grown to $119,200 by 1962. The same operations in high-multiplier stocks would have ended with a value of only $10,800; while an operation in all thirty stocks would have increased the original fund to either $35,600 or $61,000.[2]

A comparison of the same kind, and with the same general results, appeared in the *Financial Analysts Journal* for July–August 1960. The author, S. Francis Nicholson, used as his "universe" 100 common stocks of "trust-investment quality." Over the period 1939–1959, with changes in the portfolio made every five years, the consistent investor in the twenty lowest-multiplier stocks would have outperformed the buyer of the twenty highest-multipliers by over three to one.

We cannot say whether this simple method of stock selection will yield such favorable comparative results in the future. But we can recommend this general approach with confidence, because it is entirely rational, involves no surrender to the speculative enthusiasms of the day, and is backed by an impressive record of past accomplishment.

[2] In the first case the same number of shares would have been bought of each issue, corresponding to the way by which the DJIA is calculated. In the second case the same amount of money would have been placed each year in each of the issues. The better result shown by the second approach indicates that the lower-*priced* DJIA issues significantly outperformed the higher-priced ones.

One Necessary Definition

CLAUDE N. ROSENBERG, JR.

*One of the most frequently used terms in the securities
market is "price-earnings ratio." It is of utmost importance
that the investor understand the meaning of the seemingly
simple term. Claude N. Rosenberg, Jr., gives readers a
clear and understandable definition of the term, its history,
and its application.*

You should understand one basic term: the *Price-Earnings
Ratio*, or, as it is more commonly called, the Price-Earnings *Multiple*. . . . Its understanding is very simple and my definition
follows.

When you come right down to it, stock prices are but a function of two elements:

1. The earnings of the company itself.
2. What people are willing to pay for these earnings.

The first part (which can be called *profit* or *net income* as
well as *earnings*) requires no skill on your part. They (the earnings, that is) are reported to you by the company involved on
a *per-share basis*, and the only requirement is that you have a
good idea as to where these figures are going from here. Are

they likely to be sharply higher in the time ahead or are they destined to drop—and in each case, to about what degree?

The second part (what price people might be willing to pay for these earnings) does require judgment and knowledge from you. . . . Since I will refer to Price-Earnings Multiple (let's abbreviate it as *P/E*) . . . we should have the definition clear—so here we go!

The *P/E* reflects what people are willing to pay for earnings, and it is figured this way: *Market Price of the Stock ÷ Earnings Per Share = P/E.*

To illustrate, Company A's stock sells for $10 and it is currently earning $1.00 per share. Its *P/E* is 10 (10 ÷ $1.00 = 10), or, as they say in the investment business, "The stock is selling for ten times earnings."

Now suppose the same Company A, with earnings per share of $1.00, is selling for $20, not $10. What is the *P/E*?

The answer, of course, is: 20 ($20 market price ÷ $1.00 earnings per share = 20).

It is obvious that you would prefer to buy Company A at $10 instead of $20, which is simply a way of saying that *the lower the* P/E *the better.* You get more value in the way of current earnings by paying ten times earnings than by paying twenty!

Stated another way, the *P/E* shows you how many years you will have to wait to have your purchase price earned by the company involved *if there is no change in its profits in the future.* If Company A continues to earn $1.00 per share, it will take you ten years to have your $10 market price earned for you, and naturally it is better to wait only ten years than to wait twenty—which would be the case if you paid $20 for the same stock (at a *P/E* of 20).

Needless to say, chances are one thousand to one that Company A will *not* earn the same dollars year after year. It will earn way more in some years, way less in others, or perhaps it is a growth outfit which might show consistent increases as time goes by.

Most important, it is essential (although no doubt unnecessary) to point out that *a person should be willing to pay a* P/E *today*

*based on just what kind of trend in earnings might be antici-
pated for the future.* If Company A's profits soar to $2.00 per
share and then $3.00 and upward, you should be willing to pay
a much higher price for the stock than if the $1.00 profits are to
remain static or go downhill. Using our new terminology, you
should be willing to pay a higher P/E for the growth company
as opposed to the nongrowth.

By the same token, you should be ready to pay a higher P/E
for Company A growing at a rapid clip than for Company B,
which might not have the same favorable prospects.

Thus, *the P/E should be related to what the future holds.*
But since no one has a completely clear crystal ball, the P/E is
bound to be no more than what people *think* lies ahead. Thus,
sentiments and emotions and all sorts of analytical and non-
analytical assessments get involved.

The Evaluation Work Sheet—
Recording Information

WILLIAM S. HEWETT

*Most experienced investors know how important it is to
devise a method of evaluating the performance, and value,
of a company's stock in which they hope to invest.
Stockbroker William S. Hewett has developed a work sheet
which, if used consistently, would improve any portfolio's
value. Here Hewett gives several illustrations of how to set
up a work sheet and then clearly explains how to analyze
the figures, uncover significant facts, and draw invaluable
conclusions.*

*U*NCOVERING significant facts to create a desirable investment requires study and effort every week of the year. An investor can seldom capitalize on a new discovery or some other situation that suddenly causes the stock to skyrocket. Successful investors usually look for circumstances that create a high probability of capital gain to be realized over a period of months or years. This approach demands careful evaluation of stocks initially and continuous supervision once the stock is purchased. The work is continuous because not only must we buy the right stock at the proper time, but we must also sell at the proper time. The stock must then be replaced with something possessing greater potential or simply hold cash for a time.

Analysis requires comparative studies of a stock's past operations and an appraisal of its potential. Having seen growth result from a given set of facts, we create an evaluation work sheet to emphasize these points. If one made two evaluation forms each month, it would not be long before a worthwhile library of information would be accumulated. The process of selecting a security for detailed study, however, is the major time-consuming element. The *Wall Street Journal, Barron's, Forbes,* and other services provide thought starters. At the end of a month's time we may have chosen six to eight companies that merit study. An hour's perusal will generally give us reason to concentrate on two companies. The accompanying stock evaluation work sheet, Figure 1, is intended to direct concentration to critical points for consideration. This evaluation work sheet makes it possible to evaluate performance over the past several years, project probabilities and review as future estimates become current.

At the top of the work sheet the name of the company is indicated along with the date of study, its current price, yield and the Standard & Poor's quality rating. A Standard & Poor Stock Report sheet provides data about high and low prices, sales, earnings, dividends, etc. for the past ten years. The cash flow, price earnings ratio, price cash flow ratio and percent of dividend payout can then be calculated.

Next the small box related to working capital, etc. is filled in. The owner's equity percentage of capitalization gives us a clue to the leverage involved. Quarterly earnings, four-year average, and the last reported year come next. Skipping to the left-hand logarithmic chart we record sales, earnings, cash flow and book value. The beauty of this chart is that it gives a quick estimate of the rate of growth.

Having estimated the growth rate an explanation of the Growth Formula is in order. Granting that some companies grow and prosper at a more rapid pace than others, it is reasonable to expect to pay more for a dollar of the earnings of an aggressive company. Our object is to establish a standard for comparison.

Figure 1

COMPANY	QUALITY	PRICE	YIELD	DATE

Year											
High Price											
Low Price											
Sales ( )											
Net Earn ( )											
P/E ratio DJ P/E											
Cash Flow ( )											
P/C. F. ratio											
Dividend											
% of Payout											
Book Value ( )											

	H	L	Ave.	Last Year						Ave.	Last Year			
Working Cap. Ratio								M						
Inventory to Sales							Quarterly	J						
Margin of Profit							Earnings	S						
Owner's Equity % of Cap.								D						

Growth Formula - P/E ratio at zero gth. __ x __ gth. comp. 5 yrs. ____ = P/E <u>24</u> for ____ gth.
Back log % of sales _____ Opportunity in cv. pfd, cv. bds. wts? _____

Sales - Earnings Cash Flow - Book V

30%
25%
20%
15%
10%

High - Low   Price   Projection

Risk Ahead? Competition—limited customers-supply exceeding demand—new invention—labor—raw materials—power—transportation —cyclical—new or mature company—debt or com. increase—general market condition—control by individual or another company—current vol. % of outstanding stock. General Comment—Conclusion:

The average company has grown at an average of approximately 5% over a period of years. Investors in 1965 paid $18 for $1 of earnings on the average stock. Our first objective is to determine the price we might pay for earnings of a company that is not growing. Wishing to be conservative we estimate a 4% rate of growth. A projection of five years is used because this is about as long a period of time as can realistically be predicted. One dollar compounded at 4% for five years is $1.04, $1.08, $1.12, $1.17 and $1.22. To arrive at zero growth we divide the present average price earnings ratio—18—by 1.22 and conclude that 14.8 times earnings would be a reasonable price to pay for a company whose earnings might be the same five years from now. Each year zero growth must be recalculated to keep abreast of the changing psychology. Figure 2 illustrates the growth of one

Figure 2

5%	10%	15%	20%	25%	30%	35%	40%	45%
$1.05	$1.10	$1.15	$1.20	$1.25	$1.30	$1.35	$1.40	$1.45
1.10	1.21	1.32	1.44	1.56	1.69	1.82	1.96	2.10
1.16	1.33	1.52	1.73	1.95	2.20	2.46	2.74	3.04
1.22	1.46	1.75	2.08	2.44	2.86	3.32	3.84	4.41
1.28	1.61	2.01	2.50	3.05	3.70	4.48	5.38	6.39

dollar of earnings compounded at varying rates over a five-year period.

A 20% growth rate over five years will produce earnings twice as high as 5%, and 30% will generate earnings almost three times the 5% rate.

Now all of the ingredients are present for use in the Growth Formula. Assuming a 20% growth trend for net earnings, we multiply the price earnings ratio for zero growth by $2.50, the amount to which $1 of earnings will grow if the 20% growth rate continues five years. Multiplying 14.8 times 2.50 gives us approximately 37. We can reasonably expect to pay 37 times earnings for a company growing four times as fast as the average. The Growth Formula cannot be taken verbatim—it is only a means of appraising various rates of growth as related to price. Much interpolation by the investor is required. We can learn to increase or decrease the concluding figure according to such considerations as quality of the issue, the nature of the company's earnings, the potential and many other factors that might affect growth.

The right-hand chart should now be completed. Plot the year's high and low prices, connecting the points with a vertical line to create a bar chart. A 20% growth in earnings is projected in the upper section of the work sheet. Multiplying these earnings by 37 will give a price potential which can be charted.

Now let us consider "Opportunity in convertible preferred, convertible bonds, warrants" which is directly below the Growth Formula. Often an analysis of this section of a company's capitalization will uncover a more desirable medium of investment than the common stock. If the investor is fearful or uncertain about the market's future trend, a convertible bond or preferred stock might provide greater protection against loss in a declining market but equal possibility for gain in an advancing market. A speculator may choose convertible bonds because he is permitted to borrow more heavily on them than on common stock. Warrants are also intriguing to a speculator seeking additional leverage for his investment.

In the bottom part of the work sheet we analyze factors that might lessen the merit of the investment. Finally, pertinent comments and conclusions drawn from the foregoing study or from outside sources are included.

Understanding the use of this tool will not impress anyone with its capabilities unless it actually is put to use. Three companies have been shown here. Timing does not enter into the discussion. These companies have been selected because they offer diversified situations which illustrate the proper use of the evaluation work sheet.

The first study is of Black and Decker (Figure 3), a well-known manufacturer of power tools. Earnings, cash flow, book value and sales are all plotted on the ratio chart. The ten-year trend of sales and net earnings approximately follows a 15% a year growth line. It is evident the company is experiencing an

Figure 3

COMPANY Black & Decker		QUALITY A	PRICE $56			YIELD 2 4						DATE 12-31-65	
Year	1956	1957	1958	1959	1960	1961	1962	1963	1964	1965	1966	1967	1968	1969
High Price	11⁴	15³	15	21²	24⁶	36	32	32²	42¹	55⁴				
Low Price	7³	8⁴	9	13²	17⁵	20⁴	20²	25⁵	30³	37³				
Sales (15%)	49.9	52.4	43.5	52.8	60.8	67.6	75.8	85.1	101.0	119.6				
Net Earn (15%)	1.24	1.35	.79	1.12	1.19	1.23	1.38	1.54	1.92	2.37	2 73	3 13	3 80	4 14
P/E ratio DJ e/s	15 8.1	13 9.3	16 15.2	19 15.5	17 17.6	22 22.6	18 18.8	19 18.8	20 18.8	18 19.4				
Cash Flow (12%)	1.45	1.58	1.01	1.37	1.45	1.52	1.72	1.93	2.35					
P/CF. ratio	6.4x	8x	12x	12.6x	14.3x	18.4x	15.1x	15x	15.2x		1 25	1 50	1 80	2 10
Dividend	.26	.33	.38	.52	.75	.80	.80	.82	.92	1.10				
of Payout	21%	24.5%	48%	46%	63%	65%	58%	53%	48%	46%				
Book Value (10%)	6.44	7.43	8.21	8.82	9.48	9.90	10.45	11.17	12.15					

	H L	Ave.	Last Year					Ave.	Last Year	
Working Cap. Ratio		3.9:1	2.9:1			M	38	47		
Inventory to Sales			3.3x			Quarterly J	46	60		
Margin of Profit		20.4%	20.2%		Earnings	S	42	57		
Owner's Equity % of Cap.			98%			D	54	73		

Growth Formula — P/E ratio at zero gth. __15__ x __15%__ gth. comp. 5 years __20¢__ = P/E __30__ for __15%__ gth.
Backlog of Sales------ Opportunity in cv. pfd., cv. bds., wts ? __none__

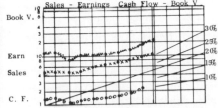

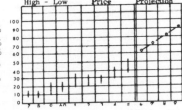

Risk Ahead? Competition—limited customers-supply exceeding demand—new invention—labor—raw materials—power—transportation —cyclical—new or mature company—debt or com. increase—general market condition—control by individual or another company—current vol. % of outstanding stock. General comment—Conclusion:

Demand in excess of capacity to produce. New facilities completed in 1965. Long-term debt, lowest in 10 years. Profit margin hurt in 1965 because of the need to subcontract some business. A 15% a year growth rate is well above average, however, manufactured tools are cyclical therefore we project a 23 P/E ratio rather than 30 times earnings. The stock is included in several growth industrial portfolios.

above-average growth rate and, therefore, justifies more thorough study. Projecting the 15% a year net earnings into the future we estimate and record earnings for the next four years. From the Growth Formula we conclude that, based on current market conditions, we might anticipate a price-earnings ratio of 30 times earnings. However, after considering the cyclical nature of the tool industry, the slower growth of book value and cash flow we adjust this to 23 times earnings. The high-low price chart is next put into use. Each year's high and low price is indicated. Then multiplying each year's projected earning by 23 we plot possible future prices. This estimate assumes there will be a continuation of the current earning trend and continuation of the public's disposition to pay $18 for $1 of earning power. The study so far would seem to encourage buying the stock, since its potential suggests a reasonable rate of future growth.

Now look at the price earnings as they relate to the Dow Industrial Average price earning ratio. The public was unwilling to pay much more than one half the Dow Industrial Average price for Black & Decker during the highs of '56 and '57. Perhaps this can be explained by the competitive nature of the industry and the fact that the company had not fully proved itself to investors. Today, however, the trade name stands out among power tools as superior equipment, and the company's past performance seems to justify a more liberal appraisal. Depreciation is not significant in this company's balance sheet; therefore, we can bypass cash flow and direct our attention to dividends. The percent of earnings paid out has varied widely in the past ten years. When the percentage has been low, however, the directors have supplemented the payout with a stock distribution. The record seems to suggest that a 50 to 60% payout is reasonable to expect and, therefore, dividend increases are likely.

Two other points are significant in this study and these are mentioned under the heading "general comment and conclusion." First, in Moody's *Handbook of Widely Held Stock* we see that management had decreased the company's indebtedness in the past ten years from $5.2 million to $2.3 million. With the substantial increase in volume of production we look with favor upon this indication of fiscal strength. Secondly, the stock appears in the portfolio of several growth-oriented mutual funds and institutional accounts. This shows that very skillful professional security management teams are favorably impressed by the company.

United States Borax (Figure 4) presents another interesting study. This company became publicly owned in 1956. It grew from a merger of the Pacific Coast Borax Co. and the U.S. Potash Co. and resulted in the world's largest producer of boron and second largest producer of potash. These products are vital to the building and agriculture industries. Also at that time with the automobile industry booming and space activity creating an element of glamor there was speculation concerning great potential in the use of boron as a fuel additive. The company suffered some setbacks with various non-recurring cost items in the ensuing years thus destroying the investors' initial attitude of high optimism.

Turning to an analysis of the company's present situation and possible future potential one becomes aware of a much more stable development in recent years. Sales and book value have steadily grown and recently a favorable trend is evident in net earnings and cash flow. A market appraisal of 8 to 10 times cash flow would seem to understate the company's potential. Investors' confidence, however, has been badly shaken by past performance and this is not quickly changed. Our Growth Formula suggests a 24 price earnings multiple but the stock currently trades at 17 times earnings. Evaluating these circumstances we select a compromise multiple of 20. Multiplying 1966 projected earnings of 2.35 times 20 we arrive at a potential price in 1966 of $46. This is approximately 40% above the current market price and would suggest a reasonable purchase. A note of caution, however: the erratic nature of this stock in the past plus its reliance on the volatile construction and agriculture industries counsels caution. Also the phasing out of its principal mine and opening of a new mine suggests this company's stock only to speculatively inclined investors.

A final study directs our attention to Kaiser Aluminum and

Figure 4

COMPANY U.S. Borax & Chem. QUALITY Bt PRICE 33 1/2 YIELD 3.2% DATE 12-31-65

Year	1956	1957	1958	1959	1960	1961	1962	1963	1964	1965	1966	1967	1968	1969
High Price	57^4	76^6	48^5	51^3	43^2	47^6	41^1	32^2	41^4	39^6				
Low Price	21^6	39	33^3	29^4	30^1	33^2	19^1	24^6	27^4	29				
Sales (8%)	50.5	51	53.1	62.2	66.7	67.8	73.6	81.7	89.8	est. 100				
Net Earn (10%)	1.47	1.15	41	1.29	1.50	1.37	1.43	1.62	2.00	2.14	2^{33}	2^{59}	2^{85}	3^{13}
P/E ratio DJ P/E	$15/27$	$13/50$	$16/100$	$19/31$	$17/24$	$22/30$	$18/21$	$19/17.5$	$20/17$	$18/17$				
Cash Flow (10%)	2.33	1.92	1.44	2.68	2.57	2.78	2.95	3.55	3.74					
P/C. F. ratio	17x	30x	28x	15x	14.5x	14.5x	10x	8x	9x					
Dividend	15	60	60	-	30	60	75	80	1.00	1.10	1^{20}	1^{30}	1^{40}	1^{55}
% of Payout	10%	52%	-	-	20%	44%	52%	49%	50%	51%				
Book Value (10%)	12.71	13.49	13.44	14.87	16.00	17.06	17.89	19.19	20.21					

	H/L	Ave.	Last Year
Working Cap. Ratio		2.4:1	3.1:1
Inventory to Sales			6.8x
Margin of Profit		21.5%	21.9%
Owner's Equity % of Cap.			

		Ave.	Last Year
	M	30	35
Quarterly Earnings	J	50	56
	S	50	57
	D	50	66

Growth Formula - P/E ratio at zero gth. 15 x 10% gth. comp. 5 yrs. 1.64 = P/E 24 for 10% gth.
Backlog % of sales ----- Opportunity in cv pfd, cv. bds, wts? none

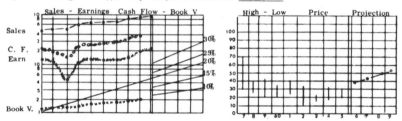

Risk Ahead? Competition—limited customers-supply exceeding demand—new invention—labor—raw materials—power—transportation —cyclical—new or mature company—debt or com. increase—general market condition—control by individual or another company—current vol. % of outstanding stock. General comment—Conclusion:

Deposits at Carlsbad, N.M. scheduled to run out about 1970. New high-grade properties now being developed in Saskatchewan. Nonrecurring costs in the past have retarded and caused earnings to fluctuate widely. A merger in 1956 and the stock being traded publicly for the first time were responsible for the wild speculative move in the price of the stock.

Chemical (Figure 5). This is one of the three major integrated aluminum companies in the United States. Its major activities are centered in the state of Washington and in West Virginia. Bauxite, its basic ore supply, comes from Jamaica and is sufficient to meet company requirements for over forty years. Kaiser is a relative newcomer in the industry and, therefore, has been forced to seek outside financing more than its competitors. About 50% of its financial needs have been met internally through a heavy depreciation allowance. With 45% of its capitalization represented by senior securities we conclude this to be a heavily leveraged situation.

Referring to a Standard and Poor's report we find that aluminum demand is increasing. Capacity is not being fully utilized and it is being projected that margins should improve and sales increase in the first half of 1966. For this reason we project a 20% increase in net earnings and using our multiple of 18 a potential price of 46 in the coming year is concluded.

Turning to a technical approach to stock analysis we note that a great deal of overhead resistance was generated in past years when the price was in the $40 to $42 range. It would seem a very considerable demand for this stock would have to be generated to push the price through the distribution area. The possibility for this development is not entirely absent. It would seem, therefore, that the prudent course for the investor might be to watch earning progress and news releases. If these developments proved encouraging and the stock breaks through the distribution area we would have a strong confirmation of much better things to be expected from this company. This obviously is not a stock for a long-term investor to hold. On the other hand, we might explore the merit of owning one of the four convertible preferred securities. The 4¾%–1957 series offers a good illustration of the merit and demerit of owning these issues. An obvious reason that would attract an investor to this security is that the current dividend yield is 4.8% versus 2.4% on the common. This convertible preferred is currently selling at approximately $98. It is convertible into common stock at a price of $47½ until May 31, 1967 and thereafter at a price of $55. In 1959 when the common stock sold at $65 or 79% above the

Figure 5

COMPANY Kaiser Alumnium & Co.   QUALITY B+   PRICE 36 5/8   YIELD 2.4%   DATE 12-31-

Year	1956	1957	1958	1959	1960	1961	1962	1963	1964	1965	1966	1967	8	1969
High Price	70 ²	46 ⁶	47 ⁶	65	54 ⁷	49 ⁴	37	42 ¹	42	41 ³				
Low Price	34 ⁷	22	23	37	32	29 ⁷	25	31 ¹	28 ⁵	28 ⁶				
Sales (4%))	343.6	391.6	408.6	435.5	406.6	424.0	444.2	437.1	515.9	est. 590	6 ²⁵			
Net Earn (0)	2.71	1.58	1.43	1.17	1.20	1.27	1.74	1.23	1.55	2.10	2 ⁵⁰			
P/E ratio DJ P/E	15 19	13 21	16 24	19 43	17 34	22 38	18 18	19 17	20 22	18 17				
Cash Flow (0)	4.96	3.85	4.28	4.33	4.50	4.41	4.79	4.00	4.12					
P/C F ratio	10x	9x	8x	8.5x	9x	9x	6.5x	9x	8.5x					
Dividend	86¢	90¢	90¢	90¢	90¢	90¢	90¢	90¢	90¢	90¢				
% of Payout	32%	57%	63%	77%	75%	71%	52%	73%	58%	43%				
Book Value (4%)	11.65	12.29	12.84	13.04	13.35	14.13	14.97	15.30	16.32					

	H	L	Ave.	Last Year
Working Cap. Ratio			27:1	3:1
Inventory to Sales				3.7x
Margin of Profit			23.5	18.5
Owner's Equity%of Cap.				45%

		Ave.	Last Year
Quarterly Earnings	M	31	43
	J	56	64
	S	35	45
	D	46	61

Growth Formula - P/E ratio at zero gth. __15x__ _4%_ gth. comp. 5 yrs. __1.21__ = P/E __18__ for _4%_ gth.
Backlog % of Sales ------ Opportunity in cv. pfd. , cv. bds. , wts ? ___Yes___

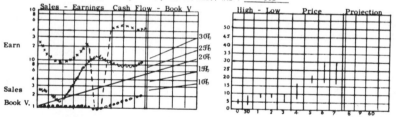

Risk Ahead? Competition—limited customers-supply exceeding demand—new invention—labor—raw materials—power—transportation—cyclical—new or mature company—debt or com. increase—general market condition—control by individual or another company—current vol. % of outstanding stock. General comment—Conclusion:

Based on increased demand for aluminum and elimination of new plant start-up expenses we estimate a 20% increase in net for 1967. High-low price chart suggests a buy at $42.50. Government seems representative to price increases in basic commodities.

current price, the preferred sold at $135 or 38% above its current level. One might have expected the preferred to advance on an equal percentage basis thereafter since the conversion price of $47½ had been exceeded. In 1962 when the common sold at $25 or 32% below the current price, the preferred held at $101 because the yield on the preferred justified investors standing pat for dividends alone. Today we have a different situation for in only a little more than a year the conversion price will be increased considerably. The preferred is therefore selling well below conversion and almost entirely on the basis of its yield. It would seem to hold little interest to the investor seeking capital appreciation. Only investors seeking above-average current income with nominal appreciation potential and very little downside risk might buy or hold this issue.

Once the investor concludes that an issue warrants purchase, he should check quarterly earning reports as they become current and compare his figures and conclusions with the new information that presents itself to his attention. A rapid advance in price, deteriorating earnings, sale of the stock by institutions—all such developments should be considered as possible reasons for selling.

Aside from analytical studies of companies an investor will profit by keeping a card catalogue or notebook to remind him of important dates such as when earnings of a company will be reported and its dividends declared by the board of directors. Investors who use a broker's custodian service will find this card catalogue a handy way of checking the dividends due to be credited to his account.

Another important set of records is of the purchase and sale of securities. This record sheet might include such data as the name of the security, date purchased, number of shares, price, commission and the offering price of a mutual fund. On the same page and line, figures related to the security's sale should be noted, such as the date of sale, number of shares, price, commission and the bid price of the mutual fund previously noted. The reason for noting the commission is for income tax calculations. A mutual fund is used for comparison purposes. The stated objective of the fund should closely resemble that of the investor.

When a security is purchased or sold the price of the fund is recorded beside it. At the end of each year the investor will be able to compare his performance with that of the fund's management.

Many investors have found themselves groping for a simple method of creating a total picture of their portfolio. Too frequently they review their accumulated holdings and find issues no longer serving their objective. They are overbalanced in one industry or issue. They lose sight of one or several issues for long periods of time. A portfolio Record Sheet may eliminate many of these deficiencies. It should include the security name, then four columns for the net earnings of past years, a column for the investor's projection of the next year's earnings, the current price of the stock, current price earnings ratio, a hoped for or projected price at which another review would be in order, and a space for various comments that might arise as a result of the study.

Securities should be grouped by industries to focus attention on the percentage of money concentration. A check of this nature might be initiated each quarter as new earnings are being reported. All this paperwork might appear to be rather formidable but once the system is put into practice it will require relatively little time.

Adventures in the Land of
the Red-Hot Tip

ELLEN WILLIAMSON

The lure of a stock market tip is a tempting one. Anything can happen when you act on one. Ellen Williamson, an investor since 1927, wittily writes of the sorrows that can beset the investor who heeds the urge to speculate.

. . . *L*ET us daringly and briefly turn to *speculation*—it's time you at least knew the terms even though you're never going to do anything so silly. Or are you?

The answer is yes. There apparently is no one who at some time or other in his or her life didn't take a flyer. The evidence is in the safe-deposit boxes of the deceased. There hasn't been a box opened yet that didn't contain, besides the stacks of gilt-edged triple-A bonds and the noble packet of first-class mortgages and the 1000-share certificate of General Motors, in an envelope marked "Worthless Securities," a limp little certificate entitling the owner to 10,000 shares of Gin Daisy Gold Mining or 5000 shares of Whammo Uranium or 1000 Lucky Perky Oil Drilling Corporation—that sort of thing.

The most staid of all my uncles died a few years ago. He

was almost saintlike in his investment policies and his name was synonymous with ultraconservatism: if Uncle Edwin had some it meant that it was safe as the Old North Church. Yet in his little old box of securities down at the bottom was a little old paper showing that he owned a piece of a night club in Las Vegas known as The Purple Powwow whose proprietor was referred to as "Dooky" Lo Scalpo. Furthermore, in the box was also an outlined plan (in Uncle Edwin's own squiggly writing)— a presentation, it could be called—to sell to the United States Government the idea of printing advertisements on the reverse side of all paper currency—items selling for $1.00, like neckties or pairs of nylons, would be on dollar bills, whiskey or a bottle of cologne or a pair of sneakers would advertise on the $5.00 bills, and automobiles, jewelry, and funeral directors would plug their merits on the bills of higher denomination. It is taking some of us years to grasp this colorful new side of Uncle Edwin.

All right! So you're maybe going to speculate a bit. Ever hear of *Puts* and *Calls*? At least they fix it so that you don't lose more than a certain prearranged amount.

Actually, a *Call* is when you rent some stock for a certain length of time, hoping that it will go up. In other words, it's an option that you take out on an amount of stock (100 shares is a unit) the way people take options on land or houses in the real estate business. You can acquire a Call from your broker for a month or six weeks, three months, or six months—whatever length of time you like, at a certain price.

For example, a six-month call on General Dynamics might cost you about $400 including the broker's commission. This really means that you are betting that General Dynamics is going to go up at least 4 points in the next six months (100 shares at $400 equals 4 points a share). If it does go up 4 points you will break even, and anything more will give you a profit of $100 a point.

If nothing much happens to General Dynamics in this six-month period of time—let's say that it was selling for 33 when you acquired the Call, and it is still 33 six months later, you have lost $400. If it had gone to 37 in the six months, you'd get your $400 back and break even, and had it risen to 57 (Oh Happy Day) you'd have made $2000 before taxes. But also let's suppose it went down to 25 or even 19—you still are only out $400, no matter how low General Dynamics goes.

A *Put* is exactly the opposite. In this case you take out an option on (or rent) a stock, betting that it will go down in a certain period of time.

I owned a Put only once. It was on 100 shares of Baltimore & Ohio. Someone "in the know" told me that the railroad's earnings for the year were going to be most disappointing, and the stock was bound to drop by many points. I paid $350 for a three-month Put and the stock was selling at 27. The following week the company did announce lower earnings and the stock went down to 24½. I got cold feet and bowed out at a loss of $100 (to come out even, remember, the stock had to go down 3½ points, or down to 23½), and I'm glad I did as the stock went up after that so that if I'd held it for the whole three months I'd have lost the whole $350—when the Put expired B & O common was up in the 30s somewhere.

Sometimes a speculator will buy both a Put and a Call at the same time on the same stock, and this is known as a *Straddle*. A purchase of each is a wise precaution in the case of a volatile stock. Remember when Xerox went down 59 points in one week? Think of the fun you'd have had, if you had decided to buy a Call on it, and then prudently changed it into a Straddle instead. You could have exercised the Put part of the Straddle that week, then held on to the Call part for six more weeks and you would have made a heap of money in both.

Ever hear of *Strips* and *Straps*? Well, a Strip is sort of a lopsided Straddle: it's a pair of Calls and a single Put, and a Strap is a Straddle and a single Call, in other words a Strap is two Puts and one Call and a Strip is two—or is it the other way around? And what are they for? The answer is *Never Mind! Skip it!*

Now then—some people spend a happy lifetime with Puts and Calls. Personally I've never done very well with them, and when I hear that something is going up I'd greatly rather own the stock outright: you'd be surprised how fast three months can speed by when you have a loss of two or three points on a Call. I can hear you complain, "Oh if I'd only waited until *now* to get the Call," or, "If I'd only taken a six-month Call," or, "If I'd just bought 10 shares of the stock instead."

About the only time that owning a Call is justifiable is when most of your money is tied up and your grandfather tells you in the utmost secrecy that his very own company, the Wet Whistle Distillers Corporation, is going to pay an extra dividend of $3.00 a share and raise the regular payment from 50¢ a quarter to $1.00, plus the common stock is going to be listed on the New York Stock Exchange, and all this is going to be announced after the next directors' meeting, which is to be held next month. Yes, in an unusual case such as this, the acquisition of a few Calls would be justified—this is, if Grandfather doesn't make a habit of sampling his own products.

Now that you are acquainted with Puts and Calls, a word about margins should follow, seeing that it is also a form of speculation.

Basically there are two kinds of accounts in brokerage firms: the *cash account* and the *margin account* (sometimes called the *general account*).

In the former, all securities are paid for in full as they are purchased, while in the latter the customers pay for only part of their securities and the brokerage firm loans them the money for the balance, charging an interest rate the way banks do.

At present, margin requirements are 70 per cent, which means that if you were to buy 100 shares of General Motors at let's say $100 a share, instead of paying $10,000 the way people do who have cash accounts, you would only pay $7000, and the firm would loan you the remaining $3000 at the current rate of about 5½ per cent. You would then have what is called a *debit balance* in your account and its amount, of course, is $3000.

In 1929 margin requirements were only 10 per cent, and in 1946 the Federal Reserve Board, which decides what the rate will be, raised it to 100 per cent. In other words, buying on margin was not allowed at all and anyone whose account already had a debit balance in it was said to be *frozen*. Why was it raised to 100 per cent? To curb credit, to act as a brake. It was right after the war, remember, and there was lots of easy money around.

The risk in buying on margin should be obvious. If disaster struck General Motors, let's suppose, and the stock went down and down to around 45 or 44, the New York Stock Exchange requires your broker to give you a *margin call*, meaning that unless you can put up more money at once your stock will be sold at the market, the brokerage firm will get its $3000 back plus its commission plus interest on the loan, and you will get the paltry leftovers of what was once $7000.

A margin requirement of 70 per cent on 100 shares of General Motors does not seem to be a very good example of wild specu-lation. Consider instead the 10 per cent of 1020, so flimsy a margin requirement that you can see how easily the whole price structure of the stock market crumbled and collapsed as margin calls that couldn't be met set off further margin calls, the chain reaction bringing the market down as easily as blowing down a house of cards.

And now that you are becoming a Sophisticated Investor, are you wise about tips? So many people have no judgment about them, and can't tell a good tip from a bad one. A good tip isn't a tip at all; it's actually sound information from a usually reliable source.

Let's say that you are on your way home from Europe on the *Nieuw Amsterdam* and you've been asked to sit at the captain's table. The man on your right is the president of Bethlehem Steel (Hi there, Mr. Cort!). During the course of the voyage you get to know him and his wife (Hi, Liza!) very well, and when he volunteers that his company is going to report record earn-ings for the current year and that its backlog of orders is the highest ever, you might just add a little Bethlehem Steel to your portfolio on your arrival home.

Similarly, in the winter of 1951 I met the nicest man at a dinner dance at the Waldorf-Astoria. I not only sat next to him at dinner but danced with him several times during the evening. He and his wife had just returned from a trip to Kuwait where they had been entertained by the ruling sheik, a man so rich from the royalties of his newly discovered oil wells that his income was— well, here's what the nice man said:

"I don't know anything about your terms of financial reference, but I can't help worrying about a man whose personal income is over $100,000 a day and tax-free."

I remember gasping at the thought of such wealth.

"And that's not the half of it," he continued, "by next year his income may be eight or even ten times as much. He is hiring a committee to help him figure out what to do with all of it. After all, you can only ride in one Rolls-Royce or Cadillac at a time, only eat so many steaks a day, and only sleep in one bed at a time."

As my dancing partner turned out to be a director of the Gulf Oil Corporation, and as Gulf Oil owned half the wells in Kuwait I figured that Gulf stood to make ten times or so more than the sheik, so the next day I trotted out and bought some Gulf, and am happy to report that one year later the stock had more than doubled in value.

However: to be wary of all tips is a word to the wise. Get them checked thoroughly before wading in.

Years ago there was a well-known big fat Wall Street trader who used to waddle down the theater aisle to a first-row seat just as the opening curtain was going up. People in the audience would nudge each other and whisper his name with reverent awe. He would stifle a sneeze or cough with a handkerchief which he'd pull out of a side pocket of his coat and at the same time a few small slips of paper would also fall out.

As the lights dimmed, people would surreptitiously pick up the slips of paper. Each one would be an order to buy 1000 shares of one or another stock at the market the next morning. Thinking they were onto a hot tip, part of the audience would rush out at the intermission and wire their brokers to buy some for them too. Meanwhile, back in Old Snake-in-the-Grass' Wall Street office, arrangements were being made to unload this same stock the following morning.

Here's a last anecdote about tips, and it concerns the common stock of The Philip Horsefall Company.

Toward the end of World War II my husband and I lived in Washington, D.C. In the October after the Normandy Invasion the Navy transferred him back to the good old U.S.A., and after a thirty-day leave, blissfully spent in Sea Island, Georgia, I found myself happily house-hunting in jam-packed over-crowded war-rationed Washington.

With good luck it wasn't too long before we discovered a dear little brick house smack next door to the empty Japanese Embassy—just the place to walk our dog, and in no time at all the movers were carting all our scratched-and-marred worldly goods (fresh from two years in storage) into the house, and Bessie, our all-time favorite cook, was unpacking pots and pans while taking little sips of tea laced with rum (sometimes in Bessie's case it was rum laced with tea).

"Madam"—Bessie was the formal type—"best if you'd find us a grocery store in the neighborhood, for soon I'll be wanting to telephone an order."

I told her that I'd go over to Magruder's (a friend had said that it was Washington's best) and establish credit—open a charge account at once.

"Madam." Bessie looked at me scornfully. "Better if you'd get us a smaller store. That Magruder sends all the best things to the embassics. We'd be lucky to get cat food from them."

"We'll be lucky to get any meat at all," I said, "we have so few red stamps. However, you're right. In a smaller store we'll be treated as more important customers. I will buzz over to Georgetown and find us something."

Bessie held up a hand in protest. "No, madam, Georgetown is also too fashionable. Go over to Columbus Avenue, find a privately owned grocery store where them big tall apartment buildings are."

She was right. I found a place there called Stein's Market and introduced myself to Mr. Stein himself, a dark harassed-looking little man in his thirties.

"Sorry, we can't take any more charge accounts," he said promptly. "The bookkeeper will leave."

"Oh come *on.*" I gave him what I hoped was a dazzling smile. "Just one more account won't hurt her; besides, we'll be very good customers. My husband is just back from two years in Great Britain where he ate nothing but Brussels sprouts. He is hungry as a wolf. Also we know lots of people here and expect to have a lot of dinner parties."

A crafty look crossed Mr. Stein's face.

"How much does your grocery bill usually run?"

I had no more idea what *any* family grocery bill would run to than a horse. After three years of camp following and living in hotels and motels and visiting and moving I didn't dare even to guess.

Again I tried the dazzling smile, and then had a dazzling idea.

"Our bill should be about the same as the Turkish Embassy's." I spoke casually.

A flash of a gold tooth and the account was opened.

I explained that we would not be able to buy any rationed meat; the few red ration points that we had would have to be used for butter (our daughter had gone off to boarding school with extra red points from us at the request of the school).

"But we don't care," I finished heartily. "We'll subsist on fish and oxtails and anything that you can supply."

At his suggestion I left our pathetic little booklets of red stamps with the bookkeeper (Mrs. Stein) to be doled out when we needed butter, and returned to the new house to unpack barrels and hang pictures and read *Forever Amber* in the coffee breaks.

A few weeks later, all settled in and acting like a native, I was lunching at the Statler with a cousin from Akron who was in Washington on business. He worked for the Quaker Oats Company, at that time in the container division, and was all excited about a new package.

"The Philip Horsefall Company," he volunteered, "has an experimental machine that can make a transparent rigid plastic box so cheaply that we are thinking of packaging puffed wheat and puffed rice and even rolled oats in them. The customer can see for himself what the cereal looks like—also can see the premium teacup or plate in the Mother's Oats package. What do you think of the idea?"

"The customer can also see a dead mouse or a boll weevil should there be one inside," I suggested. "I think it's a fine idea. Would it sell more oats?"

"We'd market-test it first and see," he said. "The Philip Horsefall people are of course wildly enthusiastic. If we decide to do it they'd make a fortune."

I said I'd never heard of them.

"It's an old company. They've made boxes and such for years and years. Their common stock sells on the Big Board—around $5 a share or less."

"Let me know what happens," I said, and he said he would.

Later that afternoon found me in Stein's Market staring fixedly at a shelf towering with packages of Quaker Oats Puffed Rice, trying to visualize them in the see-through box, and who should find me there but Mr. Stein.

"What can I do for you today—a little cereal perhaps?" he inquired.

I explained why I was staring, told him about the plastic box, and even mentioned the low-priced Philip Horsefall stock.

He seemed interested and said he'd heard of the stock but never knew what it made.

"Well, *if* the Quaker Oats Company *does* decide to use this transparent packaging, and *if* my investment man approves, I'm maybe going to buy some Philip Horsefall stock and make enough money to rent the Japanese Embassy," I told him.

"Let me know if you do," he said, and I saw the gold tooth gleam as he turned away.

The next time that I was in New York I asked Tom about the stock.

"Listen," he said, "that's a *terrible* company. No matter what kind of an order they'd get or what kind of a package they'd turn out they wouldn't make any money—they've been trying for years and years and nothing happens—leave them alone."

I promptly forgot about Philip Horsefall for several weeks until I noticed that the stock was going up. It crept quietly from 4½ to 5 one week, then maddeningly rose to 5½ the following week and 6 the next. I was so irritated by it that I resolved not to look at any stocks beginning with "P" for the rest of the year. However I couldn't help peeking now and then, and sure enough—there was old Philip Horsefall Common selling at 7¼, and just before Christmas it went to 8.

Meanwhile, although I never did hear how many dinner parties the Turkish Embassy was giving, we were entertaining busily and I would guess that we were giving them stiff competition. With Bessie dreaming up tasty dishes in the kitchen, and an easygoing red-haired waitress named Lillian (oh those broken dishes) in the dining room, and a cleaning man known as "Smelly James" who came the following morning, we had six or eight for dinner once or twice a week all that winter.

And all the time that the Allied forces under General Patton were marching nearer and nearer the Rhine, and General MacArthur's men were getting closer and closer to Manila, and our Russian allies were approaching Berlin mile by mile from the east, we in war-rationed Washington were eating better and better—*we*, in this case meaning us and our guests—thanks to Stein's Market.

When Bessie ordered for a Saturday night dinner party, she always telephoned on Friday. Mr. Stein himself took the order.

"We have a very nice five-rib roast of beef today," he would volunteer, "how would you like to have me send it over?"

"But our red points—can we afford it?" Bessie would ask.

"Now you just let me worry about that," Mr. Stein would answer unctuously. "And how are you fixed for butter? I'd better send you an extra pound."

At first Bessie and I worried ourselves sick—we were sure that we couldn't afford such extravagances—the Ration Board would be knocking on our door any day and we'd be hauled off to jail. But nothing of the sort happened, and Mr. Stein continued to offer us delicious goody after delicious goody—bacon, soap flakes (*very* rare in those days), filets mignons, potato chips (I hadn't seen any of these for *years*) and cartons of *real* cigarettes—Luckies and Chesterfields instead of those Coffeetones and Hushpuppies—or whatever they were called that most people were trying to get along with (they tasted as if someone else had smoked them first), if they were lucky enough to find a cigar store that had some for sale.

It was not only fun for us but also a lot of fun for our guests— it was a joy to watch the incredulous expression on the faces of newly returned Navy and Army officers, especially those who'd been stationed in London, when they saw one of Bessie's succulent-looking sirloin steaks, sizzling in butter and surrounded by delicately browned mushrooms and shoestring potatoes.

We continued to eat in this Lucullan manner through the winter and into the spring. By V-E Day when no F. B. I. men had appeared to question us and no word had come from the War Ration Board denouncing us as scofflaws or black market users or whatever we were, we breathed more easily, and by V-J Day we were actually believing that in some mysterious way *our* red points either secretly multiplied when lying quietly in their books the way rock crystals do under the right circumstances, or that our blue points (there were more of them for each person than red, and I think they were for canned peaches and things like that) had in some mysterious way turned red.

It turned out to be nothing like that. A month or so after the war was over my husband was out of the Navy. We had sold the cute little brick house and were off to New York. I dropped in to pay the final grocery bill and bid Mr. Stein a fond farewell.

"Meat will still be rationed for a few more months," he told me, "so here is the name and address of a grocery firm in New York which is run by a friend of mine. I've made arrangements for him to look after you."

I thanked him enthusiastically, told him he was a real pal and that I'd never forget him, and timidly asked for the ration books. As he handed them over he remarked casually: "By the way, did you realize that you owe me 1200 red points?"

My heart sank. Of course I knew it—I'd been kidding myself for months—only what could I *do*? Furthermore it was all Mr.

Stein's fault for egging me on. I had a fast vision of myself being escorted into the paddy wagon with people throwing tomatoes and rocks at me while flashbulbs popped.

Mr. Stein's gold tooth showed itself briefly in a quick smile.

"However," he said, "I've decided to cancel the whole thing, and you don't owe me anything. You see, after you gave me the tip on Philip Horsefall I bought 2000 shares—also bought 500 for the missis, paid a little over $4 a share for them. I figured here was a tip right from the horse's mouth for Horsefall." He laughed merrily at this show of wit and I noticed that now he had three gold teeth, not just one.

"I sold 1000 shares at 8½," he continued, "last week I sold the other 1000 at 13 and also the 500 of the missis. It sure was the best tip I ever got and the missis thanks you too. Best tip I ever got."

A Sobering Thought for Today: If Philip Horsefall had gone down to 2½, for example, instead of up to 13, would Mr. Stein have given us and all our guests ptomaine poisoning?

Don't Forget Your Gilbert and Sullivan

PHILIP A. FISHER

*To most investors, the past performance of a company has
critical bearing on deciding whether to invest in its shares
of stock. In this selection, however, investment expert
Philip A. Fisher offers his readers some unexpected and, to
many, controversial advice on how to view a company's
past performance.*

GILBERT and Sullivan are hardly considered authorities on
the stock market. Nevertheless we might keep in mind their
"flowers that bloom in the spring, tra-la" which, they tell us,
have "nothing to do with the case." There are certain superficial financial statistics which are frequently given an unde-
served degree of attention by many investors. Possibly it is an
exaggeration to say that they completely parallel Gilbert and
Sullivan's flowers that bloom in the spring. Instead of saying they
have nothing to do with the case, we might say they have very
little to do with it.

Foremost among such statistics are the price ranges at which a
stock has sold in former years. For some reason, the first thing
many investors want to see when they are considering buying
a particular stock is a table giving the highest and lowest price

at which that stock has sold in each of the past five or ten years. They go through a sort of mental mumbo-jumbo, and come up with a nice round figure which is the price they are willing to pay for the particular stock.

Is this illogical? Is it financially dangerous? The answer to both questions is emphatically yes. It is dangerous because it puts the emphasis on what does not particularly matter, and diverts attention from what does matter. This frequently causes investors to pass up a situation in which they would make big profits in order to go into one where the profits will be much smaller. To understand this we must see why the mental process is so illogical.

What makes the price at which a stock sells? It is the composite estimate *at that moment* of what all those interested think the corrective value of such shares may be. It is the composite appraisal of the outlook for this company by all potential buyers and sellers, weighted by the number of shares each buyer or seller is disposed to bid for or offer, in relation to a similar appraisal, at the same moment, of the outlook for other companies with their individual prospects. Occasionally, something like forced liquidation will produce a moderate deviation from this figure. This happens when a large holder presses stock on the market for reasons—such as liquidating an estate or paying off a loan—which may not be directly related to the seller's view of the real value of the shares. However, such pressures usually cause only moderate variation from the composite appraisal of the prevailing price of the shares, since bargain hunters normally step in to take advantage of the situation, which thereby adjusts itself.

The point which is of real significance is that the price is based on the *current* appraisal of the situation. As changes in the affairs of the company become known, these appraisals become correspondingly more or less favorable. In relation to other stocks, these particular shares then move up or down. If the factors appraised were judged correctly, the stock becomes permanently more or less valuable in relation to other stocks. The shares then stay up or down. If more of these same factors continue to develop, they in turn are recognized by the financial community. The stock then goes and stays either further up or down, as the case may be.

Therefore, the price at which the stock sold four years ago may have little or no real relationship to the price at which it sells today. The company may have developed a host of able new executives, a series of new and highly profitable products, or any number of similar desirable attributes that make the stock intrinsically worth four times as much in relation to the price of other stocks as it was worth four years ago. The company might have fallen into the hands of an inefficient management and slipped so badly in relation to competition that the only way recovery could occur would be through the raising of much new capital. This might force such a dilution of the shares that the stock today could not possibly be worth more than a quarter of the price of four years ago.

Against this background, it can be seen why investors so frequently pass up stocks which would have brought them huge future gains for ones where the gain is very much smaller. By giving heavy emphasis to the "stock that hasn't gone up yet" they are unconsciously subscribing to the delusion that all stocks go up about the same amount and that the one that has already risen a lot will not climb further, while the one that has not yet gone up has something "due" it. Nothing could be further from the truth. The fact that a stock has or has not risen in the last several years is of no significance whatsoever in determining whether it should be bought now. What does matter is whether enough improvement has taken place or is likely to take place in the future to justify importantly higher prices than those now prevailing.

Similarly, many investors will give heavy weight to the per-share earnings of the past five years in trying to decide whether a stock should be bought. To look at the per-share earnings by themselves and give the earnings of four or five years ago any significance is like trying to get useful work from an engine which is unconnected to any device to which that engine's power is supposed to be applied. Just knowing, by itself, that four or five years ago a company's per-share earnings were either four times or a quarter of this year's earnings has almost no significance in indicating whether a particular stock should be bought or sold. Again, what counts is knowledge of background conditions. An understanding of what probably will happen over the next several years is of overriding importance.

The investor is constantly being fed a diet of reports and so-called analyses largely centered around these price figures for the past five years. He should keep in mind that it is the next five years' earnings, not those of the past five years, that now matter to him. One reason he is fed such a diet of back statistics is that if this type of material is put in a report it is not hard to be sure it is correct. If more important matters are gone into, subsequent events may make the report look quite silly. Therefore, there is a strong temptation to fill up as much space as possible with indisputable facts, whether or not the facts are significant. However, many people in the financial community place emphasis on this type of prior years' statistics for a different set of reasons. They seem to be unable to grasp how great can be the change in just a few years' time in the real value of certain types of modern corporations. Therefore they emphasize these past earnings records in a sincere belief that detailed accounting descriptions of what happened last year will give a true picture of what will happen next year. This may be true for certain classes of regulated companies such as public utilities. For the type of enterprise which I believe should interest an investor desiring the best results for his money, it can be completely false.

A striking example of this centers around events with which I had the good fortune to be quite familiar. In the summer of 1956, an opportunity arose to buy a fair-sized block of shares in Texas Instruments, Inc. from its principal officers who were also its largest stockholders. Careful study of this company revealed that it rated not just well but magnificently. . . . Reason for the officers to sell appeared entirely legitimate; this occurs frequently in true growth companies. Their holdings had already advanced so much that several of them had become millionaires so far as their holdings in their own company were concerned. In contrast, their other assets were relatively negligible. Therefore, particularly since they were selling but a tiny part of the shares they owned, some diversification seemed entirely in order. The ever-present possibility of estate tax liability alone would be sufficient to make such a course prudent from the standpoint of these key executives, regardless of the future of their company.

At any rate, negotiations were completed to acquire these shares at a price of 14. This represented twenty times the anticipated 1956 per-share earnings of about 70 cents. To anyone who gave particular weight to past statistics, this seemed well beyond the bounds of prudence. Per-share earnings had been reported at 39¢, 40¢, 48¢, and 50¢ for the prior four years of 1952 to 1955 respectively—hardly an exciting growth record. Even more depressing to those who subordinate the more important factors of management and current business trends to superficial statistical comparisons, the company, through a corporate acquisition, had obtained the benefits of some loss carryforward, which had made possible subnormal income tax charges during much of this period. This made any price calculated on the basis of past statistics seem even higher. Finally, even if 1956 earnings were included in an evaluation, a superficial study of this situation might still have produced grave forebodings. True, the company was currently doing remarkably well in the promising field of transistors. But regardless of the obviously glowing future for the semi-conductor industry as a whole, how long could a company of this size be expected to maintain its strong trade position against the larger and older companies, with much stronger balance sheets, which were sure to make a major competitive effort to participate in the great growth that lay ahead for transistors?

When the usual SEC channels reported this officer selling, a rash of heavy trading broke out in Texas Instruments shares with relatively little change in price. Much of this selling, I suspect, was induced by various brokerage comments that appeared. Most of these furnished the past statistical record and commented on the historically high price, the competition that lay ahead, and the inside selling. One such bulletin went so far as to express complete agreement with the management of Texas Instruments. It reported the officers were selling and stated: "We agree with them and recommend the same course!" Major buyer during this period, I have been told, was a large and well informed institution.

What happened in the next twelve months? Texas Instruments' geophysical and military electronic business, overlooked in the flurry of controversy, continued to grow. The semi-conductor (transistor) division grew even more rapidly. More important than the growth in transistor volume were the great strides taken by this able management in research, in plans for mechanization, and in building up the distribution organization in this key semi-conductor field. As evidence piled up that 1956 results were not a flash in the pan but that this relatively small company would continue as one of the largest and lowest cost producers in what promises to be one of the fastest growing segments of American industry, the financial community began revising upward the price-earnings ratio it would pay for a chance to participate in this well-run enterprise. As the summer of 1957 came around and the management publicly estimated that year's per-share earnings at around $1.10, the 54 per cent growth in earnings had produced in just twelve months an approximate 100 per cent increase in market value.

In the original edition* I went on to say:

I suspect that if the headquarters of the principal divisions of this company were not located in Dallas and Houston, but were situated along the northern half of the Atlantic seaboard or in the Los Angeles metropolitan area—where more financial analysts and other managers of important funds could more easily learn about the company—this price-earnings ratio might have gone even higher during this period. If, as appears probable, Texas Instruments' sales and earnings continue their sharp upward trend for some years to come, it will be interesting to see whether this continued growth, of itself, does not

* Published in 1958 [eds.].

in time provide some further upward change in the price-earnings ratio. If this happens, the stock would again go up at an even faster rate than the earnings are advancing, the combination which always produces the sharpest increases in share prices.

Has this optimistic forecast been confirmed? A look at the record may jolt those who still insist that it is possible to appraise an investment by a superficial analysis of past earnings and little more. Profits rose from $1.11 per share in 1957 to $1.84 in 1958 and give promise of topping $3.50 in 1959. Since the first edition of this book was completed the company attained honors that were bound to rivet the attention of the financial community upon it. In 1958, in the face of competition from some of the generally acclaimed giants of the electronics and electrical equipment industry, International Business Machines Corporation, overwhelmingly the largest electronic calculating machine manufacturer in the world, selected Texas Instruments to be its associate for joint research effort in the application of semi-conductors to this type of equipment. Again, in 1959 Texas Instruments announced a technological breakthrough whereby it was possible to use semi-conductor material of approximately the same size as existing transistors, not alone for a transistor but for a complete electronic circuit! What this may bring about in the way of miniaturization almost staggers the imagination. As the company has grown, its unusually able product research and development groups have increased proportionately. Today few informed people have much doubt that the company's long series of technical and business "firsts" will continue in the years ahead.

How has the market price of these shares responded to all this? Has the price-earnings ratio continued to advance as, twenty-two months ago, I indicated appeared probable? The record would appear to be in the affirmative. Per-share earnings have a little more than tripled since 1957. The stock is up over five times from the price of 26¼ at which it was selling when the first edition was completed. The current price, incidentally, represents a gain of better than 1000 per cent from the price of 14, which was mentioned in the original edition as the price at which a fair-sized block of this stock had been bought less than three and one-half years before. In spite of this steep rise it will be interesting to see whether further gains in sales and earnings in the years ahead do not produce still more worthwhile appreciation.

This brings up another line of reasoning which causes some investors to pay undue attention to these unrelated statistics on past price ranges and per-share earnings. This is the belief that whatever has happened for a number of years is bound to continue indefinitely. In other words, some investors will find a stock the per-share earnings and market price of which have risen in each of the past five or ten years. They will conclude that this trend is almost certain to continue indefinitely. I will agree that this might happen. But in view of the uncertainty in timing the results of research and of the costliness of bringing out the new products that make this type of growth possible, it is quite common for even the most outstanding growth companies to have occasional one- to three-year dips in their rate of earnings. Such dips can produce sharp declines in their shares. Therefore, to give emphasis to this kind of past earning record, rather than to the background conditions that can control the future earning curve, may prove very costly.

Does all this mean that past earnings and price ranges should be completely ignored in deciding whether to buy a stock? No. It is only when given an importance they do not deserve that they become dangerous. They are helpful as long as it is realized they are only auxiliary tools to be used for specialized purposes and not major factors in deciding the attractiveness of a common stock. Thus, for example, a study of per-share earnings for various prior years will throw considerable light on how cyclical a stock may be, that is, on how much the company's profits will be affected by the varying stages of the business cycle. More important, comparing past per-share earnings with price ranges will furnish the price-earnings ratio at which the stock sold in the past. This serves as a base from which to start measuring what the price-earnings ratio may be in the future.

Here again, however, it must be kept in mind that it is the future and not the past which governs. Perhaps the shares for years have steadily sold at only eight times earnings. Now, however, changes in management, establishment of an outstanding research department, etc., are putting the company into the class that is currently selling around fifteen times earnings instead of eight. Then anyone estimating future earnings and figuring the anticipated value of the shares at only eight instead of fifteen times earnings might again be leaning too heavily on past statistics.

I titled this . . . "Don't Forget Your Gilbert and Sullivan." Perhaps I should have titled it "Don't be influenced by what doesn't matter." Statistics of former year earnings and particularly of per-share price ranges of these former years quite frequently "have nothing to do with the case."

The Low-High Spread

SAMUEL C. GREENFIELD

*An investment adviser for many years, Samuel C.
Greenfield is also a well-respected and popular lecturer and
author. His approach to investing in the stock market is
original and promising, and he treats a complex subject —
evaluating a company's value — with clarity and
thoroughness. Greenfield proposes a system for the
investor to use in order to arrive at an accurate evaluation
of a company's stock.*

The Fashion Followers

*I*T is unlikely that the crafty Cassius could have foreseen 2,000 years ago that stock market traders of the twentieth century would be blaming their losses on bad luck. The prophet was Shakespeare. He understood the frailties of human nature.

Many traders have little success with their investments. For a number of illogical reasons, they invariably buy at the wrong time. If they sold when they bought they would make fortunes. The only time their securities rise is when they contemplate buying them. Then the stocks keep going up day after day while they watch in anguish. Finally, exhausted, they can hold out no longer and succumb. From then on the stocks start falling. What demon haunts them?

There are many reasons why some people lose consistently. One of the most important is that they are the victims of the villain "fashion." The same pressure that dictates the clothing they wear and the cigarettes they smoke determines what securities they buy and when they buy them. Examine some portfolios and you can date the purchases. U.S. Steel was probably bought in 1959 and 1960, Motorola in 1966, and Monsanto Chemical in 1965. It was during these years that these enjoyed the height of their popularity. They were the topic of "smart" conversation, made the most active list, received the best press, were discussed by the finest services, and enjoyed the most bizarre rumors. They were the "in stocks." Naturally, they were bought. Then they went out of style and were replaced by new, more romantic issues. Round and round goes the market.

Buying a security should be more than calling your broker and placing an order. That is the last step in a long series of steps. For many individuals, it is the second step. The first is hearing about the stock from a friend, neighbor, or associate. The second is to rush to the phone before it is too late, and order the stock bought at the market. The last is to sell it before the year ends for a tax loss.

Low-High Spread

One of the first things to do before buying a security is to study its historic trading pattern. Is it a volatile issue whose swings are wide, or is its activity confined to a narrow range? Once that is determined, the next question is, what is the price of the security now? Is it near the high of the year or the low? Has it already increased 100% from its lowest price? My personal experience is that whenever a client calls excitedly about a security, it is at the high of the year. No one ever calls to inquire about a stock when it is at its low.

There is an easy way to study the historic trading pattern of a security. The Standard & Poor reports on listed securities indicate, among other bits of information, the highest and lowest prices at which they sold each year. The facts can be arranged in tabular form, called a Low-High Spread chart. To illustrate, examine two securities, Standard Oil of New Jersey, representing the group which normally moves within a narrow trading range, and Zenith Radio Company, representing stocks whose swings are much wider.

Chart 1 indicates the percentage increase from the low to high

Chart 1   Low-High Spread Chart from Low to High of Same Year (Adjusted for splits and stock dividends)

	Standard Oil New Jersey			Zenith Radio		
	Lowest Price Per Share	Highest Price Per Share	Percent Spread L-H	Lowest Price Per Share	Highest Price Per Share	Percent Spread L-H
1956	$50	$63	26%	$ 3	$ 4	33%
1957	48	69	43	3	4	33
1958	48	60	25	4	12	200
1959	46	59	28	10	23	130
1960	38	51	34	15	22	46
1961	41	52	27	16	41	156
1962	45	60	33	21	38	81
1963	58	77	33	26	42	62
1964	75	93	23	31	44	42
1965	74	90	22	31	61	97
1966	66	84	27	46	89	93
1967	59	71	20	48	72	50

of the *same year*. For Standard Oil of New Jersey, for example, the stock increased from $50 to $63 in 1956 or 26%. In 1957 the increase was 43%, etc.

Studying the annual percentage increase gives the investor valuable information. Standard Oil of New Jersey, for example, moved in a narrow range. During the eleven years in this study, the increase never reached 50%. In only 4 years did it rise above

30%. Under the circumstances, where the stock was purchased after it increased by as little as 25% from its low, it did not rise too much after that. It had gone just about as far as it could that year. Thereafter it started its annual descent. Many who purchased thousands of shares at or near the top must have been quite frustrated as they saw their "blue chip" fall.

Zenith presents a totally different picture. Its moves are wide. In the same eleven years its low-high spread was less than 50% in only 4 years. In 3 years it exceeded 100%. Buying it when it had increased by 30% from its low represented little risk. But when the security was purchased after it had increased 75 to 80%, the risk increased, and kept increasing as the percentage rose.

One should know whether he is buying a security whose low-high spread is narrow or wide; also how narrow and how wide. History never repeats in precisely the same way. However, the past can be a useful guide.

The investor should learn an important lesson from these two representative charts. Each security has its own individual low-high spread pattern, from which it may stray occasionally, but which characterizes it. If the security is purchased near the lower area of its annual range it will probably do well. However, if it is purchased nearer the higher area, it will probably do poorly. There are always exceptions, but don't hope for them.

In fact, it would be wise, when making the chart, to write the word DANGER in dark red, above the area where the risk increases beyond the normal.

In the case of Standard Oil of New Jersey, the risk area is reached after the security has increased 20% or more above the year's low. In the case of Zenith, it is above 40%.

The Perennial Pattern

There is an important *similarity* between the two groups that is as significant as their *difference*. Each has its winter when it falls to its lowest price of the year and its summer when it reaches its highest.

The low-high table reveals a second important piece of information. It indicates the extent to which a security falls each year after it has reached its pinnacle. For example, after Standard Oil of New Jersey reached $63 per share in 1956, it fell to $48 the next year. It then climbed to $69 only to drop to $48 in 1958. Zenith Radio pursued a similar course of action. It also rose to a high each year only to fall significantly the next, etc.

Revise Chart 1 by placing a series of oblique lines from the *high of one year* to the *low of the following year*.

The oblique lines in Chart 2 indicate the drop from the high

Chart 2 Low-High Spread Chart from High of One Year to Low of Following Year (Adjusted for stock dividends and splits)

	Standard Oil New Jersey		Zenith Radio	
	Lowest Price Per Share	Highest Price Per Share	Lowest Price Per Share	Highest Price Per Share
1956	$50 DOWN	$63	$ 3 DOWN	$ 4
1957	48	69	3	4
1958	48	60	4	12
1959	46	59	10	23
1960	38	51	15	22
1961	41	52	16	41
1962	45	60	21	38
1963	58	77	26	42
1964	75	93	31	44
1965	74	90	31	61
1966	66	84	46	89
1967	59	71	48	72

of one year to the low of the following. It's up and down, up and down, each and every year. In some years the low came first followed by the high and in others the high preceded the low.

It might be useful, at this point, to introduce still another chart on the same "Yo-Yo" pattern (Chart 3). What is the per-

Chart 3   Low-Low Spread Chart from Low of One Year to Low of the Following Year (Adjusted for splits and stock dividends)

Year	Standard Oil New Jersey		Zenith Radio	
	Lowest Price of Year	*Percent Increase or Decrease*	*Lowest Price of Year*	*Percent Increase or Decrease*
1956	$50	−4%	$ 3	0%
1957	48	0	3	33
1958	48	−4	4	150
1959	46	−17	10	50
1960	38	8	15	7
1961	41	10	16	31
1962	45	29	21	24
1963	58	29	26	19
1964	75	−1	31	0
1965	74	−11	31	48
1966	66	−12	46	5
1967	59		48	

centage increase from the low of one year to the low of the following?

In 1957 Standard Oil of New Jersey dropped to a low of $48 per share or $2 less than the low of $50 established in 1956. This represented a drop of 4%. In 1958 it fell back to its low of 1957, etc.

Combining these figures with those in Chart 1 presents an interesting conclusion. It doesn't matter how high a security rose in any one year, if it fell substantially the following year. In the case of Standard Oil of New Jersey, the spread was 26% from the *low of 1956* to the *high of the same year* (Chart 1). The very next year the stock dropped to $48, which was 4% below the low of 1956.

Zenith Radio presents a similar picture. Although the security rose by 33% from the low of 1956 to the high that year, it dropped back to its previous low in 1957. Moving down the years note 1961 when the rise that year from low to high was

156%. However, the very next year it fell back to $21 which was only 31% above the previous year's *low*.

Charts 1 and 3 can be seen best by placing the percentages alongside one another (Charts 4A and 4B).

Comparison Chart 4A   Low of One Year to High of Same Year (Chart 1) vs. Low of One Year to Low of Following Year (Chart 3)

	Standard Oil New Jersey		
Year	Percent Increase Low to High Same Year	Percent Increase or Decrease of Low of First Year to Low of Following Year	
1956	26%	−4%	1956–7
1957	43	0	1957–8
1958	25	−4	1958–9
1959	28	−17	1959–60
1960	34	8	1960–1
1961	27	10	1961–2
1962	33	29*	1962–3
1963	33	29*	1963–4
1964	23	−1	1964–5
1965	22	−11	1965–6
1966	27		
1967	20		

* Note that in every year except two the gain from low to high was reduced by more than half in the following year.

Comparison Chart 4B

	Zenith Radio		
Year	Percent Increase Low to High Same Year	Percent Increase or Decrease of Low of First Year to Low of Following Year	
1956	33%	0%	1956–7
1957	33	33*	1957–8
1958	200	150*	1958–9

* Except for two years, the drop from the low of one year to the low of the following was at least half the rise from the low to high of the same year.

Comparison Chart 4B

	Zenith Radio		
Year	Percent Increase Low to High Same Year	Percent Increase or Decrease of Low of First Year to Low of Following Year	
1959	130	50	1959–60
1960	46	7	1960–1
1961	156	31	1961–2
1962	81	24	1962–3
1963	62	19	1963–4
1964	42	0	1964–5
1965	97	48	1965–6
1966	93	5	1966–7
1967	50		

Summarizing the results of the first four tables, it can be concluded that regardless of how much these securities rose from the low to the high of the same year, they lost at least half the following year.

Low of One Year to High of the Following

The Low-High table reveals still another significant concept. There appears to be a substantial spread between the low of one year and the high reached the *following year*. This is contained in a fifth Low-High Spread chart. This time the dates are reversed, the earlier dates at the bottom followed by the succeeding years. This will be referred to as Chart 5.

Chart 5 indicates the percentage spread between the low of one year to the high of the following year. For example, Standard Oil in 1957 had a 38% increase from $50, the low of 1956, to $69, the high for 1957, etc. Trace the "up" oblique lines for both securities, and the horizontal broken lines to the percentage spread.

It should be noted that the low of one year was always lower

**Chart 5 Low-High Spread Chart from Low of One Year to
High of Following Year (Adjusted for splits and stock dividends)**

	Standard Oil New Jersey			Zenith Radio		
Year	*Lowest Price Per Share*	*Highest Price Per Share*	*Percent Spread*	*Lowest Price Per Share*	*Highest Price Per Share*	*Percent Spread*
1967	$59	$71 – – →	7%	$48	$72 – →	55%
1966	66	84 – – →13		46	89 – →186	
1965	74	90 – – →20		31	61 – → 97	
1964	75	93 – – →58		31	44 – → 69	
1963	58	77 – – →71		26	42 – →100	
1962	45	60 – – →46		21	38 – →136	
1961	41	52 – – →37		16	41 – →174	
1960	38	51 – – →11		15	22 – →120	
1959	46	59 – – →23		10	23 – →470	
1958	48	60 – – →25		4	12 – →200	
1957	48	69 – – →38		3	4 – → 33	
1956	50	63		3	4	

than the high of the following. This occurred in Standard Oil of New Jersey even during those years 1956–1961 when its market price was declining. *It seems that where a security is purchased at or near the low of one year, it should show a profit during the following year.*

This information is important only to those who, though they are not "in and outers," want to make capital gains regularly. There are times when they buy a security near the low of the year. However, peculiar adverse factors drive it lower after the purchase. Chart 5 indicates that it will probably rise during the following year and make a capital gain possible.

Future Predictions

The 5 charts contain a wealth of information, *to be studied and not merely read.* Charts 2–5 tell the same story in different ways. Essentially they say that most stocks go up—stop—and then drop, only to start the perennial cyclic pattern all over again. *The drop is normally more than half the rise.* This explains why securities that are bought after they have increased beyond the halfway mark usually result in losses, sometimes temporarily. The last 4 charts represent background information that should be recalled instantaneously when confronted with a "hot tip." This instantaneous recall should be as swift as the conditioned reflex that makes a person withdraw his hand when he accidentally touches a hot stove.

Chart 1 is the breadwinner. If understood properly and applied consistently it should increase the investor's annual yield substantially.

When to Start?

When is the best time to start a spread chart? Begin at the sound of a "tip" or "inside information." For example, start when told that an unusual earning report will soon be released or that a security will be "split." Instead of rushing to buy the stock, make a Chart 1 analysis. The analysis may deter you from making a hasty and costly purchase.

A case in point is Pan American World Airways which split its stock two shares for one in May 1967. In January the stock hovered in the $55 range, down from its 1966 high of $79 a share. By April the security was climbing with great strength and vigor in anticipation of the great event. What should have been done? The first step would have been to make a spread chart (Chart 6).

The range of the stock since 1962 was from $8 to $79. The percent spread since 1956 varied from a low of 37% in 1956 to 146% in 1963. In April 1967, at $74 a share it was 37%. A realistic spread for the year should be at least 50%. In Probable 1 it was assumed that the low would hold and that the high would reach $83 a share. In Probable 2 it was assumed that the high of $74 would hold and the low would drop further to $49 a share. (See arithmetic at end of chapter.)

Chart 6   Low-High Spread Chart

	Year	Low	High	Percent Spread	
	1956	8	11	37	
	1957	6	10	67	
	1958	6	12	100	
	1959	10	18	80	
	1960	8	12	50	
	1961	8	12	50	
	1962	8	12	50	
	1963	11	27	146	
	1964	26	43	65	
	1965	25	56	124	
	1966	40	79	98	
Actual	1967	55	74	37	(As of April)
Probable 1	(1967)	(49)	(74)	(50)	
Probable 2	(1967)	(55)	(83)	(50)	

A price-earning ratio check . . . was made which showed that the stock at $74 a share was selling at more than 20 times its three years' average earnings. This was much too high. The cautious approach was to assume that the high would not be pierced and the stock would drop below its existing low of $55 a share. We therefore discouraged the purchase. In August of 1967 the stock broke through its low. (The low for 1967 was $23 adjusted for the 2-to-1 split.)

If the analysis had been wrong, the stock would have climbed to approximately $83 a share. At $83 it would have been selling at a three-year price-earning ratio of 24 times, a very high rate.

This kind of analysis should be made before every purchase. Here are the circumstances under which it should be made.

1. Group doing well

An entire industrial group is doing well market-wise. The various tests described [earlier] indicate that one or more members should be purchased. Here is a procedure that is recommended:

Make a Chart 1 spread test for each member of the group. If the group is doing well market-wise, the probability is that the lows of the year will hold. Assume a reasonable percentage spread from low to high of the same year based on past experience. Is there room for a substantial rise? . . . Example: Stock A, which is reasonably priced as determined by the tests, has a 10-year Chart 1 spread of from 30 to 65%. The range thus far this year has been 37 to 41 and the stock is currently selling at 39. Make Chart 7.

Chart 7

	Year	Current Range		Percent Spread Low to High
Actual	1968	37	41	11
Probable 1	(1968)	(37)	(48)	(30)
Probable 2	(1968)	(31)	(41)	(30)

The actual spread, thus far, from low to high has been 11%. The spread has been at least 30% during the past decade. It is not unreasonable to assume that the spread will be at least 30% before the year ends. This will occur in one of three ways:

Condition 1. The low of 37 will hold, and the stock will pierce the high of 41 on the upside.

Condition 2. The high of 41 will not be pierced on the upside, but the low of 37 will drop further.

Condition 3. Both the low and the high will give way and thus establish the minimum 30% spread.

It is possible that this year's spread will be an exception to the previous pattern and will not be 30%. This anomaly is rare and will be ignored.

If Condition 1 prevails, and the low of 37 holds for the balance of the year, the high will be forced upward to 48. This figure is obtained by multiplying the low 37 by 130% or 1.30. This is indicated in Probable 1.

If Condition 2 prevails, and the high of 41 remains intact for the rest of the year, the low will have to drop to 31 to establish a 30% spread. The figure 31 is obtained by dividing the high of 41 by 130% or 1.30. This is indicated in Probable 2.

Condition 3 is not expected (at least not at this time) because the security selected is in a group that is doing well. The two possibilities are summarized in Chart 8.

Chart 8

	Year	Range This Year		Percentage Spread
1.	1968	37	48	30%
or				
2.	1968	31	41	30% (approx.)

Will it be 1 or 2? If our judgment is correct, and the group will continue to do well, the range will probably be 1, and the high reach at least $48 a share.

2. Group doing poorly

Even when a group is not doing well, it is possible to purchase a security near its lowest price of the year and let the normal Chart 1 spread yield a substantial profit.

First and foremost, the best securities [should be] selected, though they are doing poorly market-wise. Make a Chart 1 spread and note the normal range for the last 10 years. Assume it is from 30 to 65%. The stock is currently selling at $39 a share. This year's spread has been 37 to 41. The current spread is only 11%. It should be at least 30%. Either the stock will rise above $41 or the low of $37 will be pierced and it will plummet to $31 or lower. There is no need to hurry. Make a daily chart . . . and watch the stock, each and every day. *You may have to wait months before making the purchase.* If the purchase is made at the right time, the rewards will be substantial and gratifying.

3. Stock doing badly

Hardly a day goes by without one or more securities making a low for the year. This calls for an immediate investigation. A spread chart should be made. If the percent spread, when the low is made, is substantially higher than the norm established during the last decade, it merits special attention, and daily watching. . . .

A case in point is Insurance Company of North America, which is one of the finest in its industry. After reaching its high of $88¾ early in 1967 it began a significant descent reaching a low point of $52 a share in November 1967. This made the range to that date $52–88¾, a spread of 70%. In none of the previous 12 years was the spread as large. In 1958 it was $45–69, or 54%. In 1962 it was $66–107, or 62%. In one year, it was 48%, from $76 to 112. Chart 9 is a Low-High Spread Chart of the company.

Chart 9 Insurance Company of North America
(Adjusted for splits and stock dividends)

Year	Low	High	Percent Increase
1956	41	52	27
1957	41	55	34
1958	45	69	54
1959	57	74	30
1960	60	79	32
1961	76	112	48
1962	66	107	62
1963	87	103	19
1964	86	100	35
1965	72	99	37
1966	68	91	34
1967	52	89	70

Because of the 70% spread from low to high the probability was that the security would not drop too significantly below $52. Inasmuch as the low was made in November, year-end tax selling was near its final phase. The procedure was to [follow] the daily movement of the stock until the technical pattern indicated that the low would probably hold. That determined, the stock could be bought confidently.

Timing Is Important

Is the investor making his analysis during the first six months of the year or during the last six months?

If it is made during the early months, before earning reports have been published, many assumptions will have to be made.

Will the economy do well? Will the industry do well? Which companies will be best?

If the stock has done well market-wise the previous year, the probability is there should be profit-taking. These securities should be avoided. On the other hand, there are usually many good quality securities that did poorly the previous year, closing near their lowest prices in December. They should be favored as candidates for purchase.

If the analysis is made during the second half of the year, the investor knows the percentage spread that has already been made. This should be quite helpful. in the case of Insurance Company of North America, just mentioned, a percentage spread of 70% had been made by November 1967 after a series of lows. The stock could have been purchased on this basis alone. This does not mean that the low for the year had been reached. End-of-year tax selling could depress it further. A daily chart should be made. . . . This will help determine when the selling pressure has been overbalanced by aggressive buying. This should pinpoint the price when the stock may be purchased with reasonable assurance that the low for the year had been established.

More Tests Ahead

While the spread chart is very important, it is only one of the tests that should be made. It may be considered an excellent "governor" reducing the risk factor.

The percentage spread varies considerably for each security. When making predictions for the probable lows and highs one should not be too rigid. They should serve as guides only, subject to market and economic conditions.

It should not be concluded that successful investing consists simply of making several charts and following a few rules mechanically. These were introduced as the *first* of a series of guidelines before investing. The charts should dissuade those who act hastily and repent slowly. They represent boundaries within which most securities move, some to high levels, others to lower ones. They are determined not so much by economic factors as by emotional ones. The economic forces determine the long-term trend of a security; the emotional ones, the perennial rhythmic "Yo-Yo" fluctuations. A governor or safety valve is necessary to prevent a "blowout." The Low-High charts perform that function.

The mathematics of probability applies to investments as it does to astronomy, physics, chemistry, insurance, and even psychology. If past patterns are applied to future situations the probability of their repetition is increased when the number of cases is large. Therefore, it should be applied to many securities, and not limited to a few.

Diversification of investments must or should be an essential part of our thinking. With all the care in the world, there will be anomalies here and there. However, if a great many securities are purchased as recommended in this book, the overall results should be good—in some cases, excellent.

Homework

One learns by doing. Making charts of every security owned provides good experience. More important, charts should be made of prospective purchases. This will provide valuable information, which will prevent hasty judgments.

Arithmetic

For those who have forgotten how to obtain percentage increase, this is a review.

Problem: What is the percent increase when a security rises from 21 to 38?

Step 1. Subtract 21 from 38, or 38 — 21 equals 17.

Step 2. Divide 17 by 21, or 17/21 equals .81 or 81%.

The division can be done easily by using a slide rule.

Summary

Consistent profits result from logic, not luck. Pitfalls surround all investments. There are several guidelines that should be understood and followed. The first is to understand the fluctuation pattern of the security you plan to buy.

What to Avoid in Over-the-Counter Securities

FRANK B. DIAMOND

There is a continually growing demand for information on over-the-counter securities. Author Frank B. Diamond raises some important issues on the reliability and stability of these stocks.

THE over-the-counter market actually dwarfs the New York Stock Exchange in sheer size, but it's a very tricky area and requires the most careful selection of securities. No one knows precisely how many companies are traded in the vast over-the-counter market, but it is estimated that there are over 100,000 different issues as against less than 1300 on the New York Stock Exchange. More investors have lost money in this market, without ever knowing what happened, than in all of the stock exchanges put together.

Because literally thousands of individual issues are traded over the counter it is impossible for the newspapers to list the daily prices of all of them. *Without exception avoid buying stock in companies whose prices are not listed in the daily newspapers.* There are several cogent reasons for this. First of all, the buyer will thus avoid the overwhelming majority of "promotions." These are fraudulent situations which crop up regularly. Since the prices are never listed in the papers, unscrupulous promoters can manipulate the prices of these securities almost at will.

But even more important to the investor is the danger that investors may decide to invest in over-the-counter stocks in which there is little trading. This can reflect buyer apathy, a small supply of floating stock, lack of dealer interest, etc. Whatever the reason, it is a dangerous place to find yourself if you ever wish to *sell* your stock. If, moreover, you plan to sell during a period of market decline, it is often next to impossible to find a buyer. Consequently, large losses are incurred because investors decided to invest in over-the-counter stocks which are not listed in the newspapers. It is also true in that you may find yourself obligated to pay more for stocks when the prices don't appear because the supply is so limited.

Avoid buying stocks in the over-the-counter market where the stock in question is issued by a *strictly local company*. During periods of market exuberance, people often get carried away with their general success in investing and become very interested when someone calls their attention to a fine local company whose stock is traded. Even when the balance sheet turns out to be quite respectable, as it frequently is, these stocks are speculations. In our highly competitive economic world local companies are generally not sufficiently progressive to make enough money for investors. You, as the investor, may also be confronted with problems of family ownership and family management, which can conceivably cause the interests of management to be different from the interests of outside stockholders. For instance, a profitable local company may be family dominated and therefore *not choose to pay dividends* for years since the family is on the payroll, and their dividends would largely be lost in income taxes!

Lastly, *avoid low-priced securities which are traded over-the-counter whether they are listed daily or not*. This is an experienced judgment based on the irrefutable fact that most people lose money on low-priced over-the-counter stocks. It is true that Xerox and Polaroid at one time traded over-the-counter as low-priced stocks, and people who bought them and held on to them made fabulous profits. But thousands of low-priced stocks have passed out of existence and tens of thousands are still languishing at the bottom with no interest and little movement.

I would like to point out at this time that there are substantial numbers of excellent *investments* available in this vast over-the-counter market. Almost all bank stocks and almost all insurance stocks are traded over the counter. Mutual funds are also traded over the counter and all municipal bonds are dealt with in this area. In addition many find industrial and utility issues help to comprise the over-the-counter market. If you are dealing with a responsible broker, he will be careful to call your attention only to the quality over-the-counter stocks, for he is always on his guard in this category.

Key Points

1. "Thin" Markets are too dangerous for the average investor.
2. Confine your over-the-counter investments to *national* companies for maximum profit opportunity.

Bull Markets and Bare Knees

IRA U. COBLEIGH

Ira U. Cobleigh, economist and financial editor of The Commercial and Financial Chronicle, *is also the highly successful author of* Happiness Is a Stock That Doubles in a Year. *Included in Cobleigh's informative and lively book is a delightful (and thus far accurate) analysis of the stock market, in which he draws comparisons between the market's up-and-down trends and women's hemlines.*

OFF and on during the past forty years, there have appeared in the financial press or in market letters of brokerage houses recurrent conjectures or whimsical observations that there exists a definite relationship between the height of the hemline of women's dresses in any given year and the levels of stock prices.

Skirts and National Income

Since 1958, the H. W. Gossard Company, a renowned maker of ladies' corsets and lingerie, has published annually a chart featuring the trendline of national income since 1900, accompanied by sketches of young ladies dressed in the prevailing fashions of each era. These sketches appear above the high and low points on the chart when national income reached a new historic peak and when it fell back to a cyclical bottom in transition years. The Gossard theory also asserts that tight waists accompany lower hemlines.

This chart, available from Gossard, has attracted considerable attention. It tends to validate the general theory that hemlines rise in good times and fall in recessions. This study, however newsworthy and provocative of comment, makes no precise correlations, since it does not portray models and hemlines for successive calendar years. Moreover, it is geared to the national income statistical series, not nearly as sensitive or widely followed as the Dow-Jones Industrial Stock Average covering the same years.

On December 15, 1964, Mr. Vermont Royster, editor of the *Wall Street Journal,* published a merry column entitled "Boom or Bust," which reflected on the possible relationship between hemlines and buoyant markets. He concluded: "Hemlines vary directly with the rise and fall of GNP."

In May, 1967, Harris Upham & Company, a leading nationwide brokerage firm, presented in its market letter a chart showing the yearly Dow-Jones Industrial Average from 1897 to date, with sketches of young women, in the mode of the year, above or below key high or low points on the stock trendline. These pictures document fairly well, visually, the idea that skirts rise in a manner somewhat parallel to stocks in bull markets; and plunge downward when stocks do. For example, in 1929, stocks and dresses were both high; in 1932, they were both just off the floor.

This was all jolly good fun, and the Harris Upham Hemline Indicator inspired many comments in the daily and weekly financial press.

In fact, somewhat earlier (July, 1965), the Economics Department of McGraw-Hill, Inc., publishers of *Business Week,* had issued a three-page report, without charts, highlighting high hemlines as a recurrent phenomenon of prosperous times—and vice versa—but without any specific reference to stocks.

Up and Down Together

And there the matter has stood until I could endure the uncertainty no longer. I simply had to find out if there was any sense at all to this hemline theory. Have skirts indeed gone up historically when stocks did? Did they go relatively higher or lower than stocks? And, most particularly, which came first, the rise in hemlines or in stocks? In other words, will the real market barometer please stand up?

To answer properly these nagging questions, I obviously had to have something more substantial than pictures to rely on. The Dow-Jones Industrial Average chart could of course be plotted accurately from actual sales prices of stocks, day after day and year after year. But how could I present a hemline curve that could be drawn on the same chart and in some sort of comparative relationship with DJIA? If the theory was valid, obviously the two lines should look much alike.

Accordingly I did some research. I designed a novel chart expressing annual hemline variations in inches off the floor.

With appropriate humility, I present in this chapter, in chart form, the answer to the question: "Skirts and Stocks—Up and Down Together?" While I certainly do not claim to have originated this theory (I don't think anyone knows who did), I am the first to chart its linear proof—to convert conjecture into credibility!

The Natural Affinity Between Fashion and Finance

Before this earth-shaking, or at least hip-shaking, chart is unveiled, however, it may be well to see how dresses and stocks ever became linked in the first place. The relationship derives from a long-term affinity between fashion and money.

When somebody mentions the word "fashion," it seems invariably to refer to the current popular style in women's apparel. Actually, however, fashion—the new mode, the "in" thing —is all about us. In addition to miniskirts and bikinis, and pipe-stem trousers for men, current fashion embraces equally our whole way of life cookouts, op and pop art, hippies, color TV, shaggy-haired young men, performance stocks, tall socks, rock-and-roll, condominiums, scuba diving, surfing, credit cards, and Everett Dirksen!

To be more precise, fashion is a concomitant of money pos-session, which makes possible leisure time, a thirst for culture, and a social compulsion to keep up with or, better yet, to top someone. Cadillacs beat Chevies, chinchilla beats mink, a brownstone beats a penthouse, and the Mets beat nobody!

Women's fashions are actually a comparatively modern phe-nomenon, and for our purposes they did not become significant until after World War I. We are principally interested in the past fifty years of fashion, 1917–1966. Why this period? Because be-fore that ladies' fashions were a minor influence in our economy, and the only women who really spent any time and money at it were women of royalty or the theater; or women socially im-portant because of their relationship to men of position, power, or opulence, often as mistresses as well as wives.

Further, it should be observed that high fashion did not in-volve the excitement of radically changing hemlines until well into the twentieth century. Almost all stylish skirts until 1914 had hemlines dragging along the floor or perhaps two or three inches above. Equally, until after 1915, stock prices were, with few exceptions, attracting very little popular attention or following. Holders of common stocks were probably only a little more numerous than ladies who could afford, and sported, high fashion.

New York City: Fashion and Finance Center

It is in part for these reasons that the chart midstream in this chapter, around which the whole theory is developed, begins in 1917 and not before. At or about that year, two economic institutions had become solidly established. They document and refine our theory about the affinity between fashion and finance. These twin phenomena were the confirmed position of New York as (1) the financial center of America and (2) the ladies' fashion center of America. The rising statures of both as (1) big business and (2) daily topics of conversation and discussion in American homes increased as wealth became diffused, and per-capita incomes steadily rose.

Higher incomes have indeed placed new millions of women each decade in a position to be patrons of fashion and of Wall Street; and the garment industry accommodated them by designing fashionable ready-made dresses, manufactured in volume, and within the budget of middle- and lower-middle class families. The arrival and concentration in New York City of thousands of emigrants from Central and Eastern Europe, many of them tailors by trade, built in due course a vast garment industry on "Seventh Avenue," an industry that today sells annually well over $5 billion wholesale in women's dresses, suits, coats, sportswear, and blouses—not including uniforms, undergarments, and children's wear.

On the financial side, there were in 1917 only 613 stocks listed on the New York Stock Exchange, with total value below $30 billion. Today there are 1,700 issues listed, worth, at the 1967 year end, $605.8 billion. In 1917, there were approximately 500,000 stockholders in America. Today there are 24 million (more than 50 percent women), plus 4% million holders of mutual funds, and probably 100 million others who own stocks indirectly through their interests in insurance policies, pension, welfare or retirement funds.

Limits

We have gathered the above data to establish a background relationship between fashion and finance, skirts and stocks. We admit, however, to having narrowed the fields a little to suit our purposes. Obviously fashion is something more than skirts.

It's also fabrics, silhouettes, sportswear, furs, handbags, shoes, gloves, and hats. But we can't measure all these phenomena against stock prices. If, for instance, we used bikinis as a gauge, we'd have the Dow-Jones Industrial Average at 3,000 right now; and at 3,500 for topless models!

Equally, finance is more than stocks. It's bank loans and deposits, mortgages, bonds, leaseholds, royalties, trust funds, etc. But again, stock prices are clearly measurable and volatile and newsworthy; and they do display vertical action, long thought to be similar in time and relative extent to the varying altitudes of skirts.

On the style side, it's just too bad we couldn't work into the chart such eye-catching fashion phenomena as waistlines and necklines, but frankly, there appears to be no coherent or measurable trend in these. There is a little evidence, however, that plunging necklines and plunging stock markets occur in the same general time period—sort of a peek and valley theory!

Levity aside, we're now about to introduce our long-awaited chart, with just one additional explanation. In plotting hemline heights, we got the altitude figures from models of daytime dresses in style in each of the fifty years; and the distances off the ground relate to a woman of average height, about 5'7" approximately the size twelve misses' dress that is standard in the trade.

Now, here for the first time is a chart designed to answer the question of the hour:

Skirts and Stocks—
Up and Down Together?
Yes!

Bull Markets . . . and Bare Knees!

(Introducing The Hemline Index of Stock Prices)

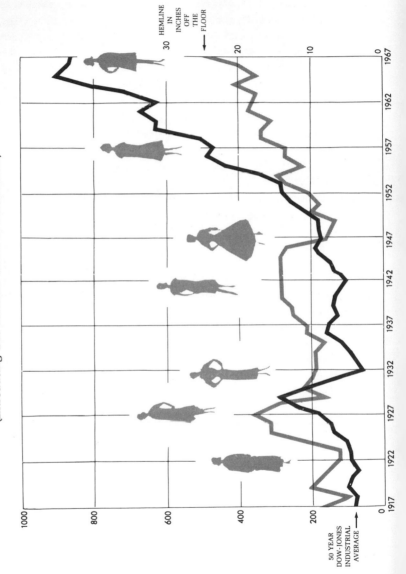

Commenting on the Chart

By starting with the year 1917, we can present a fifty-year comparison; and that year marks approximately the beginning of broad national share markets, and of consumer spending on fashions in such volume as to affect and reflect national growth and prosperity. That year was, moreover, the start of war prosperity, with rising wages and a broadening investor class getting its introduction to marketable securities through purchase of Liberty Bonds.

Business had actually begun to improve and stocks had begun a rising trend in 1915. This upswing appears to have been foretold by shorter skirts, so that in 1915 there appeared for the first time in this century hemlines 8 inches off the floor. They continued to rise, along with stocks, until 1919.

Then hemlines started down somewhat ahead of stocks in anticipation of the 1920–21 depression; after which both stocks and hems reversed. Between 1925 and 1926, skirts reached knee length, the highest altitude up to that time.

If we seek to apply hemlines as a prophetic barometer for stock prices, 1927 is a good year to analyze. There were, in that year of prosperity, speakeasies, a new car named the Chrysler, flappers, and a definite trend to longer dresses. This downtrend in hemlines was, in effect, a strong signal of declining stock prices to come, and preceded, by about two and a half years, the topping out of the stock market in October, 1929. Had the hemline chart been available then, perhaps it would have prevented, for tens of thousands, the financial baths they were otherwise doomed to take between 1929 and 1932.

Turning Points

There was a gradual but definite uptrend in skirt lines beginning in late 1932 and extending, with a pause for the slowdown in 1936–37, to 8 inches off the ground again in 1939, and reaching the ogling level of 15 inches in 1940. Here again was another powerful directional signal, although this time not given so far in advance as in 1927.

The war period put style on the sidelines. Millions of women became war workers, and their styles of dress were consequently heavily functional. Shorter skirts were dictated by two necessities. First there was the need for greater mobility in feminine action—riding buses to work, operating at workbenches and assembly lines, where flowing dresses and fancy sleeves would have been inconvenient or hazardous. The second factor limiting the free play of fashion trends during the war was a government restriction on production of civilian fabrics, which limited garments to 3½ yards of cloth, and skirt widths to 64 inches; and fashion stood still for almost five years. The plain lines of the shirtwaist dress became the mode, and slacks and overalls were almost a uniform for women factory workers.

After World War II, the pent-up desires of women to look more feminine and to spend a larger percentage of individual and family incomes on clothes led to an eager resurgence of fashion consciousness. Return to a civilian economy took a little time; the stock market was in a tentative and generally negative trend. Correspondingly, hemlines declined from wartime levels—a trend authenticated in 1947 with the introduction of the "New Look," featuring curvaceous silhouettes, longer and more flowing skirts, and pinched-in waists. These lower skirt lines foretold the lower stock market of 1949 with considerable advance notice.

The 1950's witnessed a general rise in the Dow-Jones Industrial Average, checked in 1953, and again in 1956. The hemlines rather accurately reflected this uptrend, with the long dresses of 1950–51 giving place to rising hemlines, especially noticeable in 1954 (indicating the end of the short recession of 1953), and continuing higher until 1958, when hemlines descended moderately, as did stocks, for a couple of years. In October, 1961, skirts were close to knee high again, which seemed to say that the dip in stock prices occurring ten months later was by no means the end of the long-term bull market. Thus skirts continued to rise, topping off with the miniskirt, which first appeared at about the time the DJIA reached an all-time closing high of 995.15 on February 9, 1966. Hemlines continued to rise and so did the market in the period between October, 1966, and summer, 1967—which brings our chart comparison almost to the present.

Reviewing the charts, we can now state with considerable assurance that there does exist a demonstrable relationship between skirts and stocks and, in general, hemlines are the "lead" barometer.

Future Altitudes and Attitudes

The future of the skirt-line chart and its validity and acceptance as a respected market barometer are clouded by the near-ceiling represented by mid-1967 hemlines. The prevailing fanny-high minidress leaves little room for the hemline to rise on the chart, to correspond with, say, a 1,500 figure on the DJIA. By historic hem-price relationships, stock prices "have gone about as far as they can go." The next indicated phase should be downward because (1) skirt lines cannot decently go higher and (2) indicated styles promulgated by certain fashion designers for fall, 1967, call for longer dresses. Indeed, we may have established a new Wall Street slogan to guide market decisions of avid traders: "Don't sell till you see the heights of their thighs!"

A decline in hemlines preceding, or accompanied by, a decline in stock prices can of course be accommodated within the limits of the present chart. We do, however, face a problem for the future. Granted that we have, over a fifty-year period, established a plausible relationship between stocks and skirts, how can we portray this relationship graphically if or when the DJIA advances to 1,500 or higher? While there is no theoretical ceiling on stock prices, there is an obvious ceiling on dress heights. Skirts and stocks may well continue to go up and down in some sort of parallel relationship in the years ahead, so we have developed an adjusted formula to correlate hemlines to DJIA if that average rises above 1,100.

This revised formula would not destroy the validity of our theory, but would simply reflect hemlines on a more sensitive scale —and keep them from zooming upward off the chart! The comparative result would be quite like the use of logarithmic paper for plotting bar charts.

Psychological Background

So far, we have treated these two exciting phenomena, skirts and stock variations, as cold statistical data like spring-wheat or pig-iron prices, tied together only by the fact that both are money oriented. The extensive purchase of fashionwear and stock occurs only in opulent societies. (Incidentally, in 1966, American women spent $7 billion on clothes; men, less than half that!)

On reflection, and with a modicum of research, we can conclude that there are powerful psychological forces making skirts and stocks go up and down together. Market swings and fashion changes are both motivated quite as much by emotional factors as by money logic. Both may well be expected to reflect happiness, confidence, and hope, as well as fear, anxiety, and gloom. Hence, in good times we see confidence reflected in a nationwide amorous zeal, or at least more animated girl watching. We know this to be true because, in civilized countries, birth rates rise during prosperity and fall during depressions. This romantic zest is no doubt stimulated by possession or acquisition of more money (rising income and speculative profits), making possible more extravagant expenditures on feminine plumage, and fashions tending toward higher skirts to sustain and encourage wolfish ogling. Perhaps, too, the fashion turn to lower skirts is a necessity in economic declines, tending to make men pay more attention to business.

Another observable phenomenon is that higher skirts, symbolizing euphoria, confidence, and hope, are linked emotionally to brighter, livelier colors. If you doubt this, think of the miniskirts of 1967. Were there ever assembled on the female form such dazzling arrays of gaudy colors—pastels, pinks, yellows, reds, purples? As a by-product, business prosperity is promoted by higher stocks and a greater assortment of designs and fabric, not to mention underthings, which must be bought because of their occasional visibility and their corresponding need to match, or blend with, outerthings. The short-dress fashion economy is also stimulated by the need for larger handbags, to serve as "modesty panels" discreetly deployed across the knees of ladies, particularly when riding buses!

If psychological spurs can be found to account for rising trends in skirts and stocks, they can influence attitudes just as well in reverse—in recessions or depressions. As skirts go down, quite possibly romantic enthusiasms cool down accordingly. And the longer skirts are invariably made of heavier fabrics, and in darker, less lively colors—browns, blacks, dark grays. In 1932, as the chart shows, stocks were very low, skirts were very low, and the fashionable colors of the year were somber—some almost funereal.

Projection

Ultimately the pendulum will swing. It always has. Women tire of the same style, colors, and fabrics, and in due course they will demand a change, if only out of caprice or boredom. Men, too, welcome a change in their women. This psychological or emotional urge to change (from fashions in stocks as well as fashions in clothes) may in fact be the key to our entire theory. If indeed women's styles do change their trendlines ahead of stocks, then we should be most vigilant in observing whether the current fashionable dress designs, or those projected for the next spring or fall, are going up or down. Whichever way they are headed may well indicate the direction of stock prices in the months ahead and influence market decisions.

In the first quarter of 1968, we had a kind of schizophrenia in skirts. The young, the jet, and the hippie set wore miniskirts of maximum brevity, 28 inches off the floor. At the same time, matrons and younger matrons displayed at many exclusive social events hemlines lowered to the knee or midcalf, which hinders calculation of the 1968 formula. Dress styles may now have become dual, and an average between them may in the future be needed to correlate with stock prices. In any event, it would be our opinion in summer, 1968, that miniskirts are still the dominant factor and that accordingly there will be a rising and roaring bull market in 1969, carrying Dow-Jones to 1,200. Hemlines precede, in their motion and direction, the rise or fall of stocks.

Mutual Funds

COLLEEN MOORE

Colleen Moore was one of Hollywood's biggest stars of the silent screen and has once again had a hit with her best-selling How Women Can Make Money in the Stock Market. *An experienced investor, she takes a fresh look, and a knowledgeable one, at a timely subject.*

*T*HIS is . . . written by a do-it-yourself investor for do-it-yourself investors, and right at this point I feel that I have to say something about the opposite of do-it-yourself investing: mutual funds.

It isn't enough just to say that much about them and go on to another subject. Funds are lighting up the financial sky these days, and if somebody hasn't already told you that the simplest and most sensible thing to do with your money is to put it into one, you can be sure that someone will be getting in touch with you very soon with that very thing in mind. . . .

So let's have a look at mutual funds.

A mutual fund is a company whose sole business is investing in the securities of other companies. Originally, *mutual fund* referred to only one of the two kinds of investment companies, but now the term pretty much covers them all.

The two varieties are the *closed-end* and the *open-end.*

Like a lot of Wall Street terms, these strike me as a little frustrating because one brings up a picture of something bottled up tight and the other of things dribbling out of both ends, and it isn't that way at all. I think *limited* and *unlimited* would be far more descriptive.

Anyway, a *closed-end* fund has a limited number of shares of stock outstanding—like the vast majority of corporations. If you want to buy stock in a closed-end fund, you have to find somebody who has some to sell. A few closed-end funds are listed on various exchanges and there is no problem. Some of the unlisted ones may be harder to find. . . .

An *open-end* fund will sell stock at any time to anybody who wants to buy it, and there is no limit to the number of shares you can buy. The price you pay is determined by dividing the total net assets of the fund by the number of shares outstanding. All the assets of a mutual fund—except for any uninvested cash that happens to be lying around—are the securities in its portfolio. As the prices of stocks change on the market, naturally the value of the fund's portfolio changes too. The number of shares in the fund is constantly changing. So the value per share is computed twice daily, and the price you pay is the value per share at the latest computation.

Since the title of this book is *How Women Can Make Money in the Stock Market,* the real reason for having a look at mutual funds is to see if you can make money by investing in one.

You can. The record proves it. I don't say any old fund—you have to look into them the way you do any other corporation you might invest in—but there are hundreds of funds and among them are a lot which would have doubled your money in the last ten years.

On the other hand, if you took a typical common stock and compared its performance over the past ten years with a typical mutual fund, you probably wouldn't find a great deal of difference. The most difficult part of that experiment would be finding a stock and a mutual fund that any two people would agree were typical.

And you can find funds that have performed better than some common stocks, and you can find stocks that have outperformed some funds.

Earlier I said that investing in a mutual fund was one way of getting someone else to take over the responsibility—and the fussing around with details—of making your money grow. I didn't make it sound like a good thing to do.

However, the funds consider this one of their two strongest selling points. They emphasize that you get professional management of your money. And you do. The fee for this service varies, but most typically each share is assessed ½ of 1% a year as management fee. You don't get a bill for this: it is computed on a specified date and taken out of the fund's assets.

Some people feel this is high. But it is what an investment counselor would charge you—and an investment counselor won't take responsibility for a portfolio under $50,000 and many of them insist on $100,000. You can become part of many mutual funds for the price of one share, and you can look at the financial page of your daily paper, under the heading MUTUAL FUNDS and see that, while the price per share varies, the highest is still an awful lot less than $250, which is ½ of 1% of $50,000.

In all fairness, I must tell you that a way exists to get professional management for no extra charge at all. You can open, with your broker (if he agrees), what is called a *discretionary account*. This means your broker uses his discretion about what to do with your portfolio—and when to do it—and you won't have to know any more about what is going on than you would in a fund. With your broker, though, you can find out if you want to. With a fund, you can't. The only charge in a discretionary account is the standard commission on each transaction, which you would pay anyhow.

I should add here that many brokers will not accept a discretionary account.

The second of the mutual funds' big selling points is that, for the price of one share, you get diversification you can't get in do-it-yourself investing for less than several thousand dollars. The fund's portfolio has dozens of securities in it and if you have a share in the fund, the argument goes, you have diversification too.

I don't agree with this, because if you have just *one* security in your portfolio, I insist that is not diversification, even if the one share is a share in a fund. . . .

Critics of mutual funds usually bring up the *loading charge*. It sounds unpleasant—as if they were charging you something for piling a load on you. Actually, it is just the commission the fund charges for accepting your money. It is most often 8%. I have seen it as high as 8½%, and I have been told that some funds charge 9%. In any case, it is deducted from the amount you put into the fund before you get any shares. For example, if the price of a fund's shares is $10 and you invest $1000, you don't get 100 shares; $80 is subtracted from the $1000 first. That leaves $920. At $10 a share, you get 92 shares.

Of course there is also a deduction when you buy listed stocks through a broker—his commission. So if you gave your broker $1000 and asked him to buy stock for you which is priced at $10 a share, you wouldn't get 100 shares either. But you'd get more shares than you would in a fund. The broker's commission on a $1000 transaction is $17; 17 from 1000 is 983. At $10 a share, you would get 98.3 shares.

Now, 8% does seem like a lot just for taking your money. The salesman's commission comes out of that and one reason the funds have the most enthusiastic salesmen around is very likely that they get 75% of the loading charge. In the transaction described above, it would be $60.

I have seen funds advertised which do not have loading charges. This means only that no salesmen are employed who have to be paid commissions.

As this is being written, there are discussions involving a congressional committee, the S.E.C., and the New York Stock Exchange about having the loading charge reduced to 5%. It doesn't seem to me that change is likely very soon, because the funds don't want it and the public doesn't care. Which is understandable—if you can more than double your money in, say, ten years, as has happened in a number of funds, you forget all about the commission you paid to get started. I know I would anyway.

Another point to be considered is that when you sell through a broker, you pay another commission, whereas most funds don't charge you for taking money out.

(Just to keep things straight; I am talking about the open-end type of fund, and will be from now on. If you buy or sell stock in a listed closed-end fund, you pay a broker's commission just as you would if you bought any other listed stock.)

If you've ever had a yearning to be part of what newspapers like to call a "power structure," buying shares in a mutual fund is the way to do it. On Wall Street, money is a five-letter word meaning power. And mutual funds do have money. They'll tell you so, individually and collectively, but they're getting it so fast that by the time they tell you how much they have they'll have a lot more than when they last counted.

Where volume of money is concerned, they are on a level with pension funds, insurance companies, endowment funds and bank trusts. The last four have always been in the conservative class of investors. It is among the mutual funds that you find the swingers. The conservative group have to be safe; they invest for dependable income to get cash for the payments they are obliged to make. Mutual funds want income too, but they also have to manage a steady increase in the value of their net assets—and, as I have said, the net assets are mostly the securities in their portfolios. There is only one way to keep this value moving up constantly at a good pace: take profits on the rise; reinvest for a rise, take the profits, and so on. This is trading.

If you own shares in a mutual fund and hold them no matter how tirelessly the fund's managers dance in and out of the market, I don't think that makes you a trader any more than I think your single-stock portfolio is diversified because the portfolio of the fund your single share represents is diversified. But you do share in the effects of the trading, so maybe you ought to know a little more about it.

Funds in general don't like the trader image. I have the prospectus of one of the more conservative on my desk now.

"The sole investment objective of the fund," it says, "is to seek capital appreciation." It says the same thing for two more sentences, then continues, "It is not the policy of the fund to trade in securities for the purpose of making short-term profits, but the fund expects to act quickly in disposing of all or part of its position in the security if for any reason such action is deemed advisable regardless of the length of time it has been held."

Of course you wouldn't have much confidence in them if they did anything else. In practice, however, what that passage means is: it is a fund devoted to long-term growth, but the managers will trade if and when they feel like it.

At the end of each three months or annually, the fund makes two per-share distributions: one from income and one from capital gains. The fund I am speaking of, having increased its net assets by $17,500,000 in three months, distributed $1.20 per share in capital gains—that is, profits it made by selling securities. It distributed nothing at all in income—that is, dividends received from securities.

A salesman for this fund might claim that these gains were all long-term, that is, from securities held more than six months. If so, it would seem that there should have been dividends from the seventy of so securities the fund has in its portfolio. I'm afraid there was a bit of trading there.

So when I read, "It is not the policy of the fund to trade in securities for the purpose of making short-term profits," my response is "Uh-huh" even before I read the rest of the sentence.

However, you can be sure that if I owned shares in a fund and they went up in value, I wouldn't carp about a little double-talk in the prospectus.

But I would worry a little about the way the funds are trading these days—and I do even though I don't own any fund shares.

I am bothered because I like to feel free to do my own investing under the law of supply and demand, and the funds are beginning to make that a little difficult. I'm not the only one who is concerned. The consequences of what the funds are doing are bringing new furrows to some of the more experienced and thoughtful brows in the financial world. For a long time, the brokerage houses have been advertising for the small investors' business, and the number of individual stockholders in this country is now over 24,000,000.

I have before me an article by John Cunniff, an Associated Press staff writer, published October 29, 1967. I quote:

Despite warnings from Federal Reserve Board Chairman William McChesney Martin, in-out trading by funds has been steadily increasing. Martin chose the 175th anniversary celebration of the New York Stock Exchange this year to warn of "poisonous" speculation by some funds. He suggested that investors might be abused by such activity and that the entire securities industry could be damaged "disastrously."

Because the power with which they trade is sometimes hundreds of times that of random public orders, institutions in many instances determine the immediate direction of the price of many stocks.

"Anyone who invests must realize it is a different business than it was 15 years ago," said Ted Lyman, senior vice president of Putnam Management Co., which administers several large mutual funds.

Lyman calls these individual investors, those who choose to buy stocks directly rather than through shares of mutual funds, "do-it-yourself investors."

Somehow I get the feeling that Mr. Lyman doesn't think we do-it-yourself investors are very important.

The assets of all the mutual funds together are around forty billion dollars and growing every day. Forty billion dollars is a lot of power.

In many instances, a dozen or so funds have owned an effective proportion of a company's stock amongst them, sometimes as high as 30%; 30% is not legal control, but unless 51% of the remaining 70% is organized, 30% can accomplish just about anything the funds who own it feel like accomplishing. The law says that no single fund can own more than 10% of any corporation's voting stock.

In the days before the S.E.C. really got its heels dug in, there were *pools*. Some people are afraid the funds may be tending toward pool-hood. There is no evidence that any group of them wants to get control of a company's stock for the purpose of manipulating the price, which is what the pools did, but those who view the situation with alarm wish the S.E.C. would find a way to put temptation out of the funds' reach, the way they did with the pools.

Mr. Cunniff gives an example of the impact funds can have. On November 18, 1966, 562,000 shares of Fairchild Camera and Instrument Company were sold within a few hours and the price went down 19 points. Selling by funds was the major factor in the drop.

Fairchild later regained the loss. I imagine there were a lot of do-it-yourself investors who knew enough about Fairchild to know that it was a bargain after its 19-point tumble. But anyone who didn't know why the stock went down in the first place would have been justified in thinking some disaster had happened inside the company.

The S.E.C. would like a little more control of the funds. The easiest way to avoid such control is self-regulation, but there is no compelling incentive for the funds to do anything but what they are doing. They aren't breaking any laws, and in fact a lot that they do, like the loading charge and management fee, is specifically permitted under a law passed in 1940—the Investment Company Act.

In the article I have referred to there is this: "Francis Williams, chairman of the Investment Company institute, a mutual fund trade association, says, 'We don't think the activities of the mutual funds and other institutional investors have a substantial impact on the stock market.' It certainly would take a study to prove otherwise."

You may find it remarkable, as I do, that a man in Mr. Williams' position doesn't know what everybody else in the financial world knows: that buying and selling has an effect on the prices of stocks and that buying and selling massive blocks of stocks can cause prices to change noticeably, sometimes drastically.

As far as the study "to prove otherwise" is concerned, Mr. Williams is on safe ground. There doesn't seem to be any money to finance it.

You can put your investment into a mutual fund and it will probably grow fast enough to keep ahead of the inexorable 3% to 4% advance of inflation. As to how that compares with what you could do on your own, a friend showed me recently the report of a study made in 1962 by the Wharton School of Finance at the University of Pennsylvania. This passage seemed interesting:

"With respect to the performance of mutual funds, it was found that, on the average, it did not differ appreciably from what would have been achieved by an unmanaged portfolio consisting of the same proportions of common stocks, corporate bonds, government securities, and other assets as the composite fund portfolios."

There you are. An impartial, objective study shows that there is no magic in mutual funds. So how do you choose—funds or do-it-yourself?

I choose do-it-yourself for two reasons:

First, I know it is possible to find, without too much effort, stocks that will do better for you than a mutual fund.

Second, I think the funds are going to have to stop swinging and adjust to the market rather than the other way around.

All of which, of course, is one do-it-yourselfer's opinion. But I am a do-it-yourselfer by conviction, and the conviction is the result of having made more money managing my own portfolio than I would have made in any mutual fund I have ever heard about.

Buy on the Rumor: Sell on the News

BURTON CRANE

Rumors are frequent on Wall Street, although they are discouraged by all responsible stock market regulatory agencies and firms. However, they still circulate and investors' ears are always alert to "unconfirmed" news. Burton Crane was a correspondent for the Wall Street Journal *and the London* Financial Times, *and until his death he covered the stock market for the* New York Times. *He analyzes the nature, and reliability, of the Wall Street rumor and gives his advice on when to take advantage of rumors and when to ignore them.*

You make more money in the market on rumors than you do on news. You also lose more, unless you bring a little common sense to the business.

Don't be too eager to get in on the ground floor. Sacrifice a little of the profit to make sure that somebody else believes what you've been told. In other words, let volume and price go up a bit before you buy.

Rumors about big companies are more likely to be true but less likely to be profitable than rumors about small companies. The "fast movers" who start rumors for their own advantage know that widely held companies don't move fast or far enough on tips to give adequate profits.

If you are willing to go in and out, like a trader, you may assume that any rumor that moves a stock has some truth behind it. It may not be the truth you've been told, but somebody knows something.

Increased price and volume are the only confirmations that matter. If you wait for official confirmation, you will lose money. Buy at once if you're going to buy at all.

Our study of the stock market divides fairly neatly into market analysis and security analysis. Market analysis, in which we are now engaged, splits easily into the short-term and the long-term. We are tackling the short-term first, because most investors are almost completely ignorant of it. They do not realize that their relatively low income-tax brackets let them take short-term profits that the big earner must avoid.

[At a prior time] we took up two mechanical methods of playing the market, the new-high method and the Clayton method. As we went through them we asked no questions whatever about the value of a security. We bought because a stock had made a new high on good volume or because it had increased volume at a rising price. In many cases we were buying the wrong stock at the right time but both methods proved profitable, and a combination of the two proved even more so.

[At another time] we shall talk about the techniques of the floor traders on the New York Stock Exchange and the men who run the trading desks for its firms. Often they too buy a stock merely because it is moving well, not because they know anything about it. There is even one trader who calls me up now and again to say, "I've just bought some So-and-So because it looks good on the tape. Do you know anything about it?"

I don't know about you, but I always feel uncomfortable when I risk actual money with no rationale other than a tape movement. This chapter, therefore, is an attempt to quiet the abdominal butterflies, by discussing the various ways of handling news and rumors.

Generally speaking, you buy on the rumor and sell on the confirmation—but make sure you're not the only one buying.

You take some risk when you're doing this, of course. Now and again insiders (or somebody) will see bad news coming up and circulate good rumors. For example, a sugar company was driven up to a new high in August 1958 just before it announced a dividend slash. This kind of thing, however, is not quite so common as in the past, thanks to the vigilance of the Securities and Exchange Commission and the stock exchanges themselves.

Mergers and splits always seem to send stocks higher, although neither necessarily does the company any good.

Regardless of this, investors seem to think a merger is going to be invariably helpful. Stocks go up—at least, the stock of one of the merger partners is pretty sure to go up. The reason for this, I believe, is a kind of race memory. Without thinking things through, we somehow expect the surviving company to gain monopolistic advantages or, perhaps, some of the sheer bullying advantages of bigness. Whatever these gains may be, it has been demonstrated that they are not always big enough to offset the handicaps.

How about stock splits and 100 per cent stock dividends? Here the chances for the investor are a little better. The company will remain unchanged instead of deteriorating, as it might in a merger. Here we have a company with 100 shares outstanding, selling at $100 a share earning $10 a share. It declares a 100 per cent stock dividend. Now there are 200 shares, each earning $5. Why should it sell for more than $50 a share? Or it splits 4 for 1. Why should it sell for more than $25? But it does. There is always the chance that the company may increase the dividend. But in that case, of course, the important news is the decision to increase the dividend, not the decision to split.

There may be good business reasons for splitting some stocks. A man who owns Chrysler and only Chrysler among the motor stocks is far more likely to buy a Dodge than an Oldsmobile— or so the marketing experts tell us. But I am quite sure that Mrs. Crane doesn't stop to consider whether she owns B. T. Babbitt, Colgate-Palmolive or Procter & Gamble before buying

Bab-O, Ajax or Tide. And I doubt that most other stockholders do either. (Our daughter, however, insists that when she and her husband owned Scott Paper, she suffered excruciating guilt feelings every time she bought a box of Kleenex.)

For some years I had noticed—or thought I had noticed—that stocks about to merge or split went up ahead of any announcement of such an intention and then did little. In March 1957 I decided to test out the accuracy of this observation. I dug into all the New York Stock Exchange issues that had had splits since the end of the previous June. This was an excellent period for the test, because stock prices, on the whole, were about the same at either end of this period.

In all, there were forty-three splits or 100 per cent stock dividends, but fifteen were not complete by March 20, when I made the study. I examined the other twenty-eight stocks.

How was I to know when the rumor first got around in each of these stocks? There was no way. I couldn't consult my column in the *Times*. Many stock-split rumors go unprinted for days, sometimes because they seem unlikely, sometimes because I don't hear the story in at least two trustworthy places, most often because the stock makes no one-day move big enough to match the rumor.

The best way seemed to be to assume that the rumor got under way in the three months that preceded its announcement. Directors' meetings are commonly three months apart. I took prices on these dates:

1. The day before the directors' meeting that announced the split of 100 per cent stock dividend (there were six of the latter). *Directors*, in table that follows.

2. A date three months before Item 1. *Rumor*.

3. The day before the shareholders' meeting that approved the suggestion of the directors. (Not necessary for the 100 per cent stock dividends, so that identical prices for these were noted under *Directors* and *Shareholders*.)

4. The *Distribution* of the new stock.

5. A *Recent* date. This was three months after the shareholders' meeting for twenty stocks. At the close on March 20,

1957, not quite three months had elapsed for the other eight, so the March 20 closing price was used.

Table 1 shows how the twenty-eight stocks behaved.

Table 1

	Rose	Fell	No Change
Rumor to *Directors*	23	4	1
Directors to *Shareholders*	9	12	7*
Shareholders to *Distribution*	10	18	0
Rumor to *Shareholders*	20	7	1

* Including six stock dividends.

It was clearly profitable to buy stocks when they started moving on split rumors, but how profitable? How much of that upsurge between *Rumor* and *Directors*, for example, might have been caused by the strength of the general market? Table 2 shows the figures, compared with the *New York Times* industrial average.

Table 2   Action on Split Rumors
(In percentages)

	28 Stocks	N.Y. Times Industrial Average
Rumor to *Directors*	+10.85	+0.53
Directors to *Shareholders*	+4.20	−0.54
Shareholders to *Distribution*	−1.82	−0.90
Distribution to *Recent*	−1.15	−2.09
Rumor to *Shareholders*	+15.51	−0.01
Rumor to *Recent*	+12.09	−2.99
Directors to *Recent*	+1.12	−3.50

The first four entries make clear that the only profits worth trying for are those made preceding the directors' meeting. In fact, the day before that meeting might be an awfully good time to sell. If the split is not voted, the stock will fall as disappointed holders sell. If it *is* voted, Wall Street professionals will be taking their profits. The old rule is to "buy on the rumor and sell on the news." You can see for yourself in the first table that you'd have a better chance to lose money than to make money if you hung on.

Your problem now is the fact that you would be taking a short-term capital gain. In every case you would have to add more than three months to the holding period in order to turn it into a long-term gain. There are things you can do. . . . But I am afraid that the real decision rests with you and your own view of the future.

In all honesty, however, I don't feel that anybody whose tax bracket is higher than 40 or (at most) 50 per cent belongs in this kind of speculation. The rumor, if such a man follows it, should promise something of more intrinsic value than a merger or a split.

The average gains are possibly a little better than I have indicated above. For example, El Paso Natural Gas, Louisville Gas and Electric and Panhandle Eastern Pipe Line declined in the whole Rumor-to-Directors period. Rhodesian Selection Trust also declined, due to a crumbling in world copper prices. Royal Dutch Petroleum held even, affected by trouble over Suez. Since these stocks did not rise on the split rumors, you would not have bought them and their losses would not have diminished your profits. Some of the profits were pretty good. Table 3 shows the issues that had the more violent movements.

Table 3

	Rumor	*Directors*	*Recent**
Boeing Airplane	77¾	89½	108¼
Crescent Corp.	65	79	74⅜
Gardner-Denver	58⅜	70¾	71½
Georgia-Pacific	54⅝	80⅜	59
Greenfield Tap & Die	34¾	44⅜	37½
Jaeger Machine	36½	57	49¼
National Supply	77¼	93	93¾

* Prices "unsplit" to provide comparison.

There is one thing, of course, that is missing in all this calculation: I have said nothing about the number of splits and mergers that are rumored but don't come off. There are plenty of those, believe me! One day in late 1957 I listed the names of six companies that had been mentioned *that day only* as possible merger partners for Gulf Oil. Five years later all were still waiting at the church.

A. Wilfred May, executive editor of the *Commercial and Financial Chronicle*, has done a great deal of research on these lines. Early in 1957 he examined the eighty stocks that split 2 for 1 or more in 1956. Between the admission of the new shares to trading and the end of 1956 only forty-three of the eighty out-performed the remaining companies in their respective industry groups.

Mr. May then took the sixty-six stocks that split in the first eleven months of 1955. Of these, only twenty-one out-performed the Dow-Jones industrial average up to the end of 1955 and only twenty-four did so up to the end of 1956.

In another examination of the eighty issues that split in 1956, he found that seventy-two out-performed the market in the one-month period before the directors met and only thirty-six issues did so from then until the new shares were admitted to trading.

All these data bear out my conclusions, although I prefer the dates I have chosen to those used by Mr. May.

In going over the first edition of this book* to see where he might provide updated material for the present revision, a representative of the New York Stock Exchange pointed to the title of this chapter and said, "You'll find we don't have this trouble with rumors so much nowadays." He then produced a letter from Stock Exchange President Keith Funston to the presidents of all listed companies sternly reminding them that prompt disclosure of any corporate news that might affect the price of securities is a requisite of their listing agreement. "When unusual market activity in a security accompanied by a substantial

---

* The first edition of Burton Crane's *The Sophisticated Investor* was published in 1959. This selection was taken from the revised and expanded 1964 edition.

price change occurs shortly before the announcement of an important corporate action or development," wrote Mr. Funston, "it is extremely embarrassing and may work a disservice to shareowners and to the public."

In fairness to the Exchange, without whose assistance this revision would have been enormously more difficult, it must be said that Mr. Funston's letter was aimed chiefly at public-relations officers who had been sending out corporate news on a "Hold for Release" basis to newspapers, brokerage offices and the like, giving all sorts of people plenty of time to get into or out of a security before the publication date.

Has it affected the sort of rumor we have been discussing? Table 4 shows the action in a number of issues which were split in the first six months of 1963.

Table 4

	Rumor	*Directors*	*Share-holders*	*Distribu-tion*	*Recent*
Beatrice Foods	52	56	61¼	62	62¾
Chrysler	63⅝	82⅞	109⅜	107	128½
Cleveland Electric Illuminating	61	67¼	65	65	67
Inspiration Consolidated Copper	53½	62¼	63½	69¾	70¼
Long Island Lighting	47⅜	56⅜	58⅞	62¾	63¾
Magma Copper	63	75	77½	80	76½
Singer Manufacturing	107	111⅛	136½	136	151½
Sterling Drug	65¼	77	84⅛	79	81
Sunshine Biscuits	97¾	103	110	110¾	106
Union Electric	46¼	51¾	53⅜	55½	54½
Virginia Electric & Power	57⅝	62⅞	64⅝	65¼	63½

The stocks were chosen at random. While Chrysler and Singer do not precisely prove our point, there still does not seem to be much of a case for dropping this chapter from the book.

What interests you most, I take it, is whether you ought to speculate on the rumors that a company is about to merge or split its stock. For a little while, anyhow, the stock will be higher. Why not apply these three simple tests?

1. Is the market action right? Has the stock moved in the right direction on appropriate volume? If it has, perhaps you don't need to worry too much about the truth of this rumor. *Something is happening.*

2. Is the rumor reasonable or is it something to the effect that American Home Products has discovered a cure for Rumpel-meyer's Disease? (Since there are only twenty known victims of Rumpelmeyer's disease in the world and thirteen of these are on county poor farms, this is hardly likely to mean an increased dividend, is it?) Or had you heard that Owens-Corning Fiberglas is making both the glamshishes for the TGBM—trans-galactic ballistic missile—that is to make the trip to Alpha Centauri and back? (Alpha Centauri is four light-years away and, even at ultimate speed, at least nine years must pass before we know whether these glamshishes are any good. Maybe Haveg Industries will get the 1970 contract, after all.)

This razzberry attitude may cost you a good speculation now and then but it will save you more bad ones. After all, why—within limits—should you care how many you miss? There are always plenty more.

3. As I said, there are lots of rumors about lots of stocks. Why not, then, take special interest in stocks that seem likely to do pretty well even if the rumor should not be true? Then, if the rumor happens to be true and you have a pleasant profit at the end of three months, you can hold on for another three months with less quivering behind the belt buckle.

Shall we talk about lies? The earlier pages . . . have given the impression that Wall Street rumors are true if enough people believe them. This is not correct, as you may have guessed, but from the point of view of the speculator it may be correct enough. Perhaps he can take his profit and leave before the rest of the customers start looking for the escape hatch.

There are some brokers who would like to "buy stock at 8 times earnings and drive it up to 50." There are others who—perhaps from too much anxiety to please—have an annoying habit of promoting possibilities into rumors. I have found still others who seemed a trifle overanxious to persuade me that such-and-such a stock was a gorgeous buy. Their customers had probably bought on their recommendations and they wanted to make those recommendations stand up.

Perhaps these practices are not quite up to the best Sunday School standards but I do not criticize them. When a broker is accepting a commission to sell an already listed stock—and could make just as big a commission by selling almost any other stock—you can put this kind of thing down to boyish enthusiasm. It is "just his way." If he doesn't tout the stock and drive it up beyond the limits of safety, somebody else will.

I do object, however, when the same man is acting as a salesman. Your broker should represent *you* all the time. If he is hawking a new issue or a secondary distribution of an already listed stock he is using your broker-customer relationship in a way that can be easily misunderstood. He certainly is not representing you. He is representing the issuing corporation or the owners of secondary-distribution stock who are trying to get out from under by paying more than the regular commission.

How would you like your doctor to take kickbacks from the drug manufacturers? The broker is obliged to recite a little formula when he suddenly turns into a salesman. Perhaps he is "acting as a principal" or there is "no commission to be paid by you." But what he says is apt to be so perfunctory that it is ignored or not understood.

Most of the liars who affect us in Wall Street are, I am afraid, corporation officials, not brokers. Time after time I have had company presidents deny that their concern was considering a merger with Watsis, Inc., "or with any other company," only to have the same solid citizen announce a merger with another company a week or so later.

According to Revelation 21:8, all liars "shall have their part in the lake which burneth with fire and brimstone: which is the second death."

If I could only be sure of that!

Tip to the Investor:
Always Write It Down

GERALD M. LOEB

Gerald M. Loeb, one of the most astute writers on
investing, has for many years had his market interpretations
widely published in newspapers and periodicals, and heard
on radio and television. There are certainly many tips on the
stock market, but none more helpful to the investor than
the one that follows.

WRITING down your cogent reasons for making an investment—what you expect to make, what you expect to risk, the
reasons why—should save you many a dollar.

Years ago, in the early Twenties, I was initiated into writing
down my reasons pro and con before making a purchase or a
sale. This was suggested to me by an investor who had amassed
many millions.

During about forty years of investing in stocks my major suc-
cesses were invariably preceded by a type of written analysis.
Sudden emotional decisions have generally been disappoint-
ments.

Writing things down before you do them can keep you out of
trouble. It can bring you peace of mind after you have made

your decision. It also gives you tangible material for reference to evaluate the whys and wherefores of your profits or losses.

Quality Not Quantity

I have seen many analyses, some involving many pages of information. In practice, quantity doesn't make quality. When all is said and done, there is invariably one ruling reason why a particular security transaction can be expected to show profit.

Writing it down will help you find it. It will help you judge whether it is really as important as your first inclination suggests. Are you buying just because something "acts well"? Is it a technical reason—a coming increase in earnings or dividend not yet discounted in the market price, a change of management, a promising new product, an expected improvement in the market's valuation of earnings? In any given case you will find that one factor will almost certainly be more important than all the rest put together.

Writing it down will help you estimate what you expect to make. It is important that this be worthwhile.

Of course, you will want to decide how much you can afford to lose. There will be a level at which you will decide that things have not worked out and where you will sell. Your risk is the difference between your cost and this sell point; it ought to be substantially less than your hopes for profit. You certainly want to feel that the odds as you see them are in your favor.

Much More Difficult

All this self-interrogation will help you immeasurably in the much more difficult decision: when to close a commitment.

When you open a commitment, whether it is a purchase or a short sale, you are, so to speak, on your home ground. Unless everything suits you, you don't play. But when you are called upon to close a commitment, then you have to make decisions, whether you see the answer clearly or not. The latter situation is like being stuck on a railway crossing with the train approaching. You don't know what to do—but you have to do something. Go backward, go forward—or jump out.

If you know clearly why you bought a stock it will help you to know when to sell it. The major factor which you recognized when you bought a security will either work out or not work out. Once you can say definitely that it has worked or not worked, the security should be sold.

One of the greatest causes of loss in security transactions is to open a commitment for a particular reason, and then fail to close it when the reason proves to be invalid.

Write it down—and you will be less likely to find yourself making irrelevant excuses for holding a security long after it should have been sold. Better still, a stock well bought is far more than half the battle.

What Price Growth?

CLAUDE N. ROSENBERG, JR.

What price should an investor be willing to pay for a promising growth stock? Investment and financial adviser Claude N. Rosenberg, Jr., has developed some valuable guides to assessing the value of a growth company. This is the subject for his Profit-Aid 6 (Rosenberg has 28 Profit-Aids useful to both the novice and experienced investor) that follows.

I AM sure I will encounter no argument when I state that it is extremely beneficial to investors to buy and own stocks of companies which will show consistent increases in earnings (*per share*) over the years. The theory behind buying so-called "growth companies" is virtually undisputed! The difference of opinion lies with the decision of what price a person should be willing to pay for growth.

Naturally, there is no single formula for answering this question: What price for what growth? I could make a strong argument to convince you that a range of ten to fifteen times earnings is ample for a 5-percent-growth company, that fifteen to twenty times is suitable for a 10-percent-growth outfit, and that a progression upward of about an additional five in the multiple for each additional 5 percent of growth is justified. This mathematical thinking alone, however, would hardly provide you with the right market price for securities in general. There are too many other considerations which have to be thrown into the "hopper," not the least of which are institutional support (or lack of it), general market psychology, supply of stock available, and so-called "glamour image." Any one of these (and other) factors can alter your mathematical computation and lead you to a conclusion for either a higher or a lower price-earnings ratio than might seem justified by the figures alone.

Does all this mean that we should throw up our hands in despair and close our eyes to market-price evaluation? Of course not! We must base our selection and our timing on something, and the relationship between annual compound growth rates and P/E ratios as indicated in the second paragraph is as good a starting point as any.

Opponents of the growth theory of investing can, of course, throw cold water on the whole approach—by simply posing the question: "What happens if there is a reversal in public opinion and the P/E paid by investors for an individual stock, and industry group, or the market in general is lowered considerably?"

A good question, indeed! We certainly do not want to pay twenty times earnings today for a stock and find it selling at ten times earnings five years from now, *regardless of the company's growth rate in the interim*.

Or do we?

The fact is—*we may be willing to own a stock and see its P/E come down sharply, provided its rate-of-earnings growth is strong enough*. The mathematics of compounding figures are amazing; a little later on in this chapter I will show you just how amazing by proving to you that a stock like IBM can be a decent investment today at forty times earnings even if we visualize it selling at only twenty times earnings ten years hence.

Before we come to this and other illustrations which will prepare us better for determining what price we should pay for growth, we should explore and conclude just what constitutes a good investment.

Don't worry, I'm not going to bore you with a long philosophical dissertation on investments. What I am going to do is give you a simple explanation—one which will have a practical application for you.

All investments should be judged on the basis of *annual rate of return on invested capital.* Whether it be the ownership of raw land, income property, a private business, or the holding of securities, the important consideration is the average rate of return on the money invested. Naturally, this rate of return will have to include both the income received from the investment plus the appreciation (or minus the loss) on the investment over its life. Let me emphasize that you have to consider both the income and the increment in value (or loss) in arriving at the average annual rate of return. I do this because I have heard such abuses—even by very intelligent people—of what really constitutes a good rate of return. For example, I have heard people brag about investments which seemingly yield very high rates —where the owners have failed to account for the loss of capital if the investment were to be liquidated (i.e., a second mortgage). By the same token, I have heard individuals boast about the great investment they made buying that acre of Tibetan land, where their $1,000 investment in 1944 was just sold for $2,000. While doubling of investment sounds glamorous, twenty-three years is a long time to wait for it, and, as a matter of fact, such performance amounts to a compounded rate of return of only about 3 percent per year. (Naturally, any taxes paid on the property should be accounted for, and this would reduce the return further.) At any rate, a mere bond would have achieved similar results, and certainly almost any conservative common-stock investment would have achieved far superior effects.

As far as the securities market is concerned, we should approach the problem of investing wisely, just as the professional advisors do. So now we come to Profit-Aid 6, *which shows us how to weigh the merits of bonds, preferred stocks, and common stocks by computing, as closely as possible, the probable rate of return on our invested capital over the years.* It is quite simple to do this when we are considering bond investments, and fairly easy to figure in the case of preferreds. For example, assume you are considering investment in a General Motors bond which pays $3.00 a year; the bond sells at $90.00 and it will mature in ten years at $100.00. Your average rate of return on this bond will be about 4.3 percent, figured as follows:

1. Paying $90 for a $3 yearly income provides a yield of 3.3 percent per year ($3 ÷ $90 = 3.3 percent).
2. Your $90 purchase will be worth $100 in ten years, for a gain of $1 a year, or slightly over 1 percent per year.
3. The 3.3 percent as shown in (1) plus the 1 percent as figured in (2) = 4.3 percent, which is the average rate of return per year.

As a potential investor, you will want to determine whether this 4.3 percent is attractive relative to other investments and make your decision accordingly.

The analysis of a preferred stock will be similar to the General Motors bond illustration, except that there is no maturity date or price you can count on. In essence, you should figure what the current yield amounts to and make your decision based almost solely on this.

In the more interesting area of common stocks, the approach is more complicated—but it can be so wonderfully rewarding that it is worth exploring. First of all, let's consider the case of a common stock where earnings are quite predictable, i.e., the case of a good electric-utility stock. Electric utilities in a growing area should represent good investments because their product (electricity) is in steadily growing demand. But this is a bold generalization to make—mainly because we have to consider what price we have to pay in the market for this "assured" growth and because we haven't even considered what our average rate of return on investment might be. If we have to pay too high a price and our return will be very low, perhaps we're better off placing the money elsewhere.

For example, let's look at Pacific Gas & Electric Company, or any number of a host of utilities whose earnings have grown

—and should reasonably be expected to grow in the future—at 4 to 5 percent a year. Stocks such as these are selling in today's market at about fifteen times earnings, with a yield of 4 percent. Obviously this 4-percent yield figure is *not* the total rate of return on your investment. Why? Because the company's earnings are expanding 4 to 5 percent a year! Assuming the stock sells at the same P/E a year, two years, or five years from now, the 4- to 5-percent annual improvement in earnings will be directly reflected in appreciation of the stock's market price. Thus, this investment will return an average of 8 to 9 percent on your money (4-percent current yield plus 4- to 5-percent earnings growth). To be specific, here is what happens when you buy XYZ utility today at $100 per share, when its earnings are $6.65 per share (P/E of fifteen) and its dividend is $4.00 (4 percent yield). One year from today, you look back on your investment, and here is what you find:

1. You have received $4.00 in dividends, which, based on your $100 investment, amounts to a return of 4 percent.
2. XYZ's earnings per share have advanced 5 percent, from $6.65 to about $7. XYZ stock is still selling at 15 times these latter earnings and is now 105 ($15 \times $7 = 105).
3. The five-point improvement from 100 to 105 amounts to a 5-percent appreciation.
4. The 4 percent shown in 1 plus the 5 percent in 3 gives you a total 9-percent rate of return in this one year.

This is the kind of thinking you should have done when you first considered XYZ. If you had, you would have compared this projected 9-percent rate of return with, for example, the 4.3 percent from the GM bond about which we talked and with other investment possibilities. The return on XYZ was about twice that of the GM bond, and you probably would have considered this sufficient reward for taking the risk that XYZ would either:
1. Not show a 5-percent advance in net income; or
2. Not sell as high as fifteen times earnings in the future.
The exact line of reasoning prevails when considering any

stock investment. Using utility stocks again as examples, you would weigh the purchase of a rapidly growing vehicle such as Florida Power and Light as follows:

1. FPL has averaged a 10-percent growth in earnings in recent years.
2. You will have to pay twenty times earnings for FPL stock, and the yield from same is a small 2 percent.
3. If the company's growth rate remains the same and the stock's P/E is unchanged, the rate of return will be 12 percent per year (2-percent yield plus 10-percent earnings growth).
4. You must be convinced that this 12-percent return compensates you for the risk either that FPL growth slows down or that the stock's P/E drops over the years.

The interesting thing is, however, that the P/E actually can drop rather sharply and you can still have a fine investment, provided the earnings growth continues over a long enough period. As long as Florida Power and Light, for example, grows at a 10 percent rate over, say, ten years, the P/E can drop from twenty to sixteen or even lower and it can be termed an effective use of capital. A decline of P/E from twenty to sixteen, along with a 10-percent compounded earnings growth (and a 2-percent dividend payout), will still allow the stock to show a 10-percent averate rate of return, and this still compares favorably with a fixed-income investment such as a bond.

The slower-growth utilities can also experience a reduced P/E and come out well ahead as investments. A 5-percent growth company over ten years can see its P/E drop from 15 to less than 12 and (including, of course, the current yield of 4 percent) realize a 6-percent return. As a matter of fact, the P/E can drop from 15 to as low as 9 and the average rate of return over ten years will still equal 4½ percent.

All in all, I believe one can point to an average rate of return of at least 8 percent from electric-utility stocks over a long period. With this in mind, I believe we can make two important conclusions, as follows:

1. For a portfolio which has time to wait, I would prefer large holdings of electric-utility stocks rather than huge proportions of bonds and other fixed-income securities.
2. Since results from electric utilities are among the most predictable, I would expect to achieve higher than the 8-percent average rate of return from other stocks with a less predictable future. In other words, because of the uncertainties, other stocks should sell at a *lower* P/E than the electric utility with the same anticipated growth rate.

Obviously there are many non-utility companies which have shown superior consistency in earnings growth to that of the utilities. It is this all-important element of *certainty of earnings growth* which is the key to the "proper" P/E to pay for a stock.

Before we explore this certainty element further, however, let me complete the discussion of the *importance of earnings growth*. I stated at the outset . . . that IBM could prove a decent investment even if we visualized a halving of its P/E in the future. This is only true if IBM's profits continue to advance at a compounded 15-percent rate. This combination of 15-percent growth and a cutting in half of the P/E over ten years still gives an overall investment return of 8 percent (plus dividend returns) to IBM stockholders today. To further illustrate the importance of earnings growth, we could, in our search for an 8-percent return, afford only a one-third reduction in the P/E if IBM's growth averaged 12½ percent per year; and if the company's growth rate were "only" 10 percent per year, we could not stand more than a one-quarter reduction in the P/E and come out with an average of 8-percent annual return on our dollars.

Thus, while the study of investments is all tied in with mathematics, the most important considerations will come from our *judgment of what the future holds*. . . . Profit-Aid 6 has covered what constitutes the heart of all investment decisions: the annual rate of return on dollars risked. You have seen how professional advisers think—and this should give you the proper insight and a new perspective for the future use of your dollars.

Note: In reading the above, do not conclude that returns of 4½ to 8 percent per year are considered adequate or wholly satisfactory. They certainly are not! A growth investor should hardly be satisfied with less than 10–20 percent per annum. As a matter of fact, the real capital-gain-oriented investor should never buy a stock unless he can envision a return of well above such percentages. The illustrations above, however, do prove a point, and they set up a thinking process arfd an operating procedure which should be followed by security buyers regardless of objectives.

Commodity Futures Trading

JOHN W. HAZARD

*Commodity futures are a risky, but provocative, area of
investment. The commodity futures markets appeal
primarily to those individuals with a speculative bent —
and who possess nerves of steel. John W. Hazard has for
many years written articles for* Changing Times, the
Kiplinger Magazine, *and is presently its executive editor.
Hazard clearly explains just what goes at these fast-paced
markets and analyzes the potential for making profits in
this type of trading.*

HAVE you heard the one about the country boy who
wandered into the Coffee Exchange, blinked his eyes, scratched
his chin, tugged at his ear and, upon leaving, learned that he had
made $7,000?" So ran an ad some years ago in a financial news-
paper. It went on to describe commodity futures markets as
"the fastest trading markets in the world—where you operate
on as little as 10% margin—where fortunes have been made and
lost in a matter of months."

Basically, this description is true. As a young man, John May-
nard Keynes, author of the famous Keynesian theory of economics, was determined to be financially independent and never

to "relapse into salaried drudgery." So shortly after World War I he began speculating, first in foreign exchange. He sold German marks and bought U.S. dollars. But early in 1920 the dollar began to decline and the mark rose, and Keynes soon found he had lost £13,000.

He borrowed enough to keep going and plunged into the commodity futures market, trading heavily on very small margins in lead, tin, copper, zinc, rubber, wheat, sugar, linseed oil, and jute futures. Within four years he had made £58,000. During most of his life he continued to speculate in commodities and stocks, finally accumulating a £500,000 fortune.

Keynes, of course, was a genius. Unfortunately, the ordinary speculator in commodity futures may well have the opposite experience. A Department of Agriculture study some years ago indicated that three times as many small speculators lost money as made it. Still, the lure of quick riches is strong. Every large brokerage house has its contingent of men, and even women, who are trying to outguess the weather and the professional commodity traders in New York, Chicago, Minneapolis, and Kansas City. Here are the mechanics of it and the way the speculators figure their chances of success.

Hedging vs. Speculation

Suppose in early spring you overheard a wheat farmer say, "I've just planted my crop and I see that wheat is currently selling at $2 a bushel. I'd be happy to get that price for my crop when I harvest it next September."

At this point you might say to yourself, "This might be a good deal. The long-range weather forecast is for a hot, dry summer. Congress may raise the support price of wheat. By September the going price may be considerably above $2." So you say to the farmer, "Tell you what. I'll contract to take 5000 bushels next September at $2 a bushel. And I'll give you 10% down to show good faith."

If you and the farmer made this kind of deal, you would, in

effect, have bought a September wheat future and he would have sold one. Every day thousands of transactions of this kind are made. Only instead of farmers and speculators meeting face to face, they give their orders to brokers who send them by wire to traders on the floor of one of the commodity exchanges. There the orders are filled much as are orders to buy or sell stocks on the New York Stock Exchange.

Visit the Chicago Board of Trade and from the visitors' gallery you will see the pits, or trading areas, where contracts for wheat, corn, oats, rye, soybeans, and lard are constantly being bought and sold by quick signals of hand and finger. In Minneapolis there is the Grain Exchange, in Kansas City, the Board of Trade. In New York and Chicago there are the two Mercantile Exchanges, where egg and potato futures are bought and sold. At the New York Commodity Exchange it's hides, lead, rubber, copper, and zinc.

There are only two reasons why a person would buy or sell a commodity future. One is to speculate; the other is to avoid speculation, in other words, to hedge. The farmer in the example just cited was a hedger. He knew wheat was $2 a bushel right then, and he wanted to establish the price for his crop once and for all without having to worry about future fluctuations.

Other examples of hedging: In January a chain of grocery stores wants to buy 100 carloads of flour to be delivered June 1. It asks a flour mill to quote a firm price. Now the miller does not want to buy all that wheat in January and store it until June. But in order to quote a firm price on the flour, he must know the cost of raw material, as well as overhead and profit. This means he must immediately establish the price he will pay for his wheat. He can do this by buying wheat futures. Who will sell them to him? Some speculator who thinks wheat is due to go down so that by June he can buy the futures back for less and make a profit.

When a rubber manufacturer buys raw rubber, he may sell an equivalent amount of rubber futures. Since he thus buys and sells rubber at the same time, he guards himself against a loss in case the price of rubber, and rubber goods, changes while his raw material is in inventory or in process of manufacture. Once the finished goods are sold, he will cancel his hedge by buying futures. If, in the meantime, rubber has gone up, he will pay more for his futures, but he will also receive a higher price for his rubber products. Or, if rubber has gone down, he may have to sell his products for less than planned, but also he will buy back his futures for less and hence make an offsetting profit.

You can see that the speculator, by taking the other end of the deal from the hedger, is providing a public service. But that, of course, is not why the speculator is in the market. He buys and sells for only one reason, to make a profit.

Can he do it? Yes, say the brokers who handle such accounts, the speculator can profit if he has the capital, the nerve, and the will to follow certain rules of the game. But, at best, it's a risky business.

Rules of the Game

Here is how the brokers reason. In commodity futures trading, margins are very low, 5% to 10%. So while the risks are great, so are the potential profits. If a speculator buys on a 10% margin and the price rises 10%, he doubles his money. If he buys on a 5% margin and the price rises 10%, he doubles his money. And while the speculator must pay close attention to daily movements, there are not so many basic variables to watch as there are in the stock market.

The two main ingredients of the commodity market are supply and demand. And the figures on these are public information. There can't be any inside dope. Crop reports are jealously guarded against leaks until they are made public, and, once public, they are available to everyone. So are statistics on carryover, exports, stocks under government loan, and so on.

Then there are certain basic seasonal trends. Over the years, wheat prices, for example, tend to be lowest at harvest time in July and August and on the average gradually move up during the fall and winter until the new wheat comes in. Soybean prices usually hit their lows in the first two weeks in October.

Lord Keynes asserted that futures prices tend to rise 10% per year on the average. Professor Paul Cootner, of Massachusetts Institute of Technology, once made a study of the years 1954 to 1959 to determine what would have happened, if in June of each year, a speculator had bought a wheat contract calling for delivery in the subsequent May. A May wheat contract bought in June 1954 would have appreciated 9% by the time its delivery date came around in May 1955. The same future bought in subsequent years would have appreciated as follows: 11% in 1956, 1% in 1957, and 10% in 1958. But in 1959 it would have fallen 6%. The average annual speculation would have been 5%.

Considering that the speculator could have bought such a contract on a 5% margin, you might assume that, if he had averaged out, he could have doubled his money. This assumption would be dangerous, however. For one thing, prices rise and fall from day to day, and the margin trader could easily have been wiped out on a series of temporary declines. Also, if he were pyramiding his profits, he would have been wiped out in 1959 anyway.

Just the same, brokers have certain rules of thumb that they think guard against some of these dangers. In the first place, no one should even think of speculating in commodity futures unless he is prepared to take losses. Some losses are almost inevitable. But the theory is that if losses are always cut short and gains allowed to run, a speculator can make money even if he is right only 35% of the time.

Most brokers recommend that whenever a speculator takes a position in a commodity future he immediately put in a stop-loss order. If he buys a wheat future for $2 a bushel, for example, he should put in a stop-loss order 2 cents below the market. Then if wheat falls to $1.98, he will automatically be sold out and his loss limited to only 2 or 2½ cents. If he sells a future short, he should put in a stop-loss order 2 cents above the market so that if wheat rises, instead of falling, he will again be sold out before he has lost much more than 2 cents.

In this way the speculator should attempt to cut his losses short. But if by chance he catches a broad trend, then he should let his profits run. Thus if a speculator bought wheat futures at $2 and wheat began to rise, going to $2.10, he should not take a profit but should move his stop-loss order up to $2.08. Then if the upward trend continued, say to $2.20, he could move the stop loss to $2.18 and so on.

But what happens to the speculator who buys wheat at $2 and is sold out at $1.97 or $1.98? If he has bought one future, or 5000 bushels, on a 5% margin, he has put up only $500, but has lost $100 or $150. If he tries it again he may have the same luck. In fact, it may take several tries before he catches his trend. In the meantime, his capital is impaired.

That is why the larger and more conservative brokerage houses will accept as commodity trading customers only those who they think understand the risks and can afford to take them. And unless a new customer has a stock account (and on the average over half of them do), he usually must open his account with a deposit of at least $1000. Brokers generally shy away from women as customers. The reason given: Most women can't stand to take losses.

Trading in commodity futures is not expensive as far as costs and commissions go. The commission in and out for a 5000-bushel wheat contract is only $18. It figures out that a three-eighth-cent rise in the price will compensate for the commission. Everything above that is gravy, at least on paper.

A good bit of free information is available to the commodity trader. The larger brokerage houses provide a wire service giving hourly price quotations and figures on stocks on hand, crop estimates, and so on. Various advisory services also are on file in brokerage offices, or may be purchased on a subscription basis from the publishers, giving outlook and opinion on all commodity futures prices. Some brokers provide a free handbook giving an informal course in how to trade intelligently in futures.

As you see, it's easy to get into the futures market. Margin is small. Commissions are modest. And the same information is available to everyone. Then why don't more people make money at it? Here are the answers from account executives of several leading brokerage houses.

The Risks

The average trader won't make money in the long run because once he makes a few profits he begins to think he's an expert and doesn't bother taking the proper precautions, such as putting in stop-loss orders on every trade. Also, most people who trade in commodities also have previously traded in common stocks. They can't get used to the idea of cutting losses short. If the market goes against them, they tend to hold on and become stubborn. They apply stock market logic, which is that a good stock eventually is bound to come back. But this doesn't apply to commodities. The May wheat future can go inexorably down right until May. And at that point the owner must either sell and take his loss or take delivery of 5000 bushels and make payment to the seller in full.

Amateur commodity traders have other faults. They are basically optimists and tend to take the long side of the market most of the time. In practice, according to the experts, a trader should be short about half the time.

Some years ago a group of Maine potato farmers got interested in the potato futures market. In theory, their role should have been that of hedgers. If the price was good when they planted their crop, you might expect them to sell futures and fix their year's income. Instead, many of them got overenthusiastic and actually bought futures. This meant, in effect, that the potato farmers had two crops to worry about instead of one.

Taking small gains is another pitfall. The successful trader must have nerves of steel and allow his profits to run. If he chickens out and takes small profits, they will be eaten up by the inevitable small losses.

And even though the information is available to everyone the unexpected can easily happen. In the spring of 1960, eggs were firm, and the Department of Agriculture implied a short supply. But chicken farmers are not dumb. When they received this word, they simply reversed their usual practice. Instead of culling out their old hens, they let them live and keep on laying. As a result, September egg futures fell from around 38 cents a dozen to 30. And since there are 15,000 dozen eggs in a futures contract, every price drop of 1 cent meant a loss to the futures holder of $150 per contract.

Yes, it's fun to read about the country boy who wandered into the Coffee Exchange, blinked his eyes, scratched his chin, tugged at his ear, and made $7000. That's a good old Wall Street joke. But here's another story, a true one.

An unsophisticated speculator bought a couple of coffee futures contracts, putting up $1500 margin. The market turned against him and he decided to sell, but he couldn't the first day because coffee was down the allowable daily limit on the first transaction and there were no more trades that day. He put his sell order in the next day, and again futures were down the limit on the first sale and trading stopped. This went on for five days. By the time his position was liquidated, he had lost his $1500 plus nearly $10,000 more.

And that's no joke.

"Cashing In" on Population Growth

ROBERT D. MERRITT

*To some people the overwhelming growth in population is
alarming. It means less living space, more children to feed
and educate, more jobs to be created, and more elderly
people dependent on the state for support. However, the
sophisticated investor can interpret this inevitable
phenomenon in a different way. The population boom
offers investors a great potential for profits — but how and
where? Robert D. Merritt, financial editor of United
Business Service, describes this potential.*

*A*CCORDING to Census Bureau estimates, the population of
the United States is increasing at the rate of one person every
12 seconds. There is a birth every 8 seconds, a death every 21
seconds; an immigrant arrives every 2 minutes, and someone
departs for foreign stores every 24 minutes. What it all adds up
to is simply this: the United States population is now gaining at
the rate of nearly 3 million persons a year, even considering
the recently declining birthrate. It is like adding the combined
populations of Rhode Island, Delaware, Idaho, Nebraska, and
Montana—or a new city the size of Chicago *every year*! By the
time 1980 rolls around, there will be 40 or 50 million more

people in this country, which is double the entire present population of Canada. (See Figure 1.)

For business and industry, population trends are significant. They point to bigger markets for goods and services and the need for a still further enlargement of productive capacity. The more people there are in this country, the more business will be done. And the more business is done, the more corporations will earn. More people mean more customers, more schools, more roads, more homes—more of practically everything from toothpaste to television sets.

No One-Way Street

There are some sobering aspects of population growth, however, to which we as intelligent investors must not close our eyes.

Figure 1

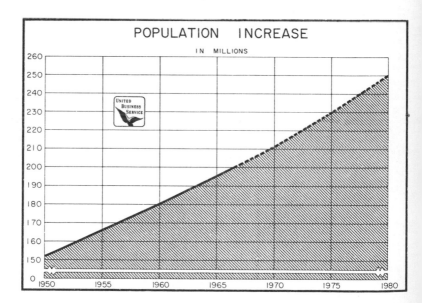

Population growth brings problems as well as benefits. The new consumers will also be potential job holders who need work. One of the fastest growing segments of the population by far will be the 20 to 24 age group. These young people will be eager to work and anxious to support their young families. But they will come streaming into the work force at a time when industry will be mechanizing more and more and learning to get along without an abundance of production workers. Encouraging in this connection is the continued growth of service industries. Nearly three-fourths of all jobs in the U.S. are now in service occupations where automation and mechanization are scarcely applicable.

The Age Mix Is Important

One of the most significant aspects of the population growth story is the age mix. In recent years a feature here has been the sharp rise in births with consequent great swelling of the school-age population. This has caused an acute shortage of classroom space, a tremendous pressure on school facilities.

As the army of adolescents moves on through high school and college, pressure on the nation's higher education facilities intensifies. High school and college enrollments are expected to soar 50% and 70%, respectively, by 1975. Textbook publishers and makers of school furniture will be among the conspicuous beneficiaries.

An added impetus in this direction will be increased awareness of the economic value of higher education and the need for trained individuals to keep abreast of Russian scientific achievements. Currently about half of the nation's adult population has a high school education. By 1970, approximately two-thirds of those aged 21 years or over will have graduated from high school, and over three times as many as ever before will go on to college. A rise in the nation's educational level always results in higher job skills, greater productivity, more wants, increased living standards.

A Boom in Family Formations

The changing mix of the age groups will eventually stimulate demands for new housing and supporting facilities. During the next decade the population in the marrying-family-forming ages 20 to 35 will grow at an extremely fast rate, while those in the 35 to 60 age group will increase very slowly if at all. This is shown dramatically in Figure 2 and the accompanying table. Very soon, in fact, we shall begin hitting the jackpot in family formations as World War II's big baby crop approaches the age of marriage. It is calculated that by 1970 there will be 60% more young people forming new households, touching off a great new wave of demand for all sorts of goods from dishwashers and bathtubs to carpets and automobiles. Initially this means great new needs for small apartments and baby food. Later will come a huge new cycle of individual home construction. These new families will also have a need for schools, hospitals, utilities, insurance, groceries, etc.

Figure 2

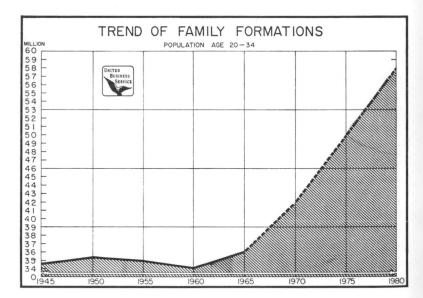

Population Changes
(000 omitted)

Age Group	1965	1980	Increase Number	%
14 and under	59,909	71,406	11,497	19.2
15–19	17,052	20,876	3,824	22.4
20–24	13,668	20,997	7,329	53.6
25–34	22,358	36,999	14,641	65.5
35–44	24,432	25,376	944	3.9
45–59	31,202	33,409	2,207	7.1
60 and over	25,965	32,833	6,868	26.5
Total Pop.	194,586	241,896	47,310	24.3

Based on Census estimates.

Virtually all leading industries will benefit to a degree from the coming tidal wave of family spending. Some fields, however, are in a special position to share directly in the setting up of households and the expenditures resulting. These include:

Apparel	Home furnishings
Appliances	Installment financing
Autos	Life insurance
Banking	Petroleum
Building	Radio-TV
Electric utilities	Retailing
Foods	Telephone

Based on this new wave of family formations, it seems safe to predict a new business boom of impressive proportions by 1970–75. Just as the decline in family formations was a factor in the nation's growth slowdown from 1955 to 1960 (Figure 2), so now we can look forward to accelerated growth. The addition of millions of new workers to the labor force will involve large expenditures for capital equipment and new machinery. Overall, the prospect is for substantial prosperity and a higher standard of living.

Another significant development has been the trend toward

decentralization. Over a million people a year are moving into the suburbs, and to a considerable extent also industry is moving out of the cities. This has been a powerful stimulus to home and industrial building. And, incidentally, it is one of the biggest boosters for the automobile industry and road building.

A Helping Hand for Automobile Industry

If government, management, and labor use their collective intelligence and a major war is avoided, we can expect by 1980 a gross national product of perhaps $1.4 trillion, almost double what it is now. Let us pause for a moment to think of what that could mean to just one industry—automobiles. Auto sales historically have closely paralleled the GNP, and profits and stock prices have followed along. Rising disposable income will be an important factor in this picture, as it stimulates multiple-car ownership. In the past decade, multiple-car households have jumped 142%, compared with a 29% gain in the total number of car-owning families. Growing population, especially in the new-driver age bracket, also boosts demand. Finally, a steadily increasing number of cars on the road will mean a rising replacement demand—scrappage is now about six million cars a year. This latter factor alone accounts for some 75% of current demand and will become even more important in the early 1970's when the large volume of cars sold in the 1962–65 peak years reach retirement age.

Thus, it seems an entirely reasonable prediction that production in a normal automobile year will reach 10 million cars by the early 1970's. By 1980 this figure may well be exceeding 15 million annually.

The best year up until now has been 9.3 million cars produced in 1965. In that year General Motors earned $7.41 a share. If X-year in the future brings a demand for, say, 15 million cars, it is not out of line to suppose that General Motors' earnings could rise at least in proportion to the industry's sales volume of 60%. This would mean around $12.00 per-share earnings and conceivably a price of 125–150 for the stock (10 to 12 times earnings).

But automobile production is a volume business and the tendency is for profits to rise even more rapidly than sales. Hence, we are being rather conservative in our estimate of $12.00 per share for General Motors and a price of 125–150 by 1980. The picture could be much brighter than we have painted.

Profiting from Area Growth

As the map shows, there will be wide differences in area growth of population. Figure 3 gives a good picture of where business is likely to develop the fastest. Those who buy the stocks of companies serving the fast-growth areas have the population factor working very much in their favor. The end result is often a profitable investment, provided enough patience is exercised. The idea is to pick the right spot for your money, and then let the waves of population growth sweep it onward and upward. Of course, you still have to seek a good product, a soundly conceived business, and alert management. Some businesses go bust even in the best locations. But other things being equal, the population-growth factor gives business a powerful shove along the road to profits.

An example of a stock which has benefited mightily from population growth is Houston Lighting and Power. The city of Houston adjoins great deposits of oil, gas, and sulphur and has become the largest community south of St. Louis, passing both Dallas and New Orleans in size. Texans are noted for the manner in which they describe things dear to them, but the Chamber of Commerce need no longer beat the drums for Houston— it is probably the fastest-growing city of its size in the United States. In 1940 it was the 26th largest municipality, and recent estimates give it sixth place. The Houston area is the site of the nation's multibillion-dollar moon-shot project. Within a century, predicts Lloyd's of London, it will become the largest city in the world.

Houston Lighting and Power Co., astride this volcano of ac-

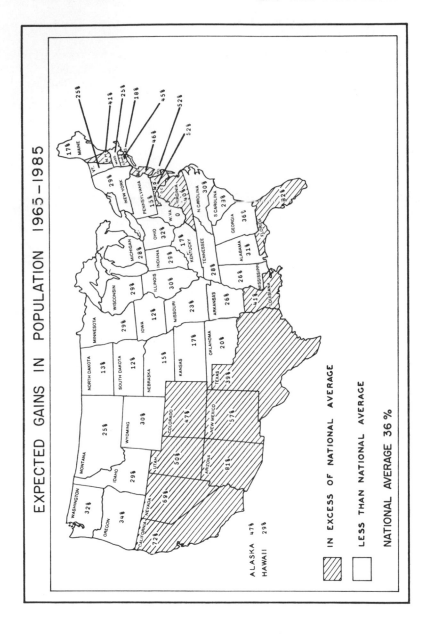

EXPECTED GAINS IN POPULATION 1965–1985

tivity, is several times blessed—by growth in customers, by a warm climate which encourages heavy use of air conditioning, by access to low-cost natural gas, by an inflow of new industries, and by relatively lenient rate regulation. The latter is important because a utility can't pull up stakes and move if it doesn't get along with the local politicians. Earnings per share have risen 120% in ten years; dividends are up 100%.

As an indication of the growth rate, the company will add 1.8 million kw to capacity in 1967–68, which represents over 50% expansion since 1966. Policy is to plow back a considerable part of earnings into the business, and the dividend payout is one of the lowest in the industry. But dividends have been boosted in seven of the past ten years. The trend is steadily up.

Fastest growth areas by far are Florida and the Pacific Coast. The center of population is still moving westward. California has nosed out New York as the most populous state and is slated for a growth of over 70% by 1985—adding some 13 million inhabitants. That increase is greater than the entire existing populations of states like Ohio, Illinois, Pennsylvania, and Texas.

New residents are continuing to pour into California at the rate of nearly 1,000 a day, or 400,000 a year. Add to that an estimated 300,000 excess of births within the state—immigration from heaven, that is—and you have a population gain of well over a half million a year. Among other things, this requires building the equivalent of one new 30-room school every day of the year. In fact, growth is so fast that the state is even behind in its jails!

The Florida Boom

Florida stands as the ninth most heavily populated state today —a decade ago it ranked only twentieth among the states. Its rate of population increase has been running about twice the national average. No longer just a land of oranges, bathing beauties, and winter vacations, the state has been attracting permanent residents recently at the rate of about 2,700 per week.

Florida has always been a big tourist mecca—about 5½ million flock there annually. New industrial plants are now being built, manufacturing payrolls are up almost twice as much as the national average, the growth in personal income has been greater than in the United States total. Whatever statistic you use— population, income, banking, trade, factory output, jobs—Florida is out in front.

Quite naturally people ask, "Is the boom sound? Can it last?" The fast pace brings uncomfortable memories of the twenties when frenzied land trading produced a giant speculative bubble. But this time the growth seems much more soundly based on population, building, industry, and farming. Banks are extremely wary about lending on undeveloped land. While land speculation has played a part in some areas, transactions are mostly for cash.

There are many reasons why Florida should continue to grow and prosper. The proportion of older, retired people in the nation will increase steadily over the next two decades, and they can live more comfortably and cheaply in the South. As a rule of thumb, every two retirees who enter the state create a job for one person. Summer tourist business promises shortly to equal the winter tourist business.

Florida has a special ringside seat at the space race. Moon rocket plans of the National Aeronautic and Space Agency call for spending billions at Cape Kennedy over the next few years. The whole state will benefit in some measure, and one visible sign is the mushrooming of new electronic and scientific plants in the area.

Ten years from now there will be only the same amount of land where one can be reasonably sure of mild weather in winter. The airlines are important in the state's development—the reduction from a 25-hour rail trip to a 3-hour jet flight has been a significant factor.

The state's natural resources are being opened up—phosphate, titanium, paper and pulp, and perhaps oil. Reliable estimates point to a near-doubling of the permanent population in the next 20 years. Florida is an exceptionally promising field for investment. People with moderate capital have been making substantial sums there in real estate, new businesses, orange groves, etc. However, it is well to remember that others have been losing through bad planning, poor location, inexperience, and insufficient capital.

Florida does offer a wealth of opportunities—but no miracles. There are risks and pitfalls. The failure rate among small business undertakings is high despite the general prosperity of the area. Speculating in land is tricky and in many cases prices have already skyrocketed. Regardless of the ballyhoo, money does not grow on bushes, there or anywhere else.

One of the best and safest ways for the average individual to participate in Florida's growth is through purchase of stocks in well-established companies—electric utilities, airlines, banks, retailers, and similar enterprises. Gains may not be immediate and spectacular, but they should be far steadier and better assured than in some of the promotions that are now attracting the savings of many individuals. Some Florida stocks are considerably inflated in price, however, and the group should be approached cautiously.

The following are examples of some companies whose fortunes are closely tied in with areas of fast population growth. Any investment action would, of course, have to depend on the relative attractiveness of prices and earnings prospects at the time of purchase.

Arizona Public Service	Gulf States Utilities
Bank of America	Houston Lighting and Power
Broadway-Hale Stores	Lucky Stores Inc.
Central & South West Corp.	Pacific Gas & Electric
Denny's Restaurants	Pacific Lighting
Eastern Airlines	Republic Nat'l Bank (Dallas)
El Paso Natural Gas	Southern Railway
First Nat'l Bank of Miami	Tampa Electric
Florida Power	Tropical Gas
Florida Power and Light	Valley Nat'l Bank (Phoenix)
Florida Telephone	Western Air Lines
Gulf Life Insurance	Winn-Dixie Stores

Five Don'ts for Investors

PHILIP A. FISHER

Philip A. Fisher has had nearly 30 years of professional investment experience and is known and respected for his unorthodox approach to the problems of investing money. He does not offer any shortcuts or formulas for making money, but instead offers his advice in terms of what not to do. In this excerpt from his national best seller Common Stocks and Uncommon Profits, *Fisher offers sage advice on how to improve your judgment and avoid several common pitfalls.*

1. Don't Buy into Promotional Companies

*C*LOSE to the very heart of successful investing is finding companies which are developing new products and processes or exploiting new markets. Companies that have just started or are about to be started are frequently attempting to do just this. Many of them are formed to develop a colorful new invention. Many are started to participate in industries, such as electronics, in which there is great growth potential. Another large group is formed to discover mineral or other natural wealth—a field where the rewards for success can be outstanding. For these reasons, young companies not yet earning a profit on their operations may at first glance appear to be of investment value.

There is another argument which frequently increases interest. This is that by buying now when the first shares are offered to the public, there is a chance to "get in on the ground floor." The successful company is now selling at several times the price at which it was originally offered. Therefore why wait and have somebody else make all this money? Instead why not use the same methods of inquiry and judgment in finding the outstanding new enterprise now being promoted as can be used in finding the outstanding established corporation?

From the investment standpoint, I believe there is a basic matter which puts any company without at least two or three years of commercial operation and one year of operating profit in a completely different category from an established company—even one so small that it may not have more than a million dollars of annual sales. In the established company, all the major functions of the business are currently operating. The investor can observe the company's production, sales, cost accounting, management teamwork, and all the other aspects of its operations. Perhaps even more important, he can obtain the opinion of other qualified observers who are in a position to observe regularly some or all of these points of relative strength or weakness in the company under consideration. In contrast, when a company is still in the promotional stage, all an investor or anyone else can do is look at a blueprint and guess what the problems and the strong points may be. This is a much more difficult thing to do. It allows a much greater probability of error in the conclusions reached.

Actually, it is so difficult to do that no matter how skillful the investor, it makes it impossible to obtain even a fraction of the "batting average" for selecting outstanding companies that can be attained if judgment is confined to established operations. All too often, young promotional companies are dominated by one or two individuals who have great talent for certain phases of business procedure but are lacking in other equally essential talents. They may be superb salesmen but lack other types of business ability. More often they are inventors or production men, totally unaware that even the best products need skillful marketing as well as manufacture. The investor is seldom in a position to convince such individuals of the skills missing in themselves or their young organizations. Usually he is even less in a position to point out to such individuals where such talents may be found.

For these reasons, no matter how appealing promotional companies may seem at first glance, I believe their financing should always be left to specialized groups. Such groups have management talent available to bolster up weak spots as unfolding operations uncover them. Those who are not in a position to supply such talent and to convince new managements of the need of taking advantage of such help will find investing in promotional companies largely a disillusioning experience. There are enough spectacular opportunities among established companies that ordinary individual investors should make it a rule never to buy into a promotional enterprise, no matter how attractive it may appear to be.

2. Don't Ignore a Good Stock Just Because It Is Traded "Over the Counter"

The attractiveness of unlisted stocks versus those listed on a stock exchange is closely related to the marketability of one group as against the other. Everyone should recognize the importance of marketability. Normally, most if not all buying should be confined to stocks which can be sold should a reason— either financial or personal—arise for such selling. However, some confusion seems to exist in the minds of investors as to what gives adequate protection in this regard and what does not. This in turn gives rise to even more confusion concerning the desirability of those stocks not listed on any exchange. Such stocks are commonly called "over-the-counter" stocks.

The reason for this confusion lies in basic changes that have come over common stock buying in the last quarter century—

changes that make the markets of the 1950's very different even from those as recent as the never-to-be-forgotten 1920's. During most of the 1920's and in all of the period before that, the stock broker had as customers a relatively small number of rather rich men. Most buying was done in large blocks, frequently in multiples of thousands of shares. The motive was usually to sell out to someone else at a higher price. Gambling rather than investment was the order of the day. Buying on margin—that is, with borrowed funds—was then the accepted method of operation. Today a very large percentage of all buying is on a cash basis.

Many things have happened to change these colorful markets of the past. High income and inheritance tax rates are one. A more important influence is the tendency toward a levelling of incomes that continues year after year in every section of the United States. The very rich and the very poor each year grow smaller in number. Each year the middle groups grow larger. This has produced a steady shrinkage of big stock buyers, and an even greater growth of small stock buyers. Along with them has come a tremendous growth in another class of stock buyer, the institutional buyer. The investment trust, the pension and profit-sharing trusts, even to some degree the trust departments of the great banks do not represent a few big buyers. Rather they are a few professional managers entrusted with handling the collective savings of innumerable small buyers.

Partly as a resut of all this, and partly as a cause helping to bring it about, basic changes have come in our laws and institutions as they affect the stock market. The Securities and Exchange Commission has been created to prevent the type of manipulation and pool operation that spurred on the rampant stock market gambling of the past. Rules are in force limiting margin buying to a fraction of what was formerly considered customary. But most important of all, the corporation of today is a very different thing from what it used to be. Today's corporation is designed to be far more suitable as an investment medium for those desiring long-range growth than as a vehicle for in-and-out trading.

All this has profoundly changed the market place. It undoubtedly represents tremendous improvement—improvement, however, at the expense of marketability. The liquidity of the average stock has decreased rather than increased. In spite of breathtaking economic growth and a seemingly endless procession of stock splits, the volume of trading on the New York Stock Exchange has declined. For the smaller exchanges it has almost vanished. The gambler, the in-and-out buyer, and even the "sucker" trying to outguess the pool manipulator were not conducive to a healthy economy. They did, however, help provide a ready market.

I do not want to get involved in semantics. Nevertheless, it must be realized that this has resulted in the gradual decline of the "stock broker" and the rise of what might be called the "stock salesman." So far as stocks are concerned, the broker works in an auction market. He takes an order from someone who has already decided on his investment course. He matches this order with an order he or some other broker has received to sell. This process is not overly time-consuming. If the orders received are for a large rather than small number of shares, the broker can operate on a very small commission for each share handled and still end the year with a handsome profit.

Contrast him with the salesman, who must go through the far more time-consuming routine of persuading the customer on the course of action to be taken. There are only a given number of hours in the day. Therefore, to make a profit commensurate with that of a broker, he must charge a higher commission for his services. This is particularly true if the salesman is serving a large number of small customers rather than a few big ones. Under today's economic conditions, small customers are the ones most salesmen must serve.

The stock exchanges are still primarily operating as a vehicle for stock brokers rather than stock salesmen. Their commission rates have gone up. They have only gone up, however, about in proportion to that of most other types of services. In contrast, the over-the-counter markets work on a quite different principle.

Each day, designated members of the National Association of Security Dealers furnish the newspapers of that region with quotations on a long list of the more active unlisted securities of interest to stockholders in that locality. These are compiled by close contact with the over-the-counter houses most active in trading each of these securities. Unlike those furnished by the stock exchanges, these quotations are not the price ranges within which transactions took place. They cannot be, for there is no central clearing house to which transactions are reported. Instead these are bid-and-ask quotations. Such quotations supposedly give the highest price at which any of the interested financial houses will bid for each of these shares and the lowest offering price at which they will sell them.

Close checking will nearly always show that the reported quotations on the bid or buy side are closely in line with what could be obtained for shares at the moment the quotation was furnished. The sales or ask side is usually higher than the bid by an amount several times greater than the equivalent stock exchange commission for shares selling at the same price. This difference is calculated to enable the over-the-counter house to buy at the bid price, pay its salesmen an appropriate commission for the time spent in selling the security, and still leave a reasonable profit after allowing for general overhead. On the other hand, if a customer, particularly a large customer, approaches the same financial house with a bid to buy this stock so that no salesman's commission is involved, he can usually buy it at the bid price plus just about the equivalent of the stock exchange commission. As one over-the-counter dealer expressed it, "We have one market on the buy side. On the selling side we have two. We have a retail and a wholesale market, depending partly on the size of the purchase and partly on the amount of selling and servicing that is involved."

This sytem in the hands of an unscrupulous dealer is subject to obvious abuse. So is any other system. But if the investor picks the over-the-counter dealer with the same care he should employ in choosing any other specialist to serve him, it works surprisingly well. The average investor has neither the time nor the ability to select his own securities. Through the close supervision dealers give the securities they permit their salesmen to offer, he is receiving in effect something closely resembling investment counsel. As such it should be worth the cost involved.

From the standpoint of the more sophisticated investor, however, the real benefits of this system are not in regard to buying. They are in regard to the increased liquidity or marketability which it produces for those unlisted stocks he may desire to own. Because the profit margin available for dealers in such stocks is large enough to make it worthwhile, a great many over-the-counter dealers keep a regular inventory of the stocks they normally handle. They usually are not at all reluctant to take on additional 500- or 1000-share lots when they become available. When larger blocks appear in their favorite issues, they will frequently hold a sales meeting and put on a special drive to move the shares that may be available. Normally they will ask a special selling commission of a point or so for doing this. However, all this means that if an over-the-counter stock is regularly dealt in by two or more high-grade over-the-counter dealers, it usually has a sufficient degree of marketability to take care of the needs of most investors. Depending on the amount offered, a special selling commission may or may not be required to move a large block. However, for what is at most a relatively small percentage of the sales price, the stock which the investor desires to sell can actually be converted into cash without breaking the market.

How does this compare with the marketability of a stock listed on a stock exchange? The answer depends largely on what stock and on what stock exchange. For the larger and more active issues listed on the New York Stock Exchange, even under today's conditions, a big enough auction market still exists so that in normal times all but the largest blocks can be moved at the low prevailing commission rates without depressing prices. For the less active stocks listed on the New York Stock Exchange, this marketability factor is still fair, but at times can sag rather badly if regular commissions are depended on when large selling orders appear. For common stocks listed on the small exchanges, it is my opinion that this marketability factor frequently becomes considerably worse.

The stock exchanges have recognized this situation and have taken steps to meet it. Nowadays, whenever a block of a listed stock appears which the exchange thinks is too big to market in the normal fashion, permission may be given for the use of devices such as "special offerings." This simply means that the offering is made known to all members, who are given a predetermined larger commission for selling these shares. In other words, when the block is too large for the brokers to handle it as brokers, they are given commissions large enough to reward them for selling as salesmen.

All this narrows the apparent gap between listed and unlisted markets in a period such as the present, when more and more purchases are being handled by salesmen rather than by brokers who just take orders. It does not mean that from the standpoint of marketability a well-known, actively traded stock on the New York Stock Exchange has no advantage over the better over-the-counter stocks. It does mean that the better of these over-the-counter stocks are frequently more liquid than the shares of many of the companies listed on the American Stock Exchange and the various regional stock exchanges. I imagine those connected with the smaller stock exchanges would sincerely disagree with this statement. Nevertheless, I believe an unprejudiced study of the facts would show it to be true. It is why a number of the more progressive of smaller and medium-size companies have in recent years refused to list their stocks on the smaller exchanges. Instead they have chosen the over-the-counter markets until their companies reach a size that would warrant "big board"—that is, New York Stock Exchange—listing.

In short, so far as over-the-counter securities are concerned, the rules for the investor are not too different from those for listed securities. First, be very sure that you have picked the right security. Then be sure you have selected an able and conscientious broker. If an investor is on sound ground in both these respects, he need have no fear of purchasing stock just because it is traded "over the counter" rather than on an exchange.

3. Don't Buy a Stock Just Because You Like the "Tone" of Its Annual Report

Investors are not always careful to analyze just what has caused them to buy one stock rather than another. If they did, they might be surprised how often they were influenced by the wording and format of the general comments in a company's annual report to stockholders. This tone of the annual report may reflect the management's philosophies, policies, or goals with as much accuracy as the audited financial statement should reflect the dollars and cents results for the period involved. The annual report may also, however, reflect little more than the skill of the company's public relations department in creating an impression about the company in the public mind. There is no way of telling whether the president has actually written the remarks in an annual report, or whether a public relations officer has written them for his signature. Attractive photographs and nicely colored charts do not necessarily reflect a close-knit and able management team working in harmony and with enthusiasm.

Allowing the general wording and tone of annual report to influence a decision to purchase a common stock is much like buying a product because of an appealing advertisement on a billboard. The product may be just as attractive as the advertisement. It also may not be. For a low-priced product it may be quite sensible to buy in this way, to find out how attractive the purchase really is. With a common stock, however, few of us are rich enough to afford impulse buying. It is well to remember that annual reports nowadays are generally designed to build up stockholder good will. It is important to go beyond them to the underlying facts. Like any other sales tool they are prone to put a corporation's "best foot forward." They seldom present balanced and complete discussions of the real problems and difficulties of the business. Often they are too optimistic.

If then, an investor should not let a favorable reaction to the tone of an annual report overly influence his subsequent action, how about the opposite? Should he let an unfavorable reaction influence him? Usually not, for again it is like trying to appraise the contents of a box by the wrapping paper on the outside. There is one important exception to this, however. This is when such reports fail to give proper information on matters of real significance to the investor. Companies which follow such policies are usually not the ones most likely to provide the background for successful investment.

4. Don't Assume That the High Price at Which a Stock May Be Selling in Relation to Earnings Is Necessarily an Indication That Further Growth in Those Earnings Has Largely Been Already Discounted in the Price

There is a costly error in investment reasoning that is common enough to make it worthy of special mention. To explain it, let us take a fictitious company. We might call it the XYZ Corporation. For three decades there has been constant growth in both sales and profits, and also there have been enough new products under development to furnish strong indication of comparable growth in the period ahead. The excellence of the company is generally appreciated throughout the financial community. Consequently for years XYZ stock has sold for from twenty to thirty times current earnings. This is nearly twice as much for each dollar earned as the sales price of the average stock that has made up, say, the Dow Jones Industrial Averages.

Today this stock is selling at just twice the price-earnings ratio of the Dow Jones averages. This means that its market price is twice as high in relation to each dollar it is earning as is the average of the stocks comprising these Dow Jones averages in relation to each dollar they are earning. The XYZ management has just issued a forecast indicating they expect to double earnings in the next five years. On the basis of the evidence at hand, the forecast looks valid.

Whereupon a surprising number of investors jump to false conclusions. They say that since XYZ is selling twice as high as stocks in general, and since it will take five years for XYZ's earnings to double, the present price of XYZ stock is discounting future earnings ahead. They are sure the stock is overpriced.

No one can argue that a stock discounting its earnings five years ahead is likely to be overpriced. The fallacy in their reasoning lies in the assumption that five years from now XYZ will be selling on the same price-earnings ratio as will the average Dow Jones stock with which they compare it. For thirty years this stock, because of all those factors which make it an outstanding company, has been selling at twice the price-earnings ratio of these other stocks. Its record has been rewarding to those who have placed their faith in it. If the same policies are continued, five years from now its management will bring out still another group of new products that in the ensuing decade will swell earnings in the same way that new products are increasing earnings now, and others did five, ten, fifteen and twenty years ago. If this happens, why shouldn't this stock sell five years from now for twice the price-earnings ratio of these more ordinary stocks just as it is doing now and has done for many years past? If it does, and if the price-earnings ratio of all stocks remain about the same, XYZ's doubling of earnings five years from now will also cause its price to be doubled in the market over this five-year period. On this basis, this stock, selling at its normal price-earnings ratio, cannot be said to be discounting future earnings at all!

Obvious, isn't it? Well, look around you and see how many supposedly sophisticated investors get themselves crossed up on this matter of what price-earnings ratio to use in considering how far ahead a stock is actually discounting future growth. This is particularly true if a change has been taking place in the background of the company being studied. Let us now consider the ABC Company instead of the XYZ Company. The two companies are almost exactly alike except that the ABC Company is much younger. Only in the last two years has its fundamental excellence been appreciated by the financial community to the point that its shares, too, are now selling at twice the price-earnings ratio of the average Dow Jones stock. It seems almost impossible for many investors to realize, in the case of a stock that in the past has not sold at a comparably high price-earnings ratio, that the price-earnings ratio at which it is now selling may be a reflection of its intrinsic quality and not an unreasonable discounting of further growth.

What is important here is thoroughly understanding the nature of the company, with particular reference to what it may be expected to do some years from now. If the earning spurt that lies ahead is a one-time matter, and the nature of the company is not such that comparable new sources of earning growth will be developed when the present one is fully exploited, that is quite a different situation. Then the high price-earnings ratio does discount future earnings. This is because, when the present spurt is over, the stock will settle back to the same selling price in relation to its earnings as run-of-the-mill shares. However, if the company is deliberately and consistently developing new sources of earning power, and if the industry is one promising to afford equal growth spurts in the future, the price-earnings ratio five or ten years in the future is rather sure to be as much above that of the average stock as it is today. Stocks of this type will frequently be found to be discounting the future much less than many investors believe. This is why some of the stocks that at first glance appear highest priced may, upon analysis, be the biggest bargains.

5. Don't Quibble Over Eighths and Quarters

I have used fictitious examples in attempting to make clear various other matters. This time I will use an actual example. A little over twenty years ago, a gentleman who in most respects has demonstrated a high order of investment ability wanted to buy one hundred shares of a stock listed on the New York Stock Exchange. On the day he decided to buy, the stock closed at 35½. On the following day it sold repeatedly at that price. But this gentleman would not pay 35½. He decided he might as well save fifty dollars. He put his order in at 35. He refused to raise it. The stock never again sold at 35. Today, almost twenty-five years later, the stock appears to have a particularly bright future. As a result of the stock dividends and splits that have occurred in the intervening years, it is now selling at over 500.

In other words, in an attempt to save fifty dollars, this investor failed to make at least $46,500. Furthermore, there is no question that this investor would have made the $46,500, because he still has other shares of this same company which he bought at even lower figures. Since $46,500 is about 930 times 50, this means that our investor would have had to save his fifty dollars 930 times just to break even. Obviously, following a course of action with this kind of odds against it borders on financial lunacy.

This particular example is by no means an extreme one. I purposely selected a stock which for a number of years was more of a market laggard than a market leader. If our investor had picked any one of perhaps fifty other growth stocks listed on the New York Stock Exchange, missing $3,500 worth of such stock in order to save $50 would have cost a great deal more than the $46,500.

For the small investor wanting to buy only a few hundred shares of a stock, the rule is very simple. If the stock seems the right one and the price seems reasonably attractive at current levels, buy "at the market." The extra eighth, or quarter, or half point that may be paid is insignificant compared to the profit that will be missed if the stock is not obtained. Should the stock not have this sort of long-range potential, I believe the investor should not have decided to buy it in the first place.

For the larger investor, wanting perhaps many thousands of shares, the problem is not quite as simple. For all but a very small minority of stocks, the available supply is usually suffi- ciently limited that an attempt to buy at the market even half of this desired amount could well cause a sizable advance in quotations. This sudden price rise might, in turn, produce two further effects, both tending to make accumulating a block of this stock even more difficult. The price spurt by itself might be enough to arouse the interest and competition of other buyers. It might also cause some of those who have been planning to sell to hold their shares off the market with the hope that the rise might continue. What then should a large buyer do to meet this situation?

He should go to his broker or securities dealer. He should disclose to him exactly how much stock he desires to buy. He should tell the broker to pick up as much stock as possible but authorize him to pass up small offerings if buying them would arouse many competitive bids. Most important, he should give his broker a completely free hand on price up to a point somewhat above the most recent sale. How much above should be decided in consultation with the broker or dealer after taking into account such factors as the size of the block desired, the normal activity of the shares, how eager the investor may be for the holding, and any other special factors that might be involved.

The investor may feel he does not have a broker or dealer upon whom he may rely as having sufficient judgment or discretion to handle something of this sort. If so, he should proceed forthwith to find a broker or dealer in whom such confidence can be placed. After all, doing exactly this sort of thing is the primary function of a broker or the trading department of a security dealer.

How to Invest
in Problem Companies

WINTHROP KNOWLTON

*Alert and sophisticated investors are always looking for
fresh investment ideas. One financial authority, Winthrop
Knowlton (presently an officer in the United States Treasury
Department) suggests that there may be profits in locating
and investing in "problem companies." Knowlton proposes
some questions for the investor to raise when investigating
these companies, and advises on how to minimize risks.*

Nobody knows de troubles ah seen.
—*Old Negro Spiritual*

MOST U.S. business concerns are problem companies.
They live in a tough, competitive world. Despite all the talk of inflation, price competition has become more intense during the last
five years than in the immediate postwar period. Ask the aluminum, the paper, the tire and rubber producers, the oil refiners,
the copper and brass fabricators, the chemical and lumber companies. Analyze their growth rates; look at the rates of return
they earned on their equity in 1963 and 1964, two of the greatest business years the nation has ever known.

Obviously, it takes a special combination of managerial, technical, and marketing skill for a company to rise above the general battle, to create and dominate large, new markets that provide continually handsome returns for entrepreneur and shareholder alike. In recent years approximately six hundred companies* have accounted for close to half of all domestic corporate profits. Eight companies have accounted for nearly a quarter of the total.

Nevertheless, there is money to be made in problem companies, and there is a place for them, on an interim basis, in your portfolio.

The problems of most major corporations are environmental; generally speaking, the typical large U.S. industrial concern is ably managed, believes in research, and has adequate financial resources. But it also has able competitors—therein the problem—who make it impossible to maintain a position of clearcut technical superiority, whether with respect to products or processes, for meaningful lengths of time. Desire to hold or increase market share results in industrywide bursts of capital spending, followed by overcapacity, price cutting, margin deterioration, and grief for all concerned (except the consumer).

Another environmental problem that plagues certain industries is federal regulation. Complicated and contradictory policies with respect to prices, routes, and rates of return appear to have produced neither orderly industry development nor optimum consumer service in such industries as the airlines, railroads, and natural gas pipelines.

In the case of these companies—in the case of all problem companies—you look for a change. Will demand for a basic commodity go up sufficiently rapidly to "firm" prices? If so, are the members of the industry likely to create their problems all over again by scrambling en masse to increase output? Will a new presidential appointment to a regulatory commission signal a more lenient policy toward a particular industry? Will the plight of certain major companies in a regulated industry become so desperate that a change in regulatory policies—such as we have seen in the last few years in the airline and railroad industries—

* Out of a total of more than 1 million corporations.

becomes necessary to avert major corporate disasters and ensuing political embarrassment?

The fundamental difference in the way you analyze a problem company and a successful company is that in the former you welcome change and in the latter you are on guard against it. In the one you look for a reversal of downward momentum; in the other, you hope that forward momentum will be sustained.

The second kind of problem company suffers from internal disorders. Its ailments include an old, high-cost plant, a stingy research effort, a weak product line, a strained balance sheet, and, inevitably, in conjunction with the foregoing, a sleepy management. Almost always you will find this kind of company in environmental difficulties as well because management (1) once lacked the wisdom to steer it into new fields and (2) now finds itself without the resources to do so.

The following suggestions are designed to help you make wise investment selection from the virtually limitless array of problem companies.

1. *Define the problems.* Are they wholly environmental and thus out of management's control, depending on improved industry supply-demand relationships? Or are they internal, depending on more aggressive capital expenditure programs, intensified research effort, or more imaginative advertising? Ask yourself how and why the company finds itself in this position and, depending on your answer, how realistic it is to expect it to extricate itself in the near future.

2. *Avoid companies with a serious financial problem.* You should be willing to take on all the other problems—environmental or internal—but the solution of these problems requires money, in addition to people and time. If a company has borrowed all the money it reasonably can, if it must raise additional common stock money at, say, five times earnings, and if it can pay no dividend while you wait for the payoff, my advice is to look elsewhere. This game is for the pros—rich, able men like Henry Crown who, as in the recent case of General Dynamics, will step in personally with money and managerial resources to

bring a corporate corpse back from the grave. I believe there are too many other investment opportunities for you to struggle with this kind of turnaround situation.

3. The other side of this coin is: *Find problem companies that reward you while you wait.* A surprising number of problem companies are in remarkably good financial condition because their managements (depending on how you look at it) have been too prudent or too timid to invest their cash resources.

In the fall of 1962 one could have bought Phelps Dodge at 47. Its $3.00 dividend provided an annual return of 6.4 per cent. The dividend could have been cut to $2.00 and still have provided an annual return of over 4.0 per cent. The strong balance sheet (current ratio more than 5 to 1; cash and equivalents nearly $140 million; long-term debt: none) and the fact that the company was not spending a great deal of money for new or expanded facilities led even a superficial observer to the conclusion the dividend could and probably would be maintained. As it turned out, the dividend held at $3.00 (it has actually since been raised to $3.40 per share), the copper business (and copper prices) improved, and the stock today—only two years later—sells at 75. An investor shrewd enough to have bought this stock has received an average annual return of over 30 per cent from dividends and capital gains combined. As recently as the summer of 1964 one could have bought Kennecott Copper on a 5 per cent yield basis, with a far more clearly defined and hopeful industry outlook than that confronting Phelps Dodge in 1962. This stock has been rewarding, too.

4. *Ask yourself whether a less problematical company in a particular industry will not do as well, or nearly as well, as the particular problem company you are considering.* By the time the Great Atlantic & Pacific Tea Company has been "turned around," if it ever is, you may find you would have made just as much money, and incurred less risk, in Winn Dixie or Kroger —both of which are subject to competitive industry conditions but have fewer internal problems. Occasionally you will conclude that the more problematical company is the more promising investment of the two—as some now believe to be the case,

for example, with Westinghouse versus General Electric. However, my experience has been that the best way to make money is often the easy way. Many investors are unnecessarily masochistic in their search for corporate obstacle courses.

5. If you are basing your hopes for change on an improvement in general business conditions, *ask yourself whether other companies will not benefit to an even greater extent from the same improvements (or to at least the same extent but with less certainty and risk).* You may be attracted to U.S. Steel as a means of implementing your optimism about the economy. First, you must decide whether this is the best steel company to buy. How do the risks and rewards compare with those provided by an investment in Armco, Inland, or National? (Your broker must have an able steel analyst to guide you here.) But even more important: Is it possible to visualize the steel industry having a really banner year without the automobile industry also having a banner year? (The auto industry consumes 20–25 per cent of all steel produced.) And if this is what you're betting on, how does General Motors compare with U.S. Steel in terms of risks and rewards? If you were wise enough to pursue this line of inquiry during the last three years, you would have found: (a) General Motors consistently selling at a lower price-earnings ratio than U.S. Steel; (b) General Motors consistently providing a higher dividend return, with the dividend more secure; (c) General Motors stock consistently out-performing U.S. Steel in the market.

6. *Don't buy a problem company because of a management change* too soon *after the management change.* Investors too frequently assume that a new president, riding like Lochinvar out of the West, will wring profit from loss, order from chaos, *immediately.* How do you know the new president is better than the last? Even if he is, it will take other new people, money, and time to effect meaningful changes. Corporations in trouble change direction grudgingly. Almost always it takes longer than new managements, or the investors who are pinning their hopes on them, expect.

The biggest rewards (and risks) are found in problem companies that suffer a number of complaints. In a multiple-problem company, you must foresee several constructive changes taking place at once. Chrysler is an example of a company that benefited from internal management changes, economic recovery, and a sharp increase in industry sales of passenger cars— all in a short period of time (during the previous decade, however, the company suffered many a false start). The railroads, similarly, have been brilliant investments the last few years because of the convergence of the following favorable trends: (1) better general economic conditions; (2) an improvement in government regulation, which permitted railroads to price their products more competitively and thus increase— for the first time in years—their share of the available transportation business; (3) favorable Interstate Commerce Commission rulings on proposed rail mergers; (4) favorable changes in corporate tax laws and depreciation allowances; (5) technological change—the developments of piggyback transportation and the use of electronic data-processing equipment—that enabled the industry to provide better service with better control of costs. (The airlines, too, have benefited from a simultaneous improvement in the regulatory climate and economic conditions.)

Generally speaking, I have tried to limit my investment in problem companies to those that provide an above-average dividend return while one waits for internal or external recovery. The great risk here is that you guess wrong, that the company's dividend is cut, and the stock moves lower. At the moment, it is almost impossible to find stocks of major companies that provide yields of over 5 per cent and where there are prospects for the kind of improvement that will make them sell on a lower yield basis. Today, you are probably on sounder ground looking for a problem company that yields you around 4 per cent, at a time when the Dow-Jones Industrials are yielding around 3 per cent, than in reaching for a stock that provides a substantially higher return. Companies of the caliber of Gillette, Reynolds Tobacco, Inland Steel, and U. S. Gypsum, as well as a number of slower-growing but less problematical utilities (like Northern States Power) today provide annual dividend returns in the range of 3.5–4.5 per cent.

Since many problem companies are in basic industries with pronounced cyclical characteristics, it is always easier to find these stocks selling at high yields at the bottom of an economic cycle than at the top. This is when their prospects are most gloomy and it takes the most courage to buy them. At the top of an economic cycle you can often do better by purchasing problem companies in industries not as directly affected by the overall trend of the industrial economy. The aerospace stocks, certain producers of nondurable consumer goods (beer, cigarettes, etc.), and selected gas and electric utilities fit into these categories.

If you invest in a problem company and its shares move up as hoped, you must keep asking yourself when the time has come to sell. Avoid the common tendency to believe that a company's problems have been permanently solved simply because its stock has become popular.

Can You "Beat the Market"?

LOUIS ENGEL

Almost every investor is familiar with the terms "dollar cost averaging" and "formula investing." But exactly what do they mean and what is their purpose? The noted Louis Engel defines these terms and how they can mean profits for you.

*I*SN'T there any system to "beat the market," any system that will protect you against price fluctuations and virtually guarantee you a profit over the long pull?

Yes, there are such systems, and some of them work pretty well. They are far from foolproof, but at least they do point out some important lessons about successful investing. They are called dollar cost averaging and formula investing.

Dollar cost averaging simply involves putting the same fixed amount of money—$200, $500, $1000—into the same stock, regardless of its price movement, at regular intervals—say, every month or every six months or so—over a long period of time. The Monthly Investment Plan is built on precisely this basis.

Following a system of investing a fixed sum of money in the same stock at regular intervals, you could have made a profit on probably 90% of the stocks listed on the New York Stock Exchange over almost any period of fifteen or twenty years you might want to pick.

Dollar cost averaging works simply because you buy more shares of a stock with your fixed amount of money when the stock is low in price than you do when it is comparatively high, and when the stock rises again, you make a profit on the greater number of shares you got at low cost.

Suppose you bought $500 worth of a particular stock when it was selling at $10 a share, another $500 worth three months later when it was $9, another $500 worth at $8, and so on, while the stock fell to $5, then rose to $15, and settled back to $10. If you then sold out, you would be able to show a profit of about 10%, ignoring both dividends and commission costs, despite the fact that you had paid an average price of $10 and sold out at exactly that same price. You don't believe it?

Don't bother to figure it out, because here's the proof (Table 1). To avoid the complication of fractional shares of stock, it is assumed that at every different price level the buyer would purchase whatever number of shares would yield a total cost nearest $500.

All told, you paid $10,495, and your holdings would be worth $11,510, a gain of $1015, or almost 10%.

Exactly the same results—again exclusive of all dividends and purchase costs—would be achieved if the stock first rose steadily from $10 to $15, then dropped to $5, then came back to $10. The figures on that are in Table 2.

There's only one significant difference between the two tables. Note that you are considerably better off all the way along the line if your stock drops first and then comes back. Thus, in the first table, after the stock had fallen to $5 and recovered to $10, you could have sold out and made a profit of $1954, or about 35%, on your money.

So if the stock you buy drops in price and you have the confidence to believe that it will come back, as stocks in general always have, you would do well to continue buying it as it slides on down. This is called *"averaging down,"* and it's a con-

Table 1

Price per Share	Number of Shares Purchased	Cost of Shares	Number of Shares Owned	Cumulative Cost of Shares	Total Value of Shares
$10	50	$500	50	$500	$500
9	56	504	106	1004	954
8	63	504	169	1508	1352
7	71	497	240	2005	1680
6	83	498	323	2503	1938
5	100	500	423	3003	2115
6	83	498	506	3501	3036
7	71	497	577	3998	4039
8	63	504	640	4502	5120
9	56	504	696	5006	6264
10	50	500	746	5506	7460
11	45	495	791	6006	8701
12	42	504	833	6505	9996
13	38	494	871	6999	11323
14	36	504	907	7503	12698
15	33	495	940	7998	14100
14	36	504	976	8502	13664
13	38	494	1014	8996	13182
12	42	504	1056	9500	12672
11	45	495	1101	9995	12111
10	50	500	1151	10495	11510

cept which the investor who thinks the market is "too high to buy right now" might well keep in mind.

While no stock could ever follow the precise pattern set in the tables, the examples do serve to demonstrate the validity of the dollar cost averaging principle.

There's only one big catch to this sytem of beating the market. You've got to have the cash—yes, and the courage, too—to buy the same dollar amount of the stock at whatever interval of time you've fixed on, be it every month or three months or a year.

And if it drops, you've got to keep right on buying, in order to pick up the low-cost shares on which you can later make

Table 2

Price per Share	Number of Shares Purchased	Cost of Shares	Number of Shares Owned	Cumulative Cost of Shares	Total Value of Shares
$10	50	$500	50	$500	$500
11	45	495	95	995	1045
12	42	504	137	1499	1644
13	38	494	175	1993	2275
14	36	504	211	2497	2954
15	33	495	244	2992	3660
14	36	504	280	3496	3920
13	38	494	318	3990	4134
12	42	504	360	4494	4320
11	45	495	405	4989	4455
10	50	500	455	5489	4550
9	56	504	511	5993	4599
8	63	504	574	6497	4592
7	71	497	645	6994	4515
6	83	498	728	7492	4368
5	100	500	828	7992	4140
6	83	498	911	8490	5466
7	71	497	982	8987	6874
8	63	504	1045	9491	8360
9	56	504	1101	9995	9909
10	50	500	1151	10495	11510

your profit. Unfortunately, when the stock market is down, the average man's bank account is likely to be down too, and so he often can't afford to buy at just the time he should. If instead of buying, he should have to sell at such a time, he might have to take a loss. This will always be true if a person has to sell at a price lower than the average cost of the shares he owns. In such circumstances, the dollar cost averaging technique will have provided no protection. Most times, it works over the long pull because the long-term trend of the stock market has been upward.

If a dollar cost averaging plan had been applied for twenty

years at an annual rate of $1000 a year to the stocks in Standard & Poor's 500-stock index, and if all dividends paid on these stocks had been reinvested, an investor by the end of 1965 would have realized a return more than four times his out-of-pocket investment. He would have achieved this result despite the fact that the market in that period suffered seven declines ranging from 15% to 28%.

The stock of the Radio Corporation of America offers a classic example of the advantages of dollar cost averaging. Let's assume that back at the beginning of 1929 you had a lump sum of $19,000 and you decided to invest it all in RCA stock. RCA was a popular stock then, highly regarded for its growth possibilities—just as it still is—and it was selling early in 1929 in the price range of $375 to $380 per share. So for your $19,000 you would have been able to buy 50 shares. Over the years, thanks to splits in the stock, those shares would have increased to 891 and you would have received a total of almost $7000 in dividend payments. As of mid-1966, when RCA was selling around $50 a share, your stock would have been worth about $44,000. This means that, together with your dividends, you would have realized a net gain of about $32,000 on your $19,000 investment.

That's not too bad, but consider how much more you would have made if you had followed the dollar cost averaging plan and put that same amount of money in RCA stock at the rate of approximately $500 a year for the same 37½ years. Here again it is assumed that the number of shares purchased (at the opening of the market each year) would have been that number which you could have bought for an amount closest to $500—sometimes a little less, sometimes a little more. By June 1966, you would have owned 5262 shares of RCA, and you would have had a net gain, after payment of all brokerage commissions on your purchases, of $280,000. Of this sum, the $40,000 you would have collected in dividends would have been more than twice the total cost of your investment.

This is an especially impressive record because of the dramatic drop in the price of RCA from its 1929 high and the opportunity you would have had to pick up RCA shares at bargain levels in ensuing years. It should also be noted, however, that we would have an entirely different story to tell if we had taken 1933 as our starting date instead of 1929; then it would have been decidedly more advantageous for you to have made a big lump-sum purchase of RCA than for you to have acquired RCA stock in units of $500 a year. If you had put $17,000 into RCA at the beginning of 1933, your investment would have been worth about $800,000 in mid-1966, counting both price appreciation and dividends, whereas if you had bought the stock at the rate of $500 a year throughout the thirty-four-year period, you would have realized just a little more than 33% of that figure—a little over $265,000. But because few people have large sums that they can put into one stock at a time, confident that it will go steadily on up, and because most stocks do fluctuate from time to time, it is generally more prudent and more profitable for an investor to follow the dollar cost averaging plan, which can make it possible for him to capitalize on price fluctuations, rather than to take one big plunge.

This is an impressive record, but it is not unlike that which can be shown for many other stocks. Table 3 shows how you would have made out by June 1966, if you had put roughly $500 a year, beginning in 1929, into several other stocks which have also proved popular with M.I.P. [Monthly Investment Plan] investors.

Of course, this is history, and no one can guarantee it is the kind of history which will repeat itself. But it does provide a convincing demonstration of the value of accumulating shares on a dollar cost averaging basis over a period of time, and this is one of the most persuasive features of the Monthly Investment Plan, which makes it possible for the small investor to follow precisely this course in buying most of the stocks listed on the New York Stock Exchange.

Formula investing is not so much a system for beating the market as it is a mechanical means for enforcing prudence and caution. There are many different formula plans—almost every expert has his own—but stripped of their technicalities, all of them can be reduced to the basic premise that an investment

Table 3 $500-a-Year Investment Program
January 1929–June 1966

In the Common Stock	Total Cost of Shares Purchased	Shares Owned	Market Value	Total Dividends Received	Total Dividends Plus Market Value of Stock	Net Gain
Aluminum Co. of America	$19,189	1450	$119,806	$30,005	$149,811	$130,622
American Tel. and Tel.	19,021	655	36,025	22,616	58,641	39,620
Caterpillar Tractor	19,271	9168	380,472	77,924	458,396	439,125
Consolidated Edison	19,258	1074	38,530	25,251	63,781	44,523
Dow Chemical	19,374	2748	181,368	65,849	247,217	227,843
DuPont (E.I.) de Nemours*	19,482	421	124,445	54,928	179,372	159,891
Eastman Kodak	19,269	2902	372,907	51,864	424,771	405,502
General Electric	19,104	1147	121,725	39,855	161,580	142,476
General Motors	19,116	1826	146,993	86,004	232,997	213,881
Goodyear Tire & Rubber	19,248	6198	315,323	87,931	403,254	384,006
Gulf Oil	19,182	2999	149,950	52,681	202,631	183,449
National Biscuit	19,363	1105	48,344	23,434	71,778	52,415
Pacific Gas & Electric	19,138	1537	46,879	29,158	76,037	56,899
Phillips Petroleum	19,148	2209	111,002	71,186	182,188	163,040
Radio Corp. of America	19,008	5262	259,811	40,481	300,292	281,284
Sears, Roebuck	19,298	4671	258,657	60,490	319,147	299,849
Standard Oil Co. (N.J.)	18,989	1645	113,094	62,092	175,186	156,197
Union Carbide	19,259	1159	68,091	37,309	105,400	86,141
United States Steel	19,110	1281	55,499	53,618	109,117	90,007
Westinghouse Electric	18,735	1408	73,674	31,451	105,125	86,385

* The last four columns include the market value ($45,402) of 564 shares of General Motors stock received as dividend between 1962 and 1965, and cash dividends of $7,028 since paid on those shares.

fund should be balanced between stocks and bonds, and that the ratio of one kind of security to the other should be changed as the market rises and falls. You buy bonds and sell stocks when the stock market gets high—on the assumption that the market becomes increasingly vulnerable as prices advance—and you reverse the procedure when the market drops.

The premise may be basically sound, but it's one that the average investor can't apply very effectively, since his investment fund is rarely large enough for a formula plan to operate without distortion. This is so because all formula plans assume that that portion of the fund which is invested in stocks will perform generally as the market average does. Obviously, the fewer stocks you can afford to own the less likely are they to perform in line with the general market; they may do significantly better or they may do significantly worse. Again, the only bonds that a small investor can generally afford are government E bonds, and he can't expect to achieve the same interest return on these bonds as he might earn on other government or corporate bonds, particularly since the return on E bonds is measurably less in the early years. Savings bank deposits can, of course, be substituted for bonds.

Basically, there are three kinds of formula plans—the constant-dollar plan, the constant-ratio plan, and the variable-ratio plan. The *constant-dollar plan* assumes that a fixed dollar amount of stocks will be held at all times. Thus, if you had $20,000, you might decide to keep $10,000—no more or no less—invested in stocks. If the dollar value of your stock portfolio rose—say, to $11,000—you would sell $1000 of stocks and put the proceeds into bonds. If your stocks declined $1000, you would sell $1000 of bonds and buy stocks. One objection to the plan is that over any long period of years stock prices are likely to advance—at least they have historically—and if your stock investments are frozen at any specified level, you won't keep up with the parade.

The *constant-ratio plan* works like the constant-dollar plan except that you determine to keep 50% of your investment fund in stocks at all times and 50% in bonds. You don't use fixed dollar amounts. The constant-ratio plan is obviously more flexible, can be adopted more readily to the shifting cycles of the stock market, and assures you of at least partial participation in the long-term growth of common stock values.

The *variable-ratio plan* operates like the constant-ratio plan, except that you decide to vary the ratio invested in common stocks as the market rises or falls. Thus, you might start out on a fifty-fifty basis, but decide to keep only 40% of your funds in common stocks whenever the market, as measured by one of the accepted averages, moved up 25%. When the market advanced 50%, you would cut back your common stock holdings to 30% of your total funds, and if it went up 75%, you would have only 20% invested in stocks. If the market fell, you would reverse the operation, buying stocks at the designated market levels and selling bonds. There are dozens and dozens of variations in the variable-ratio theme, many of them involving complicated mathematical formulas and using a variety of economic indexes as well as the market averages. They are designed to permit the investor to take maximum advantage of interim fluctuations in the market while simultaneously protecting his long-term position.

But they don't always work that way. Thus, anyone investing on a formula plan which called for reducing his commitments in common stocks as the market advanced would have lost out on the big bull market which began in 1950. That's why even many big, conservative institutions have either abandoned or modified extensively the formula plans that they initiated a decade or more ago.

While the average investor may not be able to apply any neatly devised mathematical formula to his own situation, he can profit by paying heed to the one basic precept of all these formulas: Keep an eye on those market averages, and as they rise, let them act as a brake on your buying enthusiasm. Remember, no bull-market movement lasts forever.

Timing with Trendlines

DAVID L. MARKSTEIN

Charts have proven to be of measurable help to those investors aware of what certain distinctive chart patterns mean. "Trendline" is a term that all investors should understand because it can be a tool for predicting the performance of a stock. Financial analyst and author David L. Markstein has had nearly twenty years' experience as an investment counsellor. Markstein explains how to chart trendlines, and how they should be interpreted for maximum accuracy.

*A*LL through 1963 and nearly to the end of 1964, the magic word in Wall Street was "Chrysler." Investment salesmen who had recommended "C" to their clients were the tallest citizens of Wall Street. Then suddenly the plug was pulled, and from a high of 67 Chrysler declined to 42 in nine and a half months.

Could this have been foreseen? Technical security analysts, adept in the use of a tool called the "trendline," warned only a few weeks after the top—the stock was then 58—that what was happening was no mere dip, like other dips in Chrysler's meteoric and profitable rise. This was for real; the rise, they noted, was over for a time. They based their warning on a break in the long-term trendline.

In a protracted decline from March, 1966 until October of the same year, Great Northern Paper stock had more than one-third of its value shaved away as it sank in price from 48 to 30. Along this decline, there were two tops, at 48 and again at 45 where a summer rally of that year failed. After reaching bottom at 30, Great Northern did little but trade back and forth in a narrow range. Then in March of 1967, a year after the top had been made, it suddenly spurted. Breaking through a trendline drawn to connect the tops at 48 and 45, it gave a buy signal at 40. Only seven short weeks later the stock was up 25 percent.

Westinghouse likewise gave a buy message following its own 1966 decline by soaring in October, 1966 through the trendline which had marked its long-term drop from 67 to 40. The signal came at 46. Less than a year afterward Westinghouse was selling above 76.

What is a trendline, and how does an investor recognize and use it to avoid such sags as that which overtook Chrysler? How, too, can he spot the breaking of down-trendlines and tell of new upmoves about to get under way?

A trendline is what the name implies—it defines a trend. Pick out any stock chart in which there has been a decided uptrend and then, using a straight-edge, draw a line connecting the bottoms of the shorter-term reactions which are part of the long-term rising movement. In most cases you will find that the principal bottoms all fall right along (or extremely close to) this straight line. What you have drawn is a trendline.

When an upward movement is under way analysts draw a trendline to connect the bottoms of the reactions along the movement. But when a trend is toward the bottom of the chart paper it is defined with a line connecting the tops of the small rallies which punctuate a longer-term down movement. It is important to remember this. An up-trendline connects the *bottoms* of the counter trend reactions, while a down-trendline connects the *tops* of the smaller rising rallies.

A trendline helps to establish points at which stocks should be bought and sold. Consider a long-term rise such as that which made so many Chrysler stockholders rich. As measured along the trendline, the rise in "C" was as straight as the proverbial arrow until the stock touched the trendline at 50, then zoomed suddenly up to 67 on greatly expanded volume. A slow drop of eight weeks followed until "C" once more touched the trendline, which by this time had risen to 56. Performance so far was normal.

Later, however, the price slid below the trendline—and, on a close of one full point below, a clear signal was given that the long rise was, for the time at least, over. Subsequently Chrysler declined in two waves to make a bottom at 42.

Knowledgeable technical analysts sold Chrysler on the breaking of that extended up-trend. Then as the big automaker's stock made a new intermediate top following the trendline break and once more declined, technicians drew a *down*-trendline connecting the all-time high of 67 with the secondary tops. This, in its turn, was decisively broken in September, 1965—nearly a year after the old high of 67 had been posted—when Chrysler closed outside the trendline. A signal was flashed that the down-trend of the stock probably had been stopped. This signal came at 53.

Technicians were careful to note that volume increased on the end-of-downturn signal. Confirmation of such a technical signal by an increase of volume is important. Without this increase the validity of the signal is suspect; although some such signals prove valid, the chances are too close for an adept technician to trade upon them. On the other hand, volume confirmation of a downward trendline break is not necessary, for even without active selling pressure the mere lack of orders lets a price go down. Even where there is volume confirmation, you cannot count every tiny break as valid. A good rule of thumb is to accept a trendline break only if the price closes a full point outside the trendline.

A confirmed major trendline break says that the old trend has been halted. But you cannot be sure whether there will be a quick reversal or whether the stock will "consolidate." In consolidation, a stock seesaws back and forth over a limited trading range. Consolidation represents a more-or-less even balance between buyers and sellers; no one can be certain whether the sellers are going to have more stock and so eventually force the price movement into a down-movement, or whether the bulls will get the best of it, exhaust offerings of the bears, and triumphantly carry the price movement upward.

Many technicians use "fanlines" to help determine whether a trendline break is likely to lead merely into consolidation or whether it is a for-real change in major direction. Let us assume, as an example, that we are following Whistle Missile, Inc. and that a major down-trendline has been broken. There follows a little rise and then a minor decline. We are at a crucial spot. If the price declines below the lowest point made before the trendline break, we can assume that the break was probably a false one, and we avoid purchasing Whistle Missile common. But if, as is probable, the price holds at the old bottom or stays a bit above it, and then goes into a new rise, we can begin to draw analytical fanlines.

The first fanline is the old down-trendline. Next we draw a new trendline connecting the old top with the top of our little after-the-break rise. We have two lines of the fan.

Next a slightly higher top is chalked up and after that another little down-move ensues. We draw a third fanline to connect the old top with our newest minor top and we have a fan. It consists of three trendlines, each slightly flatter than the one before.

When the last fanline has been broken on a new upside movement, an investor can establish long positions in Whistle Missile. Of course no one can be certain of any technical analytical method. The odds, however, now favor the initial trendline break as being valid and the fanline break as having established that our stock is in for a new uptrend rather than a consolidation.

As with resistance studies, experienced technical analysts do not act upon every break, but instead note carefully whether the trendline broken has major, intermediate, or only minor significance. A major movement continues for months and sometimes years. Along this movement there are likely to be two, three, sometimes six or seven intermediate moves of several weeks to several months' duration, each in turn consisting of a few minor movements. The minor trends hardly show up on charts and an investor who acted on minor movements would be leading into a whipsaw. The intermediates and, even more, the major movements carry sizable profit potential of the type which can make capital grow.

There are two other points you should check when looking at a trendline break:

1. How steep is it? A trendline which is too steep—anything steeper than a 45-degree angle can be deemed too steep to continue—is bound to break, but the break need not have major significance.

2. How many times has the trendline been tested? A major up-trend line which has three, four, or five reaction bottoms along its length, or a down-trendline touched by the tops of four or five rallies, obviously delineates a trend far better than one which connects only two points. Its breaking thus has greater importance.

Some successful investors and traders watch for a counter-trend drop that carries down to the major trendline. Then they buy. It is usually a safe assumption that odds favor the continuance of any trend. Chances are that our friend, Whistle Missile, Inc., will rally from the spot where the trendline was touched and that the purchase will have an early and, hopefully, a sizable eventual profit. Should the trendline be broken, you have a quick stop-out point with minimum loss.

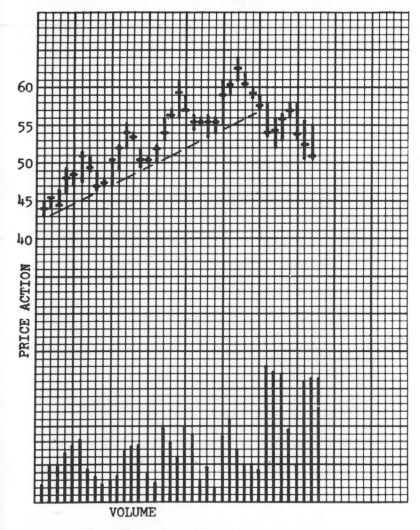

As the price of this stock rose steadily, it made the normal reactions which are to be found in every up-trend. The trendline connects the bottoms of these reactions. Its breaking signifies probable end, for a time, of the existing up-trend. Note increase of volume on trendline break, and the "pullback" to the trendline.

The Tax Dilemma

SAMUEL MITCHELL

Of importance to all investors are the tax problems encountered on the way to making — or losing — money. Even the experts cannot agree on how and when it is most advantageous to buy and sell stocks in order to minimize high taxes. Samuel Mitchell writes clearly and interestingly about his method of consistently making profits in the stock market, and he treats this confusing subject in an unorthodox and convincing manner.

*I*N prehistoric times, the strong inevitably preyed upon the weak, destroying their dwellings and carrying off their cattle and their wives, presumably in that order. As nations became more civilized, they slaughtered each other for the right to continue this practice, augmenting it in later years to the right to exact taxes. In our own democracy, the process has been somewhat refined. They continue taking our cattle but leave us our wives, compensating us for this slight irregularity by allowing us an extremely small tax deduction.

The reader may rightly assume that it is not the intention of the author to quote, even approximately, the current rate of taxation on incomes in the various brackets; I am quite sure they have not gone unnoticed. What is far more important is whether taxes should influence your stock transactions, and to what extent? And this is a subject that commands thorough exploration, no matter what bracket you are in. I have observed too many investors who focus their attention on taxes so completely they ignore other more important considerations.

I am reminded of a cartoon I saw some time ago, I believe it was in a magazine. It depicted a group of scientists in front of a huge computer complex, about three stories high, containing thousands of wheels, meters, and gadgets. One scientist is seen kneeling on the floor, exclaiming: "I found the trouble. . . . The plug had fallen out of the wall socket."

In a like manner, the income tax complex embraces many gadgets: short- and long-term profits, capital gains, cash dividends, stock dividends, losses, deductible expenses, interest payments, etc., which can be itemized and calculated very accurately by yourself, with or without the aid of your CPA, and the amount of your tax determined. All of which is academic, particularly at the time it has to be reported to the Government, i.e., anytime after the first of the year until the final day for filing, April 15.

By that time, however, the plug has fallen out of the wall socket and it is too late to activate your individual computer; it is too late to take a profit or a loss for the previous year. It is far wiser to plug in your income-tax computer and keep it activated all through the year. Of course, this puts the burden on *your* shoulders immediately, instead of putting it off until the end of the year when you must decide whether to take a profit or loss or whether to buy another hundred shares now and take a loss on the first hundred shares thirty days later or take a loss on one stock and a profit on another so that no tax will accrue, etc.

What makes these decisions so difficult is that by nature we possess an inborn hatred to pay taxes in the first place; and in the second place, as realists, we try to reduce our taxes to a minimum. And, we turn to competent CPA's for their advice, in the third place. They, being trained up to the minute in tax matters and cognizant of their client's likes and dislikes, come up with year-end recommendations (in the fourth place).

My attorney friends have a courtroom expression which I find apropos: I object to the above year-end recommendations as being "incompetent, irrelevant, and immaterial." Before my accounting friends sever their diplomatic relations with this writer, let me clarify my objections by referring to some court records. To soothe their feelings, let me add that I am not questioning the "competency" of the accountant as such, or the legality of the advice given, nor its propriety. But I do very seriously question the "relevancy" of the advice and the "material" effect it may have on one's portfolio of stocks.

I have seen too many situations where an investor, with or without the advice of a CPA, is so tax-saving-oriented that he completely overlooks the potential value of the stock he sells. One of my friends told me he sold his Photon at $17 to establish a year-end loss; it did not amount to $100, so his tax saving could not have been more than $30. (I was enjoying the warm waters and cool trade winds at Barbados, so could not reach me for my *expert* advice.) Nine months later, he would have been sitting with a profit of $8,000. This may be an unfair example, even though it is true in every detail. But even if his profit would only be a few hundred dollars, what was his reason for selling? He knows the writer for years and can certainly trust him. I advised him to buy Photon because the company was emerging from a number of years in the "red" due to the great expense of developing a new product; that the product was well thought of, the management was good and the potential exceptional for the next few years. He blames his "selling" on his accountant; in this instance, I am sure the CPA had nothing to do with it. It was simply an investor's attitude that Uncle Sam would not miss his $30.

A second case on record, an investor with a tax loss of several thousands, took a profit on one of his favorite stocks to offset his loss, thus saving the tax he would normally have to pay the following year (if he chose to sell it the following year). All of which would be "relevant" if the investor or his CPA had come to the conclusion that the stock should be sold. But this was not the case; for had they evaluated the stock with the profit, they would not have sold it. It doesn't make sense worrying about the mounting tax you will some day have to pay instead of enjoying the mounting after-tax profits you will have left.

A third situation finds an investor of modest means who had the good fortune to see a small investment run up to the two-million-dollar mark. During this period he refused to take any part of his profit primarily because he wanted to avoid paying a tax. I am confident his CPA and everyone else urged him to take a profit. Unfortunately, the stock did not stay up to expectations; a decline set in and continued for some time. Since he would not take his profit or part of his profit at the high, he held on until his profits had declined some 75 per cent and, I am informed, suffered two heart attacks. The moral of the story is pay the tax and don't speculate with your health. Personally, I would not care to evaluate (moneywise) a simple case of indigestion.

The tug-of-war continues, between the *itch* to take a profit and the *reluctance* to pay a tax. It is mostly a problem of the emotions; the individual must solve it by himself. I do not care to take part in it and suggest that CPA's follow my example. When it becomes an investment problem as to whether a stock should be sold—dependent upon its current evaluation and its potential market action—our advice may be of interest. Personally, I veer to a cold-hearted third-party approach to determine whether to buy-or-sell—totally ignoring the tax situation.

There are, of course, some gimmicks whereby you can have your cake and eat it. For example, you may have a stock at a loss; you want to establish this loss but you do not want to part with the stock. At least thirty days before you wish to *sell*, you *buy* a like amount of shares; thirty days later you sell your original holdings, thus establishing your tax loss.

In a like manner (when you have a substantial loss), you can take a substantial profit on one of your holdings by *selling* it, thus establishing a sufficient profit to offset your tax loss. Once you take a profit, the tax laws permit you to buy it back the following day. You therefore maintain your position in the stock and own it at a higher price. You pay a small premium for these procedures (the buy and sell commissions), but this is little enough "insurance" in relation to future tax savings. But, you must have good reasons for wanting to hold your position.

This writer may also be accused of avoiding taxes to the exclusion of every other consideration; but this is not so. It is true that I am still sitting with the bulk of my enormous paper profits, but . . . I am firmly convinced that my stocks should be held. My one problem is that of income, since two-million-dollars worth of my Xerox pays only one-half of one per cent dividends. I have been advised on countless occasions to sell off some Xerox, pay my 25 per cent tax, and switch to a better dividend-paying stock, bond, or tax exempts; I have resisted this type of thinking for the following reasons.

Let us say, I sell a million-dollars worth of Xerox; I will be left with $750,000 to invest in a bond at 5 per cent or even 6 per cent. This would bring me an income of $45,000, on which I would pay a tax of about 60 per cent, leaving me a net of $18,000. In lieu of this, I can sell off $50,000 worth of stock each year; the most I would have to pay is 25 per cent leaving me $37,500, or more than double the previous "net." Of course, the risk is greater in holding my common stocks, but do not think for a moment that there is no risk in tax-exempts and bonds. Several years ago, one of my friends was advised to put 30 per cent of his holdings in a safe bond and the one selected was AT&T at 4½ per cent. Since Telephone bonds are now available yielding 6 per cent, his AT&T bonds have declined over 20 per cent. Another investor bought $100,000 worth of U.S. Government long-term tax-exempts and found it expedient to take a 33⅓ per cent loss on them recently to buy some bonds at a much higher yield. Tax-exempts exempt you from taxes, but they do not exempt you from losses. The risk varies in each of these instances and it is up to the individual to take the risk he can afford. While all my figures are based on upper-bracket taxes, those in the lower-brackets should find them proportionately apropos.

Where available, stock dividends are preferred to cash dividends. Among my list of stocks, Citizen's Utilities and First Charter Finance pay stock dividends, semiannually for CU and annually for FCF. Pittston also paid a small stock dividend. These are preferable because when they are sold, the tax laws treat them as capital gains, exempting one-half of the proceeds from taxation.

The short-term trader's tax dilemma is less fathomable. In theory, I liken his operations to those of the retail discount house which thrives on small profits and quicker turnovers; this term is used by the retail merchant to calculate the number of times he is able to turn over his inventory each year. If he carries an inventory of $250,000 and can turn it five times, he reaches a volume of $1,250,000. If he is able to turn it ten times (by selling at a lower price) he achieves a volume of $2,500,000 and probably a higher net profit. Larger volume, in theory, reduces operating costs. In practice, discount operations thrive quickly and expand rapidly but, in the long run, encounter increased labor costs as well as all other costs, narrower profits due to markdowns (when you cannot sell an item at the market price, you reduce it to a price that will move it), and lower net profits despite increased volume.

This is exactly how the short-term trader works. In theory he takes a quick profit on a stock, sometimes in a week or two or more. Each time he sells, he buys another stock and if he can turn over his capital ten times in a six-month period, he may wind up with a much larger short-term profit than he would holding on to one stock for six months—the capital gains period where one-half your profit is exempted from taxation. In theory, this is quite easy; a few points here and there amount to several thousand before you know it. However, in the long run, the trader runs into the same problems as the discount house; his costs keep mounting: his buy and sell brokerage commissions keep multiplying; he must pay twice the tax the long-term investor pays and he has his markdowns, too. When he cannot sell a stock at a profit, he must sell it "below cost" and take a loss. Which is why the old-timers used to say, "Traders die broke."

Don't Be Afraid of Buying on a War Scare

PHILIP A. FISHER

A common error among investors is selling on the news of a possible war. Philip A. Fisher's thoughtful analysis of a war-time economy gives advice to readers on how best to protect their money during any inflationary economy, not just a war-time economy.

COMMON stocks are usually of greatest interest to people with imagination. Our imagination is staggered by the utter horror of modern war. The result is that every time the international stresses of our world produce either a war scare or an actual war, common stocks reflect it. This is a psychological phenomenon which makes little sense financially.

Any decent human being becomes appalled at the slaughter and suffering caused by the mass killings of war. In today's atomic age, there is added a deep personal fear for the safety of those closest to us and for ourselves. This worry, fear, and distaste for what lies ahead can often distort any appraisal of purely economic factors. The fears of mass destruction of property, almost confiscatory higher taxes, and government interference with business dominate what thinking we try to do on financial matters. People operating in such a mental climate are inclined to overlook some even more fundamental economic influences.

The results are always the same. Through the entire twentieth century, with a single exception, every time major war has broken out anywhere in the world or whenever American forces have become involved in any fighting whatever, the American stock market has always plunged sharply downward. This one exception was the outbreak of World War II in September 1939. At that time, after an abortive rally on thoughts of fat war contracts to a neutral nation, the market soon was following the typical downward course, a course which some months later resembled panic as news of German victories began piling up. Nevertheless, at the conclusion of all actual fighting—regardless of whether it was World War I, World War II, or Korea—most stocks were selling at levels vastly higher than prevailed before there was any thought of war at all. Furthermore, at least ten times in the last twenty-two years, news has come of other international crises which gave threat of major war. In every instance, stocks dipped sharply on the fear of war and rebounded sharply as the war scare subsided.

What do investors overlook that causes them to dump stocks both on the fear of war and on the arrival of war itself, even though by the end of the war stocks have always gone much higher than lower? They forget that stock prices are quotations expressed in money. Modern war always causes governments to spend far more than they can possibly collect from their taxpayers while the war is being waged. This causes a vast increase in the amount of money, so that each individual unit of money, such as a dollar, becomes worth less than it was before. It takes lots more dollars to buy the same number of shares of stock. This, of course, is the classic form of inflation.

In other words, war is always bearish on money. To sell stock at the threatened or actual outbreak of hostilities so as to get into cash is extreme financial lunacy. Actually just the opposite should be done. If an investor has about decided to buy a particular common stock and the arrival of a full-blown war scare starts knocking down the price, he should ignore the scare psychology of the moment and definitely begin buying. This is the time when having surplus cash for investment becomes least, not most, desirable. However, here a problem presents itself. How fast should he buy? How far down will the stock go? As long as the downward influence is a war scare and not war, there is no way of knowing. If actual hostilities break out, the price would undoubtedly go still lower, perhaps a lot lower. Therefore, the thing to do is to buy but buy slowly and at a scale-down on just a threat of war. If war occurs, then increase the tempo of buying significantly. Just be sure to buy into companies either with products or services the demand for which will continue in wartime, or which can convert their facilities to wartime operations. The great majority of companies can so qualify under today's conditions of total war and manufacturing flexibility.

Do stocks actually become more valuable in wartime, or is it just money which declines in value? That depends on circumstances. By the grace of God, our country has never been defeated in any war in which it has engaged. In war, particularly modern war, the money of the defeated side is likely to become completely or almost worthless, and common stocks would lose most of their value. Certainly, if the United States were to be defeated by Communist Russia, both our money and our stocks would become valueless. It would then make little difference what investors might have done.

On the other hand, if a war is won or stalemated, what happens to the real value of stocks will vary with the individual war and the individual stock. In World War I, when the enormous pre-war savings of England and France were pouring into this country, most stocks probably increased their real worth even more than might have been the case if the same years had been a period of peace. This, however, was a one-time condition that will not be repeated. Expressed in constant dollars—that is, in real value—American stocks in both World War II and the Korean period undoubtedly did fare less well than if the same period had been one of peace. Aside from the crushing taxes, there was too great a diversion of effort from the more profitable peace-time lines to abnormally narrow-margin defense work. If the magnificent research effort spent on these narrow-margin defense projects could have been channelled to normal peace-time lines, stockholders' profits would have been far greater—assuming, of course, that there would still have been a free America in which any profits could have been enjoyed at all. The reason for buying stocks on war or fear of war is not that war, in itself, is ever again likely to be profitable to American stockholders. It is just that money becomes even less desirable, so that stock prices, which are expressed in units of money, always go up.

Trading Cyclical Issues

WILLIAM S. HEWETT

William S. Hewett, stockbroker and popular lecturer, treats a difficult subject, cyclical issues, with clarity. Hewett analyzes the problematical nature of cyclical industries and acquaints the reader with the investment opportunities offered by these industries.

*I*F we were to concentrate only on growth issues, we would needlessly pass up many opportunities. It is also well to study cycles as they relate to specific industries and companies in order to avoid being drawn along by a temporary wave of optimism. We must not anticipate long-term growth in an industry that is merely riding high on a temporary bulge. Most securities have periods of growth followed by important reactions. Each industry has its own peculiarities, cycles and trends. By familiarizing himself with these factors, an investor will be better able to properly evaluate new developments and take advantage of important trends. Investor lethargy toward an industry or company at times creates an opportunity for the sharp investor. New management, new products and new promotion also create situations in which large profits can be obtained.

An important cause of wide swings in the price of a great many companies is that the product they produce is durable. Unlike food, electricity, etc., these durable items are bought to last for a period of years. Consumer buying habits fluctuate over the years. Sometimes they will discard an object after its useful life is only partially exhausted. At other times they may go to considerable pains to repair equipment so it will last many more years. Corporate management must appraise the consumers' requirements well before an actual demand. They must estimate the amount of raw materials to be inventoried, the condition and number of production machinery and the skills of employees. An understanding of the thinking and capacity of competitors, money conditions, government attitudes and plans and many other factors must be evaluated in order to be ready with just the right amount of goods that the consumer will buy one year or several years later. In order that the consumer may know the various products, manufacturers must promote their wares through vigorous advertising. The inability of any individual to make more than an educated guess at demand and supply factors with which they work explains the wide divergence in corporation profit pictures.

Of all the industries that make up the American economy, two of the most important are automobiles and housing. This is because so many industries are dependent upon the vigor of these two industrial activities. In 1963 new housing starts were at a record $22 billion and total construction at $63 billion. This created a huge demand for glass, plywood, cement, floor covering, wallboard, timber and a thousand other products. Like construction, automobile sales affect the level of prosperity of a great many different industries. It has been ascertained that over 30,000 different companies deliver materials and services to General Motors, making it possible for them to produce automobiles. The public's demand for new autos varies widely. Car sales were at a high of 7.9 million in 1955, but they declined to only 4.2 million in 1958. At the 1958 low less than 50% of the industry's capacity was in use. In 1963—7.6 million cars were sold and this figure was exceeded in both 1964 and 1965. Figure 1 shows the percentage increase or decrease in auto production and new housing starts since 1949. Figures 2 and 3 related to automobile production and home construction show the net earning swings of the various companies directly affected by the public demand in these two fields. Goodyear and Firestone were less affected by the industry's gyrations because when new car production is low they work to obtain a larger share of the replacement tire market and they have diversified into chemicals and lines other than auto tire production. The earnings of building firms fluctuated widely, partly because new facilities demanded that they sell additional stock and the profits were divided among a larger number of owners. Severe competition caused a shrinkage of profit margins and thereby affected the profit picture.

To further illustrate the nature of cyclical industries, let's look at three of our basic industries—copper, railroads and steel. All are vital to our economy and may be expected to grow as our economy grows, perhaps 4% a year. Within this long gradual trend, however, there have been and will continue to be wide price fluctuations which will give the sharp investor substantial opportunities. Referring to the three charts in Figure 4, we see that in 1949 the year ended for industrial stocks at about the same level it had begun. The copper industry, however, lost 18%. Copper and steel during the period 1950–1951 appreciated about 85% while the averages rose only 56%. The year 1955 was very fruitful for copper and steel with stock prices up 64% as against 25% for the average. Copper and railroads declined in 1956 and 1957 while most other securities advanced. The year 1959 was a very good year for basic industry and a return of investors' confidence drove railroads and steels up faster than most other issues. In 1960 and 1962 the market was hard hit with waves of pessimism. Note, in both years the cyclical industries lost more ground than the average. Obviously, an investor willing to dig for facts and risk money on his conclusions may realize very substantial profits in widely fluctuating industries. It is likewise obvious that cyclical industries offer poor opportunities for the investor that buys and holds for an indefinite period.

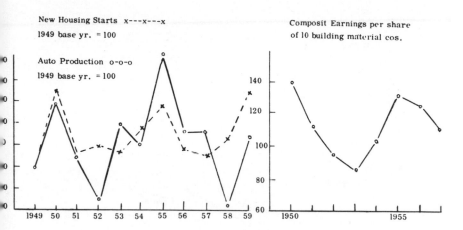

Figure 1

Figure 2 Composite earnings per share of 10 building material companies.

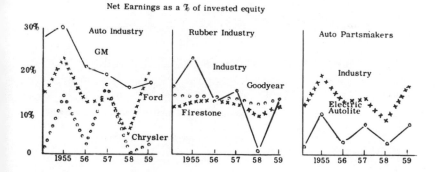

Figure 3 Net Earnings as a percent of invested equity.

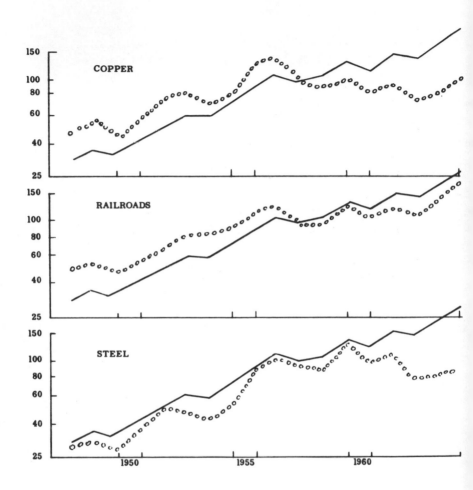

oooooo Copper, Rail or Steel price activity

———— Moody's 125 Industrials

Figure 4

Of the three industries concerned we find that copper is often considered a barometer of national productivity. About 24 pounds of copper are used in every new automobile produced, $400 worth of pipe runs through each new $20,000 home, and each new kilowatt of electricity developed for use in the United States requires nearly 115 pounds of electric wiring. If manufacturers are to produce a record number of homes and cars they must buy huge inventories of copper in advance. Hence the classification of copper as a barometer industry. Supply and demand are only partially responsible for the wide fluctuation in the price of copper. In recent years copper has fluctuated from a high of 46¢ per pound in 1956 to a low of 25¢ in 1958. South America and Africa produce the major portion of the copper consumed throughout the world. Anaconda and Kennecott control a large part of these mines. Although these companies are incorporated in the United States, they must deal with the governments in whose countries they operate. They also must compete for the copper produced by European companies. In 1954, for instance, Anaconda and Kennecott not only contended with the fantastic inflationary binge in Chile which caused a 6% loss of purchasing power each month, but they had to pay 60% of their profits to the government. The proceeds from sales in excess of 24½¢ a pound were simply confiscated by the government. One marvels that profits can be realized at all under such conditions, but comparing our worked-over mines and high labor cost to the newly exploited mines of extremely rich copper and low labor costs elsewhere in the world, we find that foreign production costs less than one half as much as domestic ore!

The high price of copper in 1956 was a result of an unusually large demand in both the United States and Europe as new highs in prosperity were reached. Supplies were inadequate and the demand for automobiles, houses and other consumer goods was at an all-time high. Fabricators, in order to meet this demand, willingly paid increasingly higher prices. Copper men were fully aware of the fact that many copper consumers were deserting to the use of aluminum and other competitive products but supply and demand factors were too far out of line for them to control the situation. Between 1957 and 1958 copper prices collapsed to 25¢ because new mines had been opened up and the recession had slowed consumer demand. During the first six months of 1959 production ran at a record rate. Strikes halted 75% of the nation's production during the third quarter and the year's total production declined 20% below 1958. Consumption was unusually high, leaving stocks of refined copper at the year end down 63% and at their lowest since before 1900. Demand increased to shore up sagging inventories and the price of copper advanced to 34¢.

Anaconda is the second largest copper producer in the world, and the number one fabricator. The company is diversified in many mining activities, including aluminum and uranium; but copper mining, smelting and fabricating represent the largest part of its enterprise. Its break-even point in 1957, so far as the price of copper was concerned, was 22¢ a pound. Kennecott and Phelps Dodge both had a lower break-even point which indicated a greater efficiency or simply lower cost operation resulting from mine location or other factors. Anaconda earnings, therefore, have fluctuated from $2.07 in 1954 to $12.85 in 1956 and $1.20 in 1957. The stock price has also moved widely. From 1949 through 1952 Anaconda appreciated 110% as compared with 45% for the Dow Industrial averages; from 1953 through 1954 a decline of 45% occurred while the averages advanced 38%; from 1955 through 1956 a booming advance of 194% took place versus 19% for the averages. A loss of nearly two-thirds of the previous rise followed from 1957 to the end of 1958 while the Dow averages advanced 21%. The years of 1959 and 1960 witnessed an 85% rise versus the averages' gain of 17%. After 1960 coppers traded in a narrow range while the averages continued to advance.

Our next study is of the railroad industry. Over the past decade the railroads have lost business to trucks and other transportation systems, particularly in inter-city commercial traffic. On the other hand, contrary to popular belief, rail traffic measured in ton miles has steadily been increasing. In 1956 it handled 650 billion ton miles—as much as all other forms of commercial transport combined. Our economy is highly dependent upon the continued operation of the railroads. The principal problems that confront the industry are State and Federal government control, labor costs and transportation of passengers. Passenger revenue represents a relatively small proportion of New York Central's business, but the net loss engendered by it has offset as much as 50% of the company's freight profits. In 1958 it was estimated that 65% of the railroad's total cost was represented by wages to labor. Several southern railroads discovered that when rates were made equal to trucks, corporations preferred truck delivery. But if rates were 1½¢ per 100 pounds lower than those for trucks, 75% of the business stayed with the rails. The lower rate was proposed to the Interstate Commerce Commission because profit could be realized at that point. The ICC limited the cut to 1¢. Often passenger runs are continued to serve only a few customers. This situation exists for one reason—because of obstinate public service commissions' insistence that the service is needed for special seasons of the year and for emergency purposes. To indulge a few communities the total cost of the service is increased.

Railroad officials have gone to considerable expense to improve their properties—conversion to diesel locomotives and piggy-back truck hauling were major steps. Today they are experimenting with light-weight passenger trains which could lessen cost. Because of electronically operated yards, in 1959 the railroads handled three-quarters the volume of carloading as they did in 1948, with just 60% of the labor force. Traffic control systems offer another avenue toward a more efficient use of assets. Electronic computers are being used to dispatch cars. All too often business has been turned away for lack of cars while empties were sitting neglected on the line.

Most railroads have income from non-rail sources. Eastern roads, particularly Pennsylvania and New York Central, own very valuable downtown real estate and air rights. Western and southern railroads own oil, gas and mineral rights. Union Pacific generates nearly 40% of its total revenue from these sources.

The chart in Figure 4 understates the normally wide fluctuations in railroad securities because of the growth nature of a few railroads such as Chesapeake & Ohio, Norfolk & Western, Great Northern, Northern Pacific, Southern Pacific and Southern Railroad. The wide swings are partially the result of heavy burdens of senior securities. In 1955 a 7% boost in the industry's operating revenue increased the net 62%. In the recession of 1958 carloadings were at a twenty-year low, down 22.7% from the preceding year. Eastern roads were hard hit but western roads fared well because of bumper farm crops and a strike of truckers.

Now let's consider the steel industry which has the capacity to produce about 140 million ingot tons a year. Demand determines the percentage of capacity at which the industry operates. Greater efficiency of operation was brought about by the introduction of oxygen jets to open-hearth furnaces, by improvements in blast furnace performance, locating new plants closer to markets and by electronic innovations. As a result of these improvements the industry has been able to operate profitably below 50% of capacity. Considerable new debt has been taken on to finance these improvements. If demand should expand to create a new record of steel shipments the companies would profit substantially.

The specter of competition from aluminum and foreign shipments is often raised when steel is being discussed. There is reason for this concern, but the dangers must be put in their proper perspective. The demand for aluminum has increased steadily over the last decade while that for steel has been rather stagnant. On the other hand, aluminum is a two-million-ton-a-year business while steel constitutes considerably over one hundred million tons a year. New thin plate steel may stop the inroads of aluminum in canning. Newly developed high quality and special purpose steels continue to find expanding markets.

Imports of steel have grown from 1% of our total consumption in 1955 to approximately 5% in 1963, and although this is a small percent of our production, steel men accept these inroads of foreign steel as an indication that new increases in price are unlikely to stick. As a result new demands from labor for higher wages are likely to meet stiffer resistance.

Knowing the specialities of the major companies in each industry might be of use to the investor. In 1957 producers of heavy steels for the petroleum, construction, shipbuilding and railroad industries rode high while lighter steel producers for the appliance and auto industries did poorly. Weight is another important factor. Steel is an expensive commodity to ship. Proximity to the market is important. Pittsburgh is a steel surplus area so companies located there—or, for that matter, nearly anywhere in the east—find competition severe. Chicago is a steel deficit area which partially explains the superior performance of Inland Steel. Many companies have been aggressively building in this part of the country.

We hope this introduction to industry study will illustrate the need for background information. Material from newspapers and various services must be placed in proper perspective.

Investing in cyclical issues is risky. One way of lessening the risk without reducing the profit potential is to consider the use of convertible preferred and debentures whenever a favorable possibility presents itself. Assume that in May of 1957 Allegheny Ludlum appeared to have promise. A convertible debenture is available which pays $40, matures in 1981 and is convertible into 18.18 shares of common. At $1200 per bond it yields 3.3%. The common $63 yields 3.5%. If the common should advance to $100 a 59% gain would have been realized. The debenture would rise to $1818, which is also a 59% gain. Bond interest is paid before taxes and common dividends and has prior claim to assets in the event of dissolution. Since gain will be the same regardless of which security we purchase, the bond would seem more desirable even though we sacrifice some dividend yield. The market break in the latter part of 1957 depressed the common to 28⅞, a 54% decline. The bond found support at $900. It resisted further decline because investors disassociated the bond from the common stock when the bond yield rose to 4½%. The bond's decline, therefore, amounted to only 25%. At the market low the investor might have become very aggressive. Using the bond as collateral he might have borrowed 80% of the purchase price. The maximum that can be borrowed on common stock is currently only 30%. In the next two years the common advanced 114% to $60.75 while the bond advanced 31% to $1182.50. The tremendous leverage that borrowed money can give is evident when we find that the 31% price advance is translated into a 156% profit. Convertible senior securities afford protection and—if the investor chooses to use them in this way—they can provide unusual leverage.

GMAC's—"The Pause That Refreshes"

FRANK B. DIAMOND

Any veteran investor knows how important it is to retain an objective perspective on the stock market — and on his own stocks, in particular. Frank B. Diamond has had many years of investment experience and he has a logical and persuasive suggestion on how periodically to reevaluate and reassess one's portfolio.

*E*VERY successful investor should enjoy the pause that refreshes and step out of the stock market occasionally with a rather sizable part of his money. There is nothing like it to renew one's perspective and to re-examine the entire market, your own portfolio and your method of operations. It is surprising how often this proves profitable and permits investors to return with a completely fresh viewpoint which quickly translates itself into greater profits and more income.

One question which always arises when this practice is recommended is: What does one do with his money during the interim? A very good answer may be found in short-term notes. These are actually promissory notes issued in either bearer or order form, payable on maturity, which may be any business day selected by the buyer, from 30 days to nine months. Many major American corporations, such as Sears, Ford, Chrysler, General Electric and General Motors, issue these short-term notes.

The General Motors Acceptance Corporation provides an excellent example. This company's entire capital stock is owned by General Motors Corporation, the world's largest and richest manufacturing concern. An ideal feature of these notes is that the investor, after calculating when he will want his money back, can lend GMAC any sum in excess of $5,000 for the precise period of time he prefers. If 76 days will suit his purpose, or 43, or whatever it may be, he selects the maturity and advises his broker. Moreover, he receives a very attractive rate of interest for every day his money is at work. This is calculated on an annual basis and normally reflects the going rate of short-term securities of the highest grade. In March 1968, for example, the rates were approximately 5⅛% for 30 to 60 days, 5¼% for 60 to 90 days and 5½% for periods extending from 90 days to nine months. Upon request, GMAC will mail offering sheets to customers following any change in rates. Of course, these interest rates fluctuate with supply and demand and are themselves an excellent barometer of the money market.

If an investor is a good customer of a brokerage firm, he will normally be charged only a tiny service charge for the handling of the transaction. If it is clear that the money is only "resting," awaiting a favorable point of re-entry into the stock market, it is quite possible that the brokerage firm will not charge any fee whatsoever and will offer the service as a courtesy. In any event, the consideration is nominal.

Since the reputation of General Motors is at stake, as well as the financial integrity of a highly successful operating subsidiary, these notes are considered by the investment fraternity to be practically riskless. The board of directors has placed stringent restrictions on the amounts of paper which can be sold at any one time. These guidelines have satisfied all banking institutions.

The general business of the company is to finance the distribution and sale of new products manufactured by General Motors and consigned to dealers for resale. In addition, GMAC helps to finance these dealers' installment sales to their millions of customers. The new products involved include all automobiles and trucks manufactured by Chevrolet, Buick, Cadillac, Oldsmobile and Pontiac; also the complete line of Frigidaire units, other household appliances, air conditioning equipment, the Delco line and many other well-known products. The business of GMAC is conducted solely with dealers who sell General Motors products, and the dealers must assume responsibility for the payment of any outstanding retail obligation in the event of a default. The continuous and rapid turnover inherent in this business provides the company with the opportunity of offering such flexible terms to investors.

United States Treasury Bills are another excellent vehicle for short-term investments of up to one year. These are short-term obligations of the United States which are sold every week by the Treasury. Although no interest is paid, the notes are sold at a discount which has the same effect as interest. For example, if $1,000 notes are offered for sale at $950 each, this will have a price equivalent to about 5% on a one-year basis. Investors actually bid for these Treasury bills every week at the government's auction. Since this weekly sale is on a year-round basis, and since there is a vital market for these bills, it is simple for the investor to select the maturity which fulfills his requirements.

The prices are quoted daily in the *Wall Street Journal* and the *New York Times*, as well as in several other places. Forty different maturities are usually quoted—certainly an ample selection for most investors. The format of the quotation is a little different at first glance, but not difficult to understand.

Mat	Bid	Ask
	DISCOUNT	
3-21	4.80	4.50

The "Mat 3–21" refers to the maturity date of March 21. The "Bid Discount" of 4.80 means that investors are willing to pay a price which will yield the equivalent of 4.80% if held until March 21. The "Ask Discount" of 4.50 indicates that sellers of these bills will accept a price equal to a 4.50% return held to maturity. Your broker will execute your order to buy Treasury bills and the commission is normally $1.25 for $1,000. This is a modest amount, since the handling of the transaction involves a somewhat more complicated procedure than in the case of commercial short-term notes. It should be noted that the normal "round lot," or unit of trading, is 25 bonds. Fewer than this amount are transacted at slightly higher prices.

The significant factor in this recommendation is that there are various safe interest-paying short-term investments available to investors where money can be invested with no anxiety. With his capital at work, but not at risk, the investor can sit back and review the entire market picture. Some of the most clarifying thoughts are likely to emerge from this quiet appraisal. It is absolutely astonishing how different certain stocks appear to the same person, when he attempts to evaluate them as a spectator as opposed to an owner! Incidentally, there is nothing which says that they may not look even more promising, and from time to time the investor will decide to resume his position with a larger number of shares.

Another favorable result of employing this periodic "withdrawal technique" is that it provides the perfect occasion for disposing of weak stocks. Some of the most experienced investment advisers strongly urge the sale each year of the poorest performing stocks in every portfolio. This is easier said than done for most investors, but sagacious advice. If the investor develops the habit of stepping out of the market from time to time, he is far more likely to use these occasions for liquidating his mistakes. He is, conversely, far more likely to increase his positions in his better acting selections. This is bound to increase his profits in the stock market.

Key Points

1. Periodically "retire" from the market to acquire a fresh viewpoint.
2. How to use short-term commercial paper to achieve maximum flexibility and greatest income.
3. Study United States Treasury Bills selling at a discount.

But What Do the Numbers Mean?

"ADAM SMITH"

The Money Game by "Adam Smith" has been a national
best seller. Along with being a witty account of the
mechanics of Wall Street, it is also very informative. To
most people the term "Annual Report" brings to mind an
image of a printed statement as reliable, accurate, and
trustworthy as a dictionary. However, "Adam Smith" comes
to his own quite opposite conclusion, and with
tongue-in-cheek he questions the intent of its authors and
the reliability of the figures it presents to the trusting
public.

You can see that there are a lot of numbers floating around
Wall Street, that the Game is played with numbers, and that with
computers more people can play with more numbers in more
combinations than anyone would have dreamed possible in the
old, archaic pre-computer days BC in 1960. But what are the
base numbers? They are the figures reported by the subject companies as sales and earnings, and earnings, in anybody's systems,
are one of the most important factors.

But what are earnings?

It really ought to be easy. You pick up the paper, and Zilch

Consolidated says its net profit for the year just ended was $1 million or $1 a share. When Zilch Consolidated puts out its annual report, the report will say the company earned $1 million or $1 a share. The report will be signed by an accounting firm, which says that it has examined the records of Zilch and "in our opinion, the accompanying balance sheet and statement of income and retained earnings present fairly the financial position of Zilch. Our examination of these statements was made in accordance with generally accepted accounting principles."

The last four words are the key. The translation of "generally accepted accounting principles" is "Zilch could have earned anywhere from fifty cents a share to $1.25 a share. If you will look at our notes 1 through 16 in the back, you will see that Zilch's earnings can be played like a guitar, depending on what we count or don't count. We picked $1. That is consistent with what other accountants are doing this year. We'll let next year take care of itself."

Numbers imply precision, so it is a bit hard to get used to the idea that a company's net profit could vary by 100 percent depending on which bunch of accountants you call in, especially when the market is going to take that earnings number and create trends, growth rates, and little flashing lights in computers from it. And all this without any kind of skulduggery you could get sent to jail for.

How can this be?

Let's say you are an airline, and you buy a brand-new, freshly painted Boeing 727. Let's say the airplane costs you $5 million. At some point in the future the airplane is going to be worth 0, because its useful life will be over. So you must charge your income each year with a fraction of the cost of your airplane. What is the life of your airplane? You say the useful life of the airplane is ten years, so on a straight-line basis you will charge your income $500,000, or 10 percent of the cost, this year. If your net income from ferrying passengers and cargo is $1 million, it will drop by half when you apply this depreciation charge. Obviously the year you buy the airplane your earnings are going to look worse than they are next year, when you have the full use of the airplane and it is shuttling back and forth all the time. Your profits will certainly look better if you are still running that airplane in eleven years, because that year there will be no charge at all for depreciation; it will have been written off.

But that is only the beginning of the complications. Right next door at the airport is another airline. It has also bought a brand-new, freshly painted Boeing 727. So you and your competitor can be compared side by side when you both report your earnings on the same day. Right?

Hardly. The airline next door says it can run an airplane twelve years. So it is depreciating its airplane over twelve years, and its depreciation charge this year is $\frac{1}{12}$, not $\frac{1}{10}$, so it has only penalized its earnings $416,666 instead of $500,000, and for this year on that basis it has made more money than you have.

Don't the accountants make everybody charge the same thing for the same airplane? No, they don't. It just makes another little bit of work for the security analysts, who have to adjust the varying depreciation rates to constants. Accountants are not some kind of super-authority, they are professionals employed by clients. If you say the life of your airplane is twelve years, you must know your business; the life is twelve years. Delta Airlines depreciates a 727 in ten years; United in sixteen.

The airplane example is, of course, a very simple one. But what about two second-generation computers, say a Honeywell H200 and something in the IBM 1400 series? Do they have the same life? They may, as far as usage is concerned, but if you are going to sell or trade up it may be easier on the IBM. Then there is an investment credit available on new equipment, a tax assist passed to encourage capital expenditures. Is the investment credit "flowed through," as the jargon says, right to the earnings the first year? Or is the investment credit spread through the whole life of the equipment?

If everybody used the same depreciation method but with different periods of use, life would be tough enough. But equipment is not always depreciated straight-line, an equal percentage for each year. Some companies use heavy charges at the beginning, say 150 percent declining. Some use a method with the charming appellation "sum-of-the-years-digits." If you really want to go into details, call up your accountant and ask *him* for definitions.

This is only the beginning. Look at inventories: Some companies value their inventories last-in, first-out. Some companies charge their research costs as they incur them, some amortize them over several years. Some companies amortize their unfunded pension costs; some do not amortize them at all. Some companies make provisions for the taxes on the profits of subsidiaries as these profits are earned; some make no provision until the subsidiary remits a dividend to the parent.

When companies purchase other companies, the accounting gets even more arcane. The acquisition can be a purchase, a pooling of interests, or a combination of the two. Good will can be amortized or not amortized. The base of depreciation can vary wildly.

In short, there is not a company anywhere whose income statement and profits cannot be changed, by the management and the accountants, by counting things one way instead of another. Not too long ago Price Waterhouse did a study captioned with the rhetorical question, "Is Generally Accepted Accounting for Income Taxes Possibly Misleading Investors?"

Generally—but not always—a real sleuth of an analyst who doesn't have to spend time answering his own phone, talking to customers, selling stock to pension funds, and attending meetings, can crack an income statement and balance sheet in a couple of days. This means real donkey work, digging out notes, making comparisons, finding the tunnels, and in general unpainting the carefully painted picture. But most analysts do have to answer their own phones, sell stocks, attend meetings—and still cover all the developments in their areas. So there are not many who can do the job. Even if every analyst could do this job, there are ten times as many brokers as analysts, and 200 times as many eager customers as brokers, so you can see the odds against Truth at any given instant, when your phone rings and a voice says, "Zilch is earning one dollar and selling at only twelve times earnings." On the other hand, as we have learned, Truth will not make Zilch go up, but the Crowd's general feeling about Zilch just might.

Most accountants are honorable men, trying to do a job. But they are hired by corporations, not by investors. Not only are they professionals hired by the corporations, but they are frequently further involved in company affairs as tax and management consultants.

For years, Wall Street accepted with religious faith an accountant's certification as the Good Housekeeping Seal of Approval, especially those of the great national accounting firms, Price Waterhouse, Haskins & Sells, Arthur Andersen, and so on. Then came a couple of cases in which corporations reported profits, had their reports audited and certified, only to come back several years later and say that the original certified reports were, for one reason or another, off by a very wide mark. In the famous and well-publicized instance of Yale Express, the corporation reported profits for the years it was sliding into bankruptcy. (It is now being reorganized under Chapter X of the bankruptcy laws.) The angry stockholders took to the courts, suing not only Yale Express, but Peat, Marwick, the Certified Public Accountants who had put their seal on Yale Express' reports. The air is now full of litigation, and it is not our purpose here to get into it. Suffice to say that with lawyers and the SEC in full cry the accountants have begun to try to thread some consistencies, but there is genuine confusion among these accountants as to what earnings really are. Corporations, they say, are not all the same, and there has to be some flexibility just to reflect the differences in businesses.

The accountants have my sympathy. But not much of it. I have a lingering skepticism about reported numbers, because I have lost money accepting the reports of accountants, and there is nothing like losing money to burn in a lesson. A leading Wall Street publication says the letters CPA do not stand for Certified Public Accountant but Certified Public Assassin.

Beware of Barbers, Beauticians, and Waiters: The Financial Press

CARTER F. HENDERSON and
ALBERT C. LASHER

Carter F. Henderson and Albert C. Lasher are both
authorities on the complex relationship between
corporations and their stockholders, and on the
relationship between all news media and the stock market.
Of utmost importance to all market analysts and investors
is the financial press — a term that encompasses the
treatment of investment news by the local daily newspaper
to the most technical financial journals. In this selection the
authors not only give you behind-the-scenes accounts of
how publicity in the news media can affect a stock, but
advise you what facts to be alert to in the financial press.

O N April 28, 1961, *Time* magazine printed a story lauding the outlook for a little-known company called Technical Animations, Inc., of Port Washington, New York, which owned rights to a process for adding animated material to film presentations. The company had never earned a penny's profit, yet rumors of the impending article boosted the price of its stock from about $6 to $9.25 a share before the story appeared, and to just over $15 a share following publication. By year's end, Technical Animations' shares had collapsed to $1.75 apiece, and the Securities and Exchange Commission had begun searching for shenanigans behind the stock's wild gyrations on the over-the-counter market.

This example of the influence the press can have on the fortunes of investors was cited by the SEC in a special report on the security industry, when it severely criticized *Time*'s business news editor for trading in the stock of Technical Animations and other companies he planned to treat in the magazine's business section. As in the case of Technical Animations, the price of the stock of these companies often would rise sharply following publication of favorable news in *Time*.

The SEC's investigation revealed that *Time*'s business news editor had purchased 2500 shares of Technical Animations' stock at an average price of about $6.25 a share before assigning a *Time* writer and researcher to the story. Not long after the article appeared, the editor sold out at a profit of some $3875—or a gain of roughly 25 per cent on his investment. According to the SEC, the editor had acquired stock in 64 different companies between 1957 and 1961, and stories about 27 of these firms had showed up in the pages of *Time*. The editor, who was eventually dismissed from *Time* for what the magazine said were other reasons, usually purchased his stock just before *Time* published an article about the company and soon after sold out at a "considerable profit," according to the SEC.

In describing the case, the SEC was careful to point out that the "publicity apparently was not generated by the issuer or its public relations man." Nevertheless, the SEC said, "It is clear that the *Time* article was the principal cause for the rise in the price of the stock."

This official testimonial to the influence a single widely read publication can have on the investment decisions of stockholders should be kept in mind by every capitalist careless enough to rely innocently on any one source of information in deciding which stocks to buy, sell, or hold.

The late Bernard M. Baruch, one of the most astute capitalists this nation has ever produced, recognized information as one of the bedrock ingredients of successful investing. He was particularly concerned about the origin, depth, reliability, and availability of data he relied on when making investment decisions—a fact which comes through loud and clear when reading Mr. Baruch's "'rules' or guidelines on how to invest or speculate wisely," published in his autobiography:

1. Don't speculate unless you can make it a full-time job.
2. Beware of barbers, beauticians, waiters—of anyone—bringing gifts of "inside" information or "tips."
3. Before you buy a security, find out everything you can about the company, its management and competitors, its earnings and possibilities for growth.
4. Don't try to buy at the bottom and sell at the top. This can't be done—except by liars.
5. Learn how to take your losses quickly and cleanly. Don't expect to be right all the time. If you have made a mistake, cut your losses as quickly as possible.
6. Don't buy too many different securities. Better to have only a few investments which can be watched.
7. Make a periodic reappraisal of all your investments to see whether changing developments have altered their prospects.
8. Study your tax position to know when you can sell to greatest advantage.
9. Always keep a good part of your capital in a cash reserve. Never invest all your funds.
10. Don't try to be a jack of all investments. Stick to the field you know best.

The ebb and flow of information is of such primary importance to the prudent capitalist that we examine the subject in some detail devoted to the press, the investment community, stockholder reports, and annual meetings. In doing this, we have gone behind the scenes whenever possible to report not only how information is communicated, but, perhaps of more significance, how this type of information is generated in the first place.

Information is food and drink to serious share owners. Opinion may vary, of course, as to what facts should be made known to the company's owners. Management, for example, may find that the immediate release of a certain piece of information, while of great significance to stockholders, may damage the company or hinder it in achieving its objectives, and therefore not serve the owners' best interests. Such is often the case in merger negotiations in which the market price of shares of the companies involved, or some other equally vital aspect of the deal, bears on whether the merger can be consummated. After Frank Freimann, president of the Magnavox Company, one summer morning told a news service reporter his company might complete a "very sizable acquisition" within the next thirty days, the price of his company's stock that day jumped by $3.125 to $42.875, and was the third most actively traded on the New York Stock Exchange. Mr. Freimann, however, apparently regretted issuing the news, because he and his public relations staff spent most of the afternoon frantically trying to stamp out the fire of speculative activity. In a series of official statements, the company said, "no merger in the immediate future is likely," and "no definite conclusion has been reached, nor has the matter been considered by the board."

In the meantime, the price of shares in the "sizable acquisition" Wall Street assumed Mr. Freimann had been talking about—General Precision Equipment Corporation—began moving ahead on the rumor. GP's stock that day rose $4.25 to $34.25 on the New York Stock Exchange, and its chairman, James W. Murray, gave the impression that he too was dancing barefoot on hot coals. He said he had spoken with Mr. Freimann about mergers in the past, but General Precision now "had no merger agreement nor tentative agreement with anyone and isn't discussing a merger with anyone."

The day closed with the busy Magnavox public relations department issuing its third statement of the afternoon confirming that General Precision was one of the companies Mr. Freimann had in mind. Whatever the facts, it is clear that at some point a merger between the two companies was under consideration, and both Mr. Freimann and Mr. Murray felt it was not in their companies' best interests to have this known—although the gyrations in the market place indicated that investors considered the news of serious import.

The premature disclosure of substantive information about new products may also work against the best interests of a company's stockholders. A classic example is the case in which reporter John Williams of the *Wall Street Journal*, on the basis of some sure-footed investigative reporting, wrote a front-page article describing new model autos months before the major manufacturers were ready to announce them, and before dealers had emptied their showrooms of the current year's models. The auto companies were furious, and General Motors promptly withdrew a king's ransom in advertising from the *Journal*. The dealers and the auto companies claimed the story and accompanying sketches resulted in the public's holding off buying current year's cars, preferring to wait a few months for the intriguing new models portrayed on page one of the nation's most widely read financial newspaper. The controversy raged for many weeks, with the newspaper holding its ground and General Motors finally reinstating its advertising.

In every industry, certain information, if made public, might lend aid and comfort to competitors, or stifle sales. This accounts for the reluctance of most companies to publish breakdowns of sales of individual products or product lines, or detailed figures on production costs or sales expense. No company need fear criticism if it refuses to discuss publicly facts which, although not themselves detrimental to the company or embarrassing to its management, would harm the company's interests if disclosed.

Management, however, traditionally is closemouthed about its business, a carry-over from the days when even publicly held companies were operated as personal fiefs. This results in a peculiar and imperious reluctance on the parts of some managements to disclose publicly vital investment information which today's aggressive newspaper reporter can ofttimes easily uncover. Webb & Knapp, Inc., once filed with the American Stock Exchange and the SEC the detailed results of a widely publicized sale of its properties which took place in the second quarter of the year. Although its report was filed with the Exchange in September, it wasn't until October 25—three days after the company's annual meeting—that it was made known to stockholders, and only then through a newspaper story which was put together by an enterprising reporter who took the trouble to check the Exchange's files.

There is general agreement that publicity has its uses, and U.S. corporations maintain massive machinery to utilize press channels of communications to gain appropriate objectives, including that of keeping stockholders up to date on the status of their investments.

The Gentlemen of the Press

The most important media group in the press spectrum is the wire services, which produce most of the news you read in the financial pages of your newspaper. They include the Dow-Jones news service, the Associated Press, and United Press International. Each of these organizations is based in New York City but has offices in many other cities. Dow-Jones, the smallest of the three in terms of personnel, nevertheless is of major importance because it is the only one which specializes in business news and is regarded by many in the financial community as a primary source of business and financial information. It has offices staffed with financial reporters in New York, Chicago, Los Angeles, and some dozen other business centers.

Both the AP and UPI have nationwide networks of offices staffed primarily by general assignment reporters, with financial staffs based mainly in New York. Most radio and television stations also subscribe to these news services. A major piece of business news sent out over the wires of these three major wire services can reach every interested investor in the United States in a matter of hours.

Daily newspapers in the nation's major business centers usually have at least one business news specialist on the staff. Some papers, such as the *New York Times*, Chicago *Tribune*, and Los

Angeles *Times*, have good-sized staffs of business reporters. These big city newspapers cover business news on a national scale, some of it taken from the wire services, or from information mailed or delivered directly to them by the company. Business news of immediate local interest to a newspaper's readers, of course, will get a much bigger play than news farther from home. The Chicago *Tribune* will devote far more space to the closing of one of the city's major meat packing plants than it will to a new defense contract received by an aerospace company in Los Angeles. The Los Angeles *Times* will handle these stories in exactly the opposite way.

Financial periodicals comprise another major medium for the dissemination of business news. The leading publication in this category is the *Wall Street Journal*. This newspaper, which is published daily, Monday through Friday, has a national daily circulation of more than 1,000,000 and its market research indicates that at least one subscription is mailed to the headquarters of every one of the top 500 corporations in the U.S. The *Wall Street Journal* is owned by Dow-Jones, which owns the Dow-Jones news service and *Barron's* magazine, a weekly business magazine with a circulation of about 150,000. All three of these media have their headquarters in New York City.

There is a host of other authoritative and widely read business publications serving the financial community. These may appear weekly, such as *Business Week, Financial World*, and *Barron's*; fortnightly, such as *Forbes* and *The Magazine of Wall Street;* monthly, as is the case with *Fortune*, and *Dun's Review & Modern Industry*, or bimonthly such as the *Analysts Journal* and the *Harvard Business Review*. The general-circulation news magazines, *Time, Newsweek* and *U.S. News & World Report*, also provide a medium for business news and, as indicated earlier, exercise considerable influence in the financial community.

One group of publications whose importance to stockholders is often overlooked is the trade press. This group includes magazines and newspapers specializing in news about companies in specific industries. Examples are *Drug Topics, Electronics News*,

Oil and Gas Journal, and *Chemical Week.* Serious stockholders would do well to subscribe to at least one publication covering each industry in which they have a major investment. Often these publications carry news of considerable financial significance long before word reaches the general public.

Among the most influential channels for financial news are publications issued by the big securities reporting services, the major stock exchanges, and large brokerage houses. These include Standard & Poor's and Moody's published services, Merrill Lynch, Pierce, Fenner & Smith's *Investor's Reader,* the New York Stock Exchange's *Exchange Magazine,* and the American Stock Exchange's *American Investor.*

There are, of course, many market advisory letters published by investment banking and brokerage houses for their customers, on a daily, weekly, or less frequent basis. These can have an important influence on market prices, although in most cases corporations do not have direct access to their pages as they have to publications sold by public subscription. For many years, one of the most prominent market letter writer's pungent commentary was followed closely by a large and loyal corps of investors. His popularity fell off at least temporarily when the SEC accused him of using his letter to tout stocks in which he and his wife held positions. He would sell his holdings, the SEC said, after publication of his own favorable comment had helped push up the price.

There is no question but that the daily press, for the vast majority of stockholders, is the major source of investment news and information. Unfortunately, space in business news departments of newspapers is limited, although papers such as the *New York Times* devote more columns of text to business news than to any other category, including foreign and national news. Many variables affect the coverage a specific company will receive. The four main determinants:

1. Geographic location of the company's operations in relation to the centers of readership of the newspaper.
2. The intrinsic interest of the company's product or service.

Control Data Corporation, a Minneapolis computer manufacturer, attracts more interest in distant New York City
than a company such as Kennecott Copper Corporation
which is headquartered only a few blocks from Times
Square.

3. Size of the company in terms of sales and profits.
4. The number of stockholders and the number of shares of
   stock outstanding.

It's easy to see, on the basis of this brief list, that small companies, and large companies in the older and more stable industries, stand less chance for space in the daily press, or in news
media generally, than do larger companies in the glamorous
industries. However, as we shall see, if your company has a
sound press relations program it can help attract its fair share
of attention in the press, and, in some cases, even more.

One of the first lessons that a corporate public relations man
learns is that the most important single factor in a successful
relationship with the press is recognizing that the newsman's
greatest love is news—not booze. To be sure, the business luncheon, the fabled press cocktail party, and the holiday gift all
have their purpose and their place. General Electric, for example, holds a "Guaranteed Annual Lunch" at Christmas time for
New York labor reporters. It offers both the reporters and G.E.'s
personnel department brass an opportunity to renew acquaintance and talk shop, cementing relationships which may become
vitally important to the company later on in the midst of sensitive labor negotiations or a strike. G.E. hands to the reporters,
as they leave the luncheon, a gift of a G.E. appliance, wrapped
neatly in plain brown paper. The *New York Times'* labor reporters, who usually turn out for the occasion, invariably pass
up the gift, primly preserving the paper's reputation for bend-
ing neither to fear nor favor.

The gamut of gifts offered reporters is extraordinary. The investment banking firm of Lehman Brothers handed out vicuna
sweaters. Florida Power distributed baskets of citrus fruits. Mag-

arete Steiff, Gmb H., the West German toy manufacturer, dispensed stuffed dwarfs. Merritt-Chapman & Scott gave away matched decks of playing cards. Other companies have piled newsmen with cases of free liquor, theater tickets, automobiles (on loan), air-conditioners, Havana cigars, and occasionally call girls.

One of the most popular gifts a company can present to a reporter is something euphemistically called the "junket." The junket is an expense-paid trip to some distant pleasure dome, ostensibly for the purpose of gathering news. Actually, the news is carefully prepared in advance and can be made available to the reporter right at his desk. The junket, however, is viewed by companies as a good way to ingratiate themselves with the press, thereby perhaps gaining more space and greater prominence for the news at hand. Reporters accept it as one of the perquisites of the journalistic profession, while their editors, with few exceptions, benignly hand out junket assignments as they would bonuses.

The junkets range far and wide. The Hilton chain of hotels invites the press to attend the opening of each of its hostelries, even in such distant places as Istanbul and Caracas; the motion picture companies think nothing of flying a planeload of Hollywood and Broadway reporters and celebrities to Tangier or Tokyo; Trans World Airlines each winter flies a gaggle of reporters to Phoenix to publicize its flights to that winter resort.

Sometimes, the junket backfires. Such was the case with a four-day visit to Miami Beach one winter sponsored by the State of Florida. With the help of a public relations firm hired expressly for the purpose, Florida was attempting to publicize its plan to turn 1800 acres of swampland ten miles north of Miami into a year-round Western Hemisphere trade fair. The long-range goal was to make Miami the trade center of the Americas. This ambitious undertaking depended on the reporters' enthusiastic response to the trade fair project, and no expense was spared in making their trip pleasant and informative. Reams of data on the project were delivered in a neat package complete with engineering studies and the testimonials of prominent New York investment bankers, including Lehman Brothers, which was eager to sell bonds to finance the project to a panting public whose appetite was to have been whetted by the stories in the nation's business press.

The peak of the party occurred on a Saturday night in the ballroom of one of Miami Beach's plushest hotels, where the city's business and civic leaders turned out to add their blandishments to the big pitch. The story was set for release the following Tuesday, to enable the reporters to return to their offices and turn in their stories at their leisure.

Overlooked by the planners of the gargantuan shindig were the local Miami reporters, not invited to participate in the four days of fun and frolic, but who could hardly overlook one of the biggest local news stories of the year. Quite properly, the Miami papers ran the story in their Sunday editions on the basis of the public presentations made by the city fathers the night before, and the major news services picked it up and carried it the same day as a brief news item. The reporters who had been invited from afar lost interest in the story since it would be old news by the time they arrived home, although several glumly phoned in a few routine paragraphs to let their editors know they weren't asleep on the job. Unfortunately for its promoters, the trade center for the Americas is yet to be built and the alligators who call the swamp site home are still able to sleep on undisturbed by progress.

Whether a reporter accepts such largesse gracefully or declines with thanks on the basis of his publisher's policy or his own misgiving, his paycheck depends on his ability to keep his readers informed and his editor convinced he's doing that job in at least passable fashion. Anything a company can do to ease his task, within the bounds of good taste, good fellowship and good business, is not only justifiable but can be considered almost obligatory. The gift a good reporter appreciates most is a piece of publishable news.

Waltzing at the Press Ball

Only a fraction of each day's business news ends up in your daily newspaper. For every annual meeting reported in the financial press, a dozen are not. Thousands of new products are reported in trade journals, but only a handful reach the public through major news media. Scores of new factories rise each year, yet small notice is taken of these in the general press. The fact remains, however, that many meetings are covered, some new products do gain notice, and some new plans do make their public debuts accompanied by photographs in the *New York Times*. Within this favored group, of course, are the giants of industry, whose every corporate hiccough is covered breathlessly by the press.

This doesn't mean that small or unglamorous outfits must be corporate wallflowers. Any company has many opportunities throughout the year to waltz at the press ball. There are periodic earnings reports, dividend announcements, executive changes, plant expansions, and new products. There are speeches by top brass, price changes in product lines. Some of these occasions may call for a formal press conference, while others can best be handled by setting up a cozy meeting with one or more of the company's officers.

With a little ingenuity, a company may generate news that might ordinarily go unnoticed. Most corporations today are substantial contributors to a wide variety of eleemosynary causes, yet rarely do corporate gifts attract more than passing notice. One noteworthy exception was an American Export Lines, Inc. contribution of $135,000 to the Metropolitan Opera of New York for the scenery and costumes for a new production of the Italian opera *Aida*. It was thought to be the first time a corporation, as such, had contributed directly to the Met. The sum, payable in equal installments over a ten-year period actually depleted the company treasury by less than $70,000, or $7000 a year, since it was a tax deductible item. If the $135,000 had been retained as profit it would have been subject to the stiff corporate income tax. For a relatively modest amount, then, American Export Lines received favorable notice in the press in the U.S. and in Italy and will continue to receive notice in the programs of every Metropolitan Opera performance of *Aida*. One objective of the gift and the attendant publicity, as explained by American Export's chairman, Admiral John M. Will, was to gain favor with opera patrons here and in Italy. These persons, he added, are prime customers for the company's luxury liners steaming between the East Coast of the U.S. and Genoa, their principal port of call in Italy, and other European cities.

The basic mechanics of dealing with the press, or "servicing" the press, are rather uncomplicated, although press custom and reporters' temperament have created what some company officials view as a stylized mating dance resembling in some respects the courtship of peacocks.

The mechanics boil down to just a handful of items, according to battle-scarred public relations men. There is, first of all, the deadline, which varies depending on the frequency of publication, and, in the case of daily newspapers, the very hour of publication. The trick here is, where possible, to prepare and distribute a press release at least a day or two in advance of the time the news should appear in the daily press. Secondly, the company should make certain that its releases go to the proper person. Thirdly, it should provide for the speedy supply of information. Reporters usually want facts immediately, if not sooner, and it's important that someone be available to provide them at a moment's notice.

It's fair to observe at this point that some publications can be influenced or coerced into modifying a story, or even dropping it entirely. The SEC has severely criticized the financial press for permitting itself to be used to mislead the investing public, and the commission chronicled a number of specific cases of this in its monumental five-part study of the securities markets, published in 1963.

Although it may be tempting for a company to do so, pressuring a publication to change what it plans to print may at best result in unwitting distortion, and at worst expose the company to criticism and possible punitive action by the SEC, the stock exchange on which its securities are traded, and in serious cases intervention by the federal or state attorney general's office.

Seeking change or retraction of an error in a matter of fact is something else again, even if the company itself was responsible for the mistake. Most publications have a set format for printing corrections even though many variables are weighed before the decision is made to print a correction.

On rare occasions, an error may create havoc, or what feels like havoc, in the newsroom as well as the executive suite. One respected business publication, for example, printed an article erroneously stating that an appliance manufacturer had discontinued one of its product lines. No printed retraction could undo the damage it suffered, the company believed, and as a result it sued the publisher for $6 million.

A face-to-face interview with the press is one of the most effective means a company can use to pump information into the financial community's news pipelines. First, it provides the opportunity to clarify ambiguities or questions concerning the "news" the company hopes to see in print. Secondly, it enables company officials and reporters to become better acquainted, thus helping build a personal relationship which, indirectly, could lead to greater understanding between the company and its stockholders.

A good example of what a valid interview or press "conference" can accomplish for a company was that held by Joy Manufacturing Company, Pittsburgh, a mining equipment manufacturer. It was called to discuss the results of the president's tour of Joy's European operations and his trip to Russia. He told the reporters at a luncheon meeting that Joy received an order for over $10 million for potash mining equipment from the Soviet Union, adding that the company had not yet received the necessary U.S. Government delivery clearance.

Joy's president, James A. Drain, said the order would supply work for 725 men for a year at the company's Franklin, Pennsylvania, plant, and probably an equal amount of work for Joy's suppliers. The Russians, he told the assembled reporters, threatened to buy the equipment from European manufacturers if Joy wasn't permitted to fill the order. In this way, presumably, Mr. Drain was able to illustrate the effects on company operations of European competition. At the same time, he was able to demonstrate the benefits of the order in terms of U.S. employment. Not incidentally, the presentation helped offset possible criticism of the company's having done business with an unpopular customer.

Mr. Drain's meeting with the press gave him a forum at which he could discuss other matters of significance to the financial community. He estimated that despite a slight drop in sales for the fiscal year, Joy's profits would rise from 53 cents a share in the previous year to at least $1.75 cents a share. He explained this was due to a pickup in new orders for coal mining equipment, enabling the company to begin building its backlog of orders after having to eat into it for some months.

A press interview often will be initiated by the press itself. Or a company will seek an interview with a representative of a specific publication, because the information it wishes to publicize fits its particular format. The business news sections of a number of large metropolitan dailies, for example, often carry brief profiles of chief executive officers. This may enable the company to have its president better known to stockholders and employees. Or it may help publicize a policy of special interest to employees or to customers who are also readers of that paper.

Regardless of who initiates the interview, it's important for both parties to have its purpose clearly in mind. It's up to the company, then, to gather pertinent data and either get them to the reporter in advance or, if this isn't feasible, have them ready for him at the interview or press conference.

But even a packet of printed data doesn't ensure that the reporter will know what a press conference is all about. He may choose not to read it until he returns to his office. If the press conference is in the late afternoon, and if the refreshments are particularly appealing, the press "kit" may not receive study until the following morning. One famed science reporter attended a General Electric press conference late one afternoon, arriving just after the formal portion of the meeting had been completed. He greeted several colleagues and G.E. friends, downed a few hors d'oeuvres, tucked a press kit under his arm, and dashed to catch his commuter's train home. He planned to read the G.E. material the next day. Late that night he learned something from a TV newscast: the press conference had been called to announce that G.E. scientists had discovered how to manufacture diamonds—one of the biggest business stories of the year.

Many reporters resent being asked to show their finished stories to the company before publication, and, in fact, some publications prohibit them from doing so. They feel such a request implies that the reporter's skills are lacking, that he is incapable of fair interpretation, or that the company is anxious to change the story to suit itself.

One reporter swore never again to permit a company to see an unpublished manuscript after his experience with a manufacturer of equipment for chemical processing plants. He had offered his manuscript for checking, on the basis that it contained a number of sections dealing with rather complicated manufacturing techniques. The effect was rather like throwing a feather pillow into an electric fan. The public relations director of the company fired off telegrams to the reporter and his editor insisting the story not be published until he returned the "corrected" manuscript. He sent a special delivery letter to the paper's advertising director asking him to use his influence to see that the corrections were made. The manuscript came in, with each paragraph numbered in sequence. Accompanying it was a corresponding manuscript, with at least one change in almost every paragraph, each numbered to correspond to the original version. There was only one actual error in the entire manuscript, and that having to do with a minor historical point in a paragraph dealing with the company's development. The "errors" which occasioned such public relations hysteria were on this order: "You describe our Mr. Anderson as grey-haired and bespectacled.' Actually he is steely-eyed and firm-muscled. . . ."

One of the most vexing and potentially destructive problems a company may face is unfounded rumor. This can directly affect the stockholders' investment and the company's welfare. Such a rumor can cause stockholders to panic and sell at a loss, or it can create undue optimism causing them to buy at an unduly high price. It can cut a company's credit rating with its banks and suppliers and ruin the sale of a new stock or bond issue. Even if a rumor temporarily benefits the company, the reaction to the disappointing truth sure to follow can adversely affect management's reputation for integrity, with all that implies in terms of the company's relationship with suppliers, customers, bankers, and stockholders.

Among the most widespread rumors in modern corporate history was one in which Teflon, a product produced by E. I. du Pont de Nemours & Company, was thought to give off poisonous fumes when heated. Teflon is a plastic resin which, when bonded to metal or ceramic cookware, enables the housewife to cook without grease. Eggs, for example, can be fried on a Teflon fry pan without using butter, bacon fat, oil, or anything else. Du Pont and other companies in the U.S. and abroad have spent untold thousands of dollars in laboratory experiments proving Teflon's safety, and thousands more attempting to dispel the rumors about Teflon, which for some still unknown reason kept popping up unexpectedly. The company finally published a special fourteen-page booklet which frankly acknowledged the rumors and refuted them point by point with scientific thoroughness.

Rumors concerning mergers, acquisitions, or tender offers may send stock prices soaring, or, on the reverse side of the coin, rumors about dividend decreases will surely send stock prices into a downward spiral.

The best policy for companies to follow in squelching harmful or embarrassing rumors, if false, is to refute them promptly. Supervisors are informed of the facts so they can respond immediately when questions arise. If a rumor has gained wide currency, and appears to have staying power, informational memos are sent to the press, and perhaps also to stockholders, employees, customers, and suppliers.

If the company's stock is listed on one of the nation's major exchanges, the exchange staff will almost certainly swing into action whenever it hears the first rumblings of a rumor. G. Keith Funston, president of the New York Stock Exchange, tells the story of how fast his staff can move when the need arises.

Shortly before noon one morning, the Exchange staff was informed of a rumor on the trading floor about a tender offer for the capital stock of Emerson Radio & Phonograph Corporation. Within minutes, the Exchange obtained confirmation from the Emerson chairman that such an offer was indeed in the works—but that the company making it, not an NYSE-listed company, did not wish to be identified until the details were set. At 12:20, the Exchange halted trading in the stock, pending an announcement—an action which, the company agreed, was appropriate under the circumstances. The last sale before the halt was at 15⅜, up ¾ from the previous day's close.

At about 3:15, the company advised the Exchange that no announcement would be possible before the 3:30 close of the market. Shortly before the close, the Dow Jones broad tape carried an item indicating that an announcement was expected before the next day's market opening. And at 9:45 A.M. the next day, the broad tape carried the details of the offer—at $18 a share—being made by National Union Electric Corporation. Trading in Emerson was resumed later in the morning and the stock opened at 16¾.

This particular situation had two most unusual aspects. First, it involved a rumor which proved to be true. And second, this was a very rare instance in which trading was halted and not resumed on the same day. But the important point is that prompt and full cooperation between the listed company and the Exchange avoided the possibility of uninformed trading being based on the unconfirmed rumor —and thus helped safeguard the interests of the investing public without premature disclosure of the facts.

Fast and accurate information is the lifeblood of successful investing. Yet it's amazing how few stockholders take even five minutes to investigate before they invest, or know more than yesterday's closing price of their company's stock once they've purchased it. The press is the fastest communications channel between your company and you, and if you ignore it you do so at your peril. But the press by itself isn't enough, because it cannot provide you with official company data in depth, or give you a chance to meet personally and question your company's management. If you want this kind of information you must read your company's reports, and attend its annual meetings. This information is there for the taking, but today's careless capitalists simply aren't interested.

About the Editors

BILL ADLER is the editor of numerous anthologies, including *The Kennedy Wit, Letters from Camp,* and *Israel: A Reader.*

CATHERINE J. GREENE is a graduate of Bennington College, Class of 1963, and did graduate work at Columbia University. She has been associated with Bill Adler since 1966. She is married to L. Bradford Greene and they reside in New York City, where Mr. Greene is a security analyst and stockbroker.